OBJECT-ORIENTED APPLICATIONS

B. MEYER
Eiffel: The Language

D. MANDRIOLI AND B. MEYER (eds)
Advances in Object-Oriented Software Engineering

D. HENDERSON-SELLERS
A Book of Object-Oriented Knowledge

M. LORENZ
Object-Oriented Software Development: A Practical Guide

P. J. ROBINSON
Hierarchical Object-Oriented Design

R. SWITZER
Eiffel: An Introduction

OBJECT-ORIENTED APPLICATIONS

EDITED BY

Bertrand Meyer

INTERACTIVE SOFTWARE ENGINEERING INC., SANTA BARBARA

AND

Jean-Marc Nerson

SOCIÉTÉ DES OUTILS DU LOGICIEL, PARIS

Prentice Hall

New York   London   Toronto   Sydney   Tokyo   Singapore

First published 1993 by
Prentice Hall International (UK) Limited
Campus 400, Maylands Avenue
Hemel Hempstead
Hertfordshire, HP2 7EZ
A division of
Simon & Schuster International Group

Printed and bound in Great Britain
by Bookcraft, Midsomer Norton

Library of Congress Cataloging-in-Publication Data

Object-oriented applications / edited by Bertrand Meyer
    and Jean-Marc Nerson.
        p.   cm.
    Includes bibliographical references.
    ISBN 0-13-013798-7
    1. Object-oriented programming.   2. Application
        software.
    I. Meyer, Bertrand, 1950–   . II. Nerson, Jean-Marc.
QA76.64.0236   1993   93–11370
005.13'3—dc20   CIP

British Library Cataloguing in Publication Data

A catalogue record for this book is available from
the British Library

ISBN 0-13-013798-7

---

1   2   3   4   5   97   96   95   94   93

Introduction

Is object-oriented technology ready to deliver on its promises? For many people who have been intellectually convinced by the arguments of principle – reusability, reliability, extendibility, elegance – this is still an open question.

Yes it looks great, but does it really work? I mean, is it going to work for me? Who else is using it? Does it scale up? What successful projects have been completed? What commercial products have been released? What are the problems (don't try to fool me, I know it can't be perfect)? Is it just for systems programming? (Read: not for the rest of us, "us" being MIS, or telecommunications, or CAD, or real-time.)

This book is an attempt to help everyone who is looking for answers to these questions. It is a detailed presentation of object-oriented technology at work, through its use in seven projects belonging to diverse fields of application.

There have been descriptions of object-oriented applications before, of course. In particular the so far eleven sessions of the TOOLS conference (Technology of Object-Oriented Languages and Systems, see reference [TOOLS 1989-1993] in the bibliography) have included many reports of O-O projects, as this is one of the major goals of the conference. The proceedings of other conferences such as ECOOP and OOPSLA, as well as the archives of the Journal of Object-Oriented Programming and other publications, also contain such reports. Yet many of these articles, informative as they may be, fall short of the expectations of someone who is in search of technical substance. Too often, an applications paper reads somewhat like this:

> *"We at L5, the Lower Leicestershire Lollipop Laboratories Ltd., have found out that, while hardware costs are decreasing, software is increasingly expensive and hard to maintain. This may be called the software crisis. The situation presents us with a difficult problem since the fabrication of lollipops relies more and more critically on computer software.* [Here, a three-page tutorial on the lollipop business.]

So we decided to use object-oriented technology. This means writing software in the form of objects that communicate through messages. [Here, a three-page, half-competent overview of object-oriented technology.] *We decided to use {Eiffel | Smalltalk | C++ | Objective C}. The program looks great because now we have an object STICK and an object CANDY. We also use inheritance, since STICK has two subclasses, WOODEN_STICK and PLASTIC_STICK. We encountered a few bugs in our use of the {compiler | interpreter | environment | libraries}, but the vendor assures us that version 53.66 release V, due in the fourth quarter of this year, has corrected them. By and large this was an extremely {pleasant painful | boring | usual | unusual | unremarkable} experience. We are now in the process of completing our prototype, and on the basis of the ensuing evaluation the L5 management will decide next month whether to apply object-oriented technology to the company's next line of new products."*

The idea behind this book was to avoid such a pattern, and provide readers with a deeper insight into what goes on when object-oriented software construction is used for significant projects. So when Jean-Marc Nerson and I wrote to a number of O-O project leaders to explore the possibility of an applications book, we included something like the above caricature to describe what we did *not* want, and precise guidelines to describe what we *did* hope to get. Quoting from our original letter to prospective contributors:

A key property of the chapters is that they should have a fair deal of technical "meat" – not just skim the surface. [...]. To make the book useful and technically relevant, we feel that the chapters should provide sound technical descriptions of the software solutions used.

This does not mean that you should publish the entire source code of your system. [...] We expect, however, that each contribution will contain some of the elements from the following non-exhaustive list:

- Interesting source code extracts.
- Short forms [i.e. full interface description] of important classes.
- System structure diagrams.
- Information about the analysis/design method used and extracts from the results of the analysis and design.
- Relevant metrics (e.g. on reuse).

Although as a reader you will be the final judge, we feel that the authors made an outstanding job of meeting these goals, sharing many important insights with other current and future users of the technology.

Technical base

Apart from this Introduction, this book consists of a technical overview and of seven chapters, each devoted to a significant O-O project.

All projects were developed using the same brand of object-oriented technology: the Eiffel language, in the implementation developed by Interactive Software Engineering Inc. (ISE), level 2.3. (Some were started with earlier releases, 2.1 or 2.2.) At the time this was the only available implementation of Eiffel, although others have appeared since, and by the time this book appears ISE itself will have released a new implementation, known as ISE Eiffel 3.

Several of the chapters describe the reasons which led the companies involved to select ISE Eiffel, in most cases over C++ or Smalltalk. Many of the lessons gained should be directly applicable to readers working with other contexts.

In many cases the authors have used Eiffel in combination with other languages, usually C. in chapter 7, Enrico Gobbetti and his colleagues from the Swiss Federal Institute of Technology explain at some length how they embedded C libraries in their application, using Eiffel's "external" mechanism. In chapter 3, Gail Murphy and her colleagues from MPR show how they interfaced their Eiffel software with the Interviews library, which is written in C++. These experiences should provide some guidance to the many teams that are trying to combine software elements written in different object-oriented languages.

Language level

Since its design in 1985, Eiffel has been a generally stable language, but some changes have proved to be necessary. In 1990-1991, as the projects described in this book were starting, the Eiffel language was undergoing a general cleanup, which was necessary for a number of reasons:

- Taking advantage of the experience accumulated through usage of Eiffel in many applications since the time of the design.

- Accounting for the existence of implementations produced by sources other than the original developer (ISE).

- Preparing the work of NICE, the Nonprofit International Consortium for Eiffel, an organization of users and developers to which control of the language was transferred in 1991.

- Transforming the original language reference manual [Meyer 1989a] into a much more extensive description published as a widely available book [Meyer 1992].

The resulting language revision, as indeed presented in that book, is known as Eiffel 3. Although there may always be room for adjustments, this version should be here for a long time.

Since software texts play an important part in this book, the question arose of what language level to use. The authors' contributions all used Eiffel 2; although the differences between the two versions are more of syntax than of substance, it would have been unpleasant to publish them in a form which would have been obsolete from the day of publication. So all submitted class texts were translated into Eiffel 3; this task was performed by the editors rather than the chapter authors.

There exists an automatic 2-to-3 translator, developed by ISE; but it was not possible to use it since the class texts were available in text form, not as actual software. So the translation had to be performed manually. Although we did the job carefully, some errors may remain; if you detect any, please blame the editors, not the chapter authors.

The contents

Chapter 1 is an overview of object-oriented technology and Eiffel. Because more in-depth presentations are available elsewhere, this chapter simply introduces the key notions briefly; but it tries to be a little more than just another O-O tutorial. Its originality comes the nature of the examples, almost all of which are borrowed from the applications described in the subsequent chapters. Besides giving the reader an early peek into these applications, this scheme provides, we hope, a more vivid and realistic description of the practice of object-oriented development than the standard pedagogical examples of object-orientation tutorials.

Chapter 2, entitled "Temporal software components", was written by Ted Lawson, Carmel Balthazaar and Alex Gray of the University of Wales. This contribution has been put first because it addresses a familiar application to which everyone can relate directly: the management of date and time. The chapter includes many complementary elements: a comprehensive presentation of the underlying notions (time, duration, interval, date); a fascinating discussion of the many difficulties that scientific, historical and cultural considerations bring to these notions; abstract data type diagrams using the ADJ notation; a description of the development method used in the project. It examines the software consequences of these issues, for example the impact of the typing policy (covariance *vs.* contravariance). The result is a set of classes which relate directly to the underlying abstractions: *ABSOLUTE_TIME, TIME_INTERVAL, DATE, DURATION, YMD_DURATION*. (Relativistic extensions are described as "an exercise left to the reader".) The chapter also describes how the classes started out in a specialized form and underwent a generalization process so as to yield truly reusable components; this discussion will be of interest to all project developers who are preoccupied with making their software reusable without sacrificing short-term needs.

Chapter 3 is the first of three chapters devoted to applications in the networking and telecommunications area – one of the fastest growing domain of application of object-oriented technology. Its title is "Engineering software with objects" and its authors are Gail Murphy, Paul Townsend, Paulin Laberge and Mike Juzenas from MPR Teltech in Vancouver, Canada, a subsidiary of British Columbia Telephone. The chapter describes the TRICS system; the initial stand for Trouble Reporting Integrator for Customer Surveillance. TRICS provides a graphical interface for monitoring networks and respond to problems before they produce damaging consequences. The system can support up to 75 different workstations and 255 simultaneous sessions. Here too the use of object-oriented modeling led to classes that closely reflect the underlying abstractions from the problem domain, for example *CIRCUIT, EQUIPMENT, ALARM_RECORD*, and four support classes whose short forms appear in the chapter: *NETWORK_MSG,*

NETWORK_ROUTER, SOCKET_INTERFACE, THRESHOLD. The development used prototyping (on which the authors express some reservations), Coad and Yourdon's OOA notation for analysis, Wirfs-Brock's responsibility-driven method for design, and relied heavily on Eiffel's assertions. In their discussion of the implementation, the authors discuss the importance of garbage collection, the persistence issues that they encountered, and the problems of interfacing Eiffel with C++ (such as guaranteeing that Eiffel objects are not garbage-collected if they are unreachable from the Eiffel side but still referenced by C++ objects). An important part of the chapter is the section entitled "metrics", which introduces some interesting measurements, showing in particular the contribution of the standard Eiffel library, which accounts for a substantial part of the overall code even though it only consists of general-purpose, application-independent code. The authors mention that a previous development in C, with substantially less functionality, had required 35,000 lines of code (to be compared with about 23,000 TRICS-related Eiffel code), and that the estimates for extending it to the functionality implemented in TRICS were "astronomical". Just to implement the presentation processes in C++ produced more than 34,000 lines of code. The discussion also covers such important problems as configuration management, project management and testing of object-oriented software, and is backed by precise diagrams of the time spent for each activity in the project. Particularly interesting is the analysis (echoing the comments of Ted Lawson and his colleagues in chapter 2) of how a particular set of classes gradually evolved into more abstract and reusable versions. Throughout the chapter, the authors offer "words of wisdom" for future users of the technology, from the voices of both management and system developers.

Chapter 4 is from another telecommunications company: Telecom Australia (as it was called at the time the chapter was written) or Telstra Corporation Ltd. (its current official international name). The author is David Giddy from Telecom Research in Melbourne. The chapter, entitled "Development of control software for an experimental Broadband ISDN switch", includes a detailed introduction to switching, signaling and B-ISDN (Broadband Integrated Services Digital Network) as well as a glossary of telecommunications vocabulary. The system it describes is an ambitious one, which is planned to include up to 100,000 lines of code when completed. The current system is built as a set of parallel processes, and the main process consists of about 50,000 lines of Eiffel. The author does an excellent job of explaining telecommunications concepts in a clear fashion and (as the MPR authors in chapter 3) to relate these concepts to the software design. Again object-oriented modeling provides a natural link, with such classes as *CALL, ROUTING_TABLE* and *CONNECTION*, whose interfaces (short forms) are given at the end of the chapter. The discussion presents the process structure of the application and its different subsystems; one of the subsystems, call control, is described in detail. Its design relied on a methodological approach similar to that used in the MPR project (Wirfs-Brock's CRC cards). The discussion shows how software design issues reflect important underlying non-software choices: making class *CALL* a direct supplier of class *PORT* would have precluded extensions to the basic notion of call, such as conference calls; therefore an intermediate class *CONNECTION* had to be introduced. This is typical of the power of object-oriented modeling, and also shows that in order to obtain software objects it does not suffice to take the objects of the physical world: many classes (object types) can only be obtained as a result of the designer's conscious decision of what deserves to be viewed as a software object, and what does not. The chapter further introduces SDL (the standard protocol specification language) and a set of classes modeling the associated finite state machines. It discusses the solutions used by the author's group to the problem of configuration management; in contrast with the MPR development which used CVS, the Telecom Australia effort relied on the older SCCS tool. As explained in chapter 1 (section 1.3.4, page 30), the Eiffel *indexing* clause, a mechanism for associating retrieval information with classes, provided some help for interfacing Eiffel with SCCS. Particular difficulties arose from having a team split over two sites; David Giddy notes that this physical separation caused some reuse opportunities to be missed. He concludes with a highly positive assessment of the technology's suitability for full-scale production developments.

Chapter 5, "Static Network Resource Allocation by Simulated Annealing", is by Paul Johnson of GEC-Marconi in England. At first the use of annealing in a chapter on networking may seem rather surprising, since annealing (a technique for heating and then cooling metals to avoid brittleness) is not something that one would want to apply to a telecommunication network. The connection comes from the physico-mathematical model of metal annealing, which yields an interesting optimization technique of wide applicability, "simulated annealing". The state of a network is identified with the arrangement of atoms in a metal, and the function to be minimized, identified with the energy, is the cost of a state. After presenting this model and its application to the problem of resource allocation in a network, the chapter explains how it was implemented, showing in particular how inheritance and redefinition facilitate extensions to the model. Once again, the modeling power of the method is clear, with such classes as *NODE, LINK, NETWORK, ANNEALER, ANNEAL_STATE*. The author discusses important design decisions, his use of the Eiffel libraries, in particular the lexical library and the parsing library – whose documentation he found to be insufficient – and the importance of a systematic use of assertions and of the "contracting" idea behind Eiffel. He also notes some mistakes that were made during the project, such as a library whose design relied on some invalid decisions and which as a consequence was not used. The chapter contains an interesting discussion of inheritance, describing the inheritance structure of the system and promoting the concept of "fine grain inheritance" which Paul Johnson originated. In discussing the debugging of the system, he once again notes the importance of assertions, which avoided many bugs that in C or C++ would have caused hard-to-debug strange behavior. He notes problems that were encountered because of limitations of ISE Eiffel 2.3: lack of advanced debugger and of system-wide type checking, slow recompilation. As is appropriate for the description of a practical application, the chapter includes performance measurements. Its conclusion notes that in spite of the need for better tools (especially for garbage collection and debugging) the author recommends Eiffel over other object-oriented environments for medium and large scale development.

Chapter 6 comes from the Netherlands and takes us to a completely different application area of engineering: the building and construction industry. Its authors are Bart Luijten and Bart Luiten, and the work was done for a combination of an engineering company (Ballast Nedam Engineering), an applied research organization (TNO) and a university (Delft). The title of their contribution is "A layered-modeling tool for the integration of computer applications". The purpose of this tool is to provide a common base for the many computer tools that are used in the CAD-CAM (computer-aided design and manufacturing) process and, more generally, product modeling. The tool is "layered" because it relies on a five-tier hierarchy of properties, from the most general to the most specific, reminiscent of the famous seven-layer ISO model used to handle networking issues. Here again object-oriented modeling appears as the natural solution. The chapter discusses four design alternatives that were considered to map the layer structure into a class-based architecture, and explains the rationale behind the most flexible one, which was finally retained; this solution implies that the Eiffel source code is not directly written by the modelers, but generated by the software from their descriptions. This design decision yields a set of classes and a sophisticated inheritance hierarchy between them; examples of classes include *BUILDING*, *GEO_OBJECT*, *PM_OBJECT* etc. Like the authors of the previous chapters, Bart Luijten and Bart Luiten have combined Eiffel with a separate analysis technique; for their part they chose NIAM (Nijssen's Information Analysis Method). It is indeed remarkable that, apart from some common use of Wirfs-Brock's method in chapters 3 and 4, each team seems to have settled on a different analysis method! The chapter then explains how Eiffel code was generated, giving detailed code examples. Here too the use of assertions, genericity and multiple inheritance is essential. The detailed description of the software architecture will be useful to anyone having to deal with similar problems. The discussion concludes with a presentation of the user interface and a description of future avenues of development.

Chapter 7 was written by a team at the Computer Graphics Laboratory of the Ecole Polytechnique Fédérale in Lausanne, Switzerland, and is entitled "Building an interactive 3D animation system". The authors are Enrico Gobbetti, Francis Balaguer, Angelo Mangili and Russell Turner. This is again an application area which appeals directly to many people, here because of the visible and impressive nature of the results. But it raises difficult software problems, and it is indeed hard, as the authors point out, to see how progress could occur in this field without the help of object-oriented technology. The authors explain why they wanted a "pure" version of the technology, as opposed to a hybrid, and describe the design method they used: division into clusters (groups of classes); description of each cluster in terms of their chosen analysis method – in this case Rumbaugh's OMT notation; use of Eiffel assertions to describe the semantic properties of classes. They provide a detailed description of each cluster, and explain how they were able to encapsulate existing and widely used numerical libraries such as BLAS (Basic Linear Algebra Subprograms) and LAPACK (Linear Algebra Package) into their product. This is a property of object-oriented technology that has perhaps not been emphasized widely enough: its chameleonic ability to adapt to various application areas by serving as a tool for repackaging existing software. This property is supported by Eiffel's external routine mechanism, illustrated by the authors in the case of a class encapsulating calls to BLAS so that the BLAS routines, although written in another language, can be used directly by the Eiffel software. The authors contrast this method with the hybrid approach used in C++ and Objective-C, which, in their opinion, fails to provide the needed separation between the object-oriented and non-object-oriented worlds. The first cluster they describe is the one in charge of animation techniques – the most impressive part of computer graphics. To achieve animation, a graphics system needs a good interpolation technique to build intermediate frames; their technique is based on B-splines, a notion which, not surprisingly, directly yields a class. Other important classes used for animation also reflect directly understandable abstractions: *ANIM_V3D, TRACK, ANIMATABLE, HISTORY*. Most of these classes are generic and many rely on the constrained genericity mechanism, which combines genericity and inheritance. The next cluster supports the graphical model, based on such classes as *CAMERA, LIGHT* (with heirs *POS_LIGHT, DIR_LIGHT, SPOT_LIGHT*), *GEOMETRY_3D* (with heirs *SM_GEOMETRY* and *RMESH_GEOMETRY*). A detailed discussion explains the relation of these abstract concepts to the actual objects being manipulated, and the design decisions taken at various stages. Another cluster is in charge of dynamics and input, addressing one of the central problems of computer graphics, how to modify graphical output in response to real-time input; the solution requires an event-driven architecture. The final system component described in the chapter is the user interface cluster, whose design was influenced by the NextStep model. For each of these clusters, the discussion follows the same order: analysis; object model; design; implementation. The chapter concludes with a detailed description of how the various pieces were put together, how the project handled the reuse goal, how it was possible to use Eiffel to achieve a high-performance graphic application, and what the prospects are for future work. An important aspect of this chapter is that it includes class extracts showing how central the use of assertions was, not just as a debugging tool (the application that is most directly visible to newcomers) but, more importantly, as a link between analysis, design and implementation, and a way for the developers to check that they are doing the right thing.

Chapter 8, the final chapter, again addresses an entirely different domain: artificial intelligence. Its describes the design of a tool called SLOT; the expansion of this acronym, "Semantic and logical object tool", also serves as chapter title. The authors are Thierry Beauchesne, Thierry Caminel, Sylvain Dupont and Lilian Druilhe, from Dialexis S.A., a company located near Toulouse and engaged in the production of knowledge-based systems. SLOT serves to represent knowledge and reason about it. It supports a number of facilities, such as propositional logic, decision trees, interfaces to C and Eiffel, forward and backward reasoning controlled on a rule-by-rule basis, fuzzy logic, belief revision, and explanation. The chapter is divided into two parts: description of SLOT; design of the system. In the first part the authors explain the advanced features that users of modern knowledge-based systems (as opposed to the simple "expert systems" of a few years ago) require. They describe the SLOT language, which was designed in response to these needs and makes it possible to describe complex semantic networks; the language, not surprisingly, is strongly influenced by object-oriented ideas. Particularly important are the support for explanations, so that users of a knowledge-based system can understand not just what conclusion the system reached for a certain problem but *why* it reached that conclusion, and the use of fuzzy logic to attach quantitative values to the conclusions reached. In describing the system design, the authors show how they combined the Unix tool LEX for lexical analysis with Eiffel, using a set of external routines; this shows once again how it is possible to interface object-oriented technology with existing tools built according to different principles. They show the implementation of the parsing mechanism, of the inference mechanism, and the importance of genericity, constrained or not, in the overall architecture. They conclude by discussing how the extendibility of the system derives from the extendibility of the underlying use of object-oriented technology.

Future work and acknowledgments

We hope you enjoy these detailed presentations of important object-oriented applications. We also hope it will be the first in a series; as object-oriented designers tackle ever more ambitious projects, there will be room for many further reports of applications of the technology.

Many people made this book possible. Foremost on the list of acknowledgments, of course, are the chapter authors, who were not only brave enough to entrust their most important projects to new tools and methods, but also patient enough to write about the results and to adopt a common set of conventions. The authors also performed extra work as reviewers of each other's chapters, of this Introduction, and of the first chapter (technology overview).

Particular gratitude is due to the managers in the authors' respective institutions. The managers' role was of course essential to authorize and support the projects in the first place; then management approval was required when the time came to publish the results in the form of this book. In the case of industrial companies, the peculiar nature of the demands we put on authors, asking them to explain the system architecture and, whenever applicable, publish actual code extracts, raised thorny problems of confidentiality and intellectual property; many thanks to the authors' managers for helping to clear these problems, enabling the results of their teams' efforts to be published so as to help others master object-oriented technology and apply it properly.

We are also grateful to Dennis Rodericks and Isabelle-Muriel Meyer for their help in the preparation of the manuscript for publication.

Santa Barbara, Milan   B.M.
May 1993

CONTENTS

THE AUTHORS[1]

Jean-Francis Balaguer

(Chapter 7)

Laboratoire d'Infographie
Ecole Polytechnique Fédérale de Lausanne
CH-1015 Lausanne
Switzerland
E-mail: <balaguer@di.epfl.ch>

Carmel Balthazaar

(Chapter 2)

University of Wales, College of Cardiff
P.O. Box 916
Cardiff, Wales CF2 4YN
United Kingdom
(On leave from Dept. of Mathematics,
University of Kelaniya,
Kelaniya, Sri Lanka.)

Thierry Beauchesne

(Chapter 8)

Dialexis S.A.
5 Place du Village d'Entreprises
B.P. 556
31324 Labège Innopole Cedex
France
E-mail: <thierry@dialexis.fr>

Thierry Caminel

(Chapter 8)

Dialexis S.A.
5 Place du Village d'Entreprises
B.P. 556
31324 Labège Innopole Cedex
France

Sylvain Dupont

(Chapter 8)

Dialexis S.A.
5 Place du Village d'Entreprises
B.P. 556
31324 Labège Innopole Cedex
France

Lilian Druilhe

(Chapter 8)

Dialexis S.A.
5 Place du Village d'Entreprises
B.P. 556
31324 Labège Innopole Cedex
France

David Giddy

(Chapter 4)

Telstra Corporation Ltd.
(Formerly Telecom Australia)
P.O. Box 249
Clayton, Victoria 3168
Australia
E-mail: <d.giddy@trl.oz.au>

Enrico Gobbetti

(Chapter 7)

Laboratoire d'Infographie
Ecole Polytechnique Fédérale de Lausanne
CH-1015 Lausanne
Switzerland
E-mail: <gobbetti@di.epfl.ch>

---

[1] The addresses given reflect the authors' affiliations at the time of publication.

Alex Gray

(Chapter 2)

University of Wales, College of Cardiff
P.O. Box 916
Cardiff, Wales CF2 4YN
United Kingdom

Paul Johnson

(Chapter 5)

GEC-Marconi Research Centre
West Hanningfield Road
Great Baddow
Chelmsford
Essex, England CM2 8HN
United Kingdom
E-mail: <paj@gec-mrc.co.uk>

Mike Juzenas

(Chapter 3)

MPR Teltech Ltd.
8999 Nelson Way
Burnaby, B.C.
Canada V5A 4B5
E-mail: <juzenas@mprgate.mpr.ca>

Paulin Laberge

(Chapter 3)

MPR Teltech Ltd.
8999 Nelson Way
Burnaby, B.C.
Canada V5A 4B5
E-mail: <laberge@mprgate.mpr.ca>

Ted Lawson

(Chapter 2)

University of Wales, College of Cardiff
P.O. Box 916
Cardiff, Wales CF2 4YN
United Kingdom
E-mail: <ted@computing-maths.cardiff.a

Bart Luijten

(Chapter 6)

TNO Building and Construction Researc
P.O. Box 49
2600 AA Delft
The Netherlands
E-mail: <Bart.Luijten@bouw.tno.nl>

Bart Luiten

(Chapter 6)

Delft University of Technology
P.O. Box 5048
2600 GA Delft
The Netherlands
E-mail: <Bart.Luiten@bouw.tno.nl>

Also: Ballast Nedam Engineering
P.O. Box 500
1180 BE Amstelveen
The Netherlands

Angelo Mangili

(Chapter 7)

Centro Svizzero di Calcolo Scientifico
CH-6928 Manno
Switzerland
E-mail: <mangili@cscs.ch>

Bertrand Meyer

(Chapter 1)

Interactive Software Engineering Inc.
270 Storke Road, Suite 7
Goleta, CA 93117
USA
E-mail: <bertrand@tools.com>

Gail C. Murphy

(Chapter 3)

MPR Teltech Ltd.
8999 Nelson Way
Burnaby, B.C.
Canada V5A 4B5
E-mail: <murphy@mprgate.mpr.ca>

Jean-Marc Nerson

Société des Outils du Logiciel
104 rue Castagnary
75015 Paris
France
E-mail: <marc@eiffel.fr>

Paul Townsend

(Chapter 3)

MPR Teltech Ltd.
8999 Nelson Way
Burnaby, B.C.
Canada V5A 4B5
E-mail: <townsend@mprgate.mpr.ca>

Russell Turner

(Chapter 7)

Laboratoire d'Infographie
Ecole Polytechnique Fédérale de Lausanne
CH-1015 Lausanne
Switzerland
E-mail: <turner@di.epfl.ch>

1

An overview of the technology

Bertrand Meyer
ISE
Santa Barbara (California)

The following chapters describe seven important systems based on object-oriented technology. They all rely on a common set of notations, techniques and tools. To facilitate understanding of the technical part of the discussion, it is appropriate to begin by summarizing these fundamental elements.

The set of properties which follows has been divided into three parts:

- *Method and language*: these two almost indistinguishable aspects cover the thought processes and the notations used to analyze and produce software. Be sure to note that (especially in object-oriented technology) the term "language" covers not just the programming language in the restricted sense, but also the notations used for analysis and design.

- *Implementation and environment*: the properties in this category describe the basic properties of the tools which enable developers to apply object-oriented ideas.

- *Libraries*: object-oriented technology is based on the reuse of software components. Properties in this category cover both the availability of basic libraries and the mechanisms needed to use libraries and produce new ones.

This division is convenient but not absolute, as some properties are significant for two or three of the categories. For example the property labeled "memory management" has been classified under method and language because a language can support or prevent garbage collection, but it also belongs to the implementation category.

1.1 METHOD AND LANGUAGE

1.1.1 Seamlessness

The object-oriented approach is ambitious: it encompasses the entire software lifecycle. It is possible to apply a consistent set of concepts and notations for analysis and design as well as implementation and maintenance. The language, in particular, should be a a vehicle for thought which will help you through all stages of your work.

Where traditional software development methods introduce significant gaps between the successive activities involved, object-oriented technology permits a **seamless** approach which emphasizes the commonalities over the differences.

The language used by the applications described in this book is Eiffel, which was intended for seamless application to the four steps listed above – analysis, design, implementation, maintenance. This helps reduce the magnitude of the transitions (sometimes called "impedance mismatches") between successive steps in the lifecycle.

In spite of the method's seamlessness, many people still feel more comfortable if they use more user-oriented notations, often graphical, at the analysis level. Several of the applications described in this book indeed used, in connection with Eiffel, an analysis method and notation:

- To model relations between time and date software components, the development described in chapter 2 relied on ADJ diagrams, an early O-O analysis notation developed in the context of work on abstract data types.
- The analysis for the network surveillance system (chapter 3) was done with the help of Coad's notation.
- The Broadband ISDN system described in chapter 4 used Wirfs-Brock's CRC cards.
- The NIAM analysis method was applied to the product-modeling tool of chapter 6.
- Some of the modeling for the graphical animation system of chapter 7 was based on the OMT notation of Rumbaugh *et al.*

Another approach to object-oriented analysis and design [Nerson 1992, 1993] provides a set of notations and tools which have been explicitly designed to be compatible with the Eiffel approach.

1.1.2 Classes

Object-oriented technology could be called **programming by abstraction**. The object-oriented software developer works by identifying important abstractions and, for each of them, building a corresponding software module, called a **class**.

The abstractions on which classes are based are **data abstractions**: in contrast with older approaches, object-oriented decomposition focuses on data (objects) rather than functions. This is the key to the method's success in ensuring extendibility and reusability.

The generality of the notion of class explains why the seamless approach discussed above is possible. Seamlessness follows from the possibility of defining classes at many levels:

- At the analysis level, classes describe abstractions from the problem domain. For example, classes in the graphical model of the Lausanne team (chapter 7) rely on the fundamental data abstractions traditionally used in the area of computer visualization, which inherited them from the film industry; so you will find such classes as *CAMERA, LIGHT* and *MATERIAL*.

- At the design level, classes describe important abstractions used to define the software architecture. For example, the SLOT system (chapter 8) has a class *SLOT*, describing the basic notion used to record knowledge and perform inferences.

- At the implementation level, classes describe data structures needed for the efficient execution of the system. Many of the projects described, for example, the product modeling tool (chapter 6) uses a class *X_HASH_TABLE*. In many cases, however, implementation classes are not built for a project in an ad hoc fashion, but reused from a general-purpose library. ISE Eiffel comes with such a general-purpose library (EiffelBase), whose classes, such as *ARRAY, LINKED_LIST, HASH_TABLE* have been used extensively by all the projects reported in this book. Libraries will be discussed in more detail below.

A note on typographical conventions: as illustrated by these examples, class names appear in *UPPER-CASE ITALICS*. The rest of software texts is also in *italics,* except for keywords, which appear in ***boldface italics***, and comments, appearing in roman. A comment begins with -- and extends to the end of the line.

1.1.3 Clusters

For a proper organization of the software development process, it is useful to gather classes into groups known as clusters. A cluster contains a set of closely related classes. The division into clusters should minimize the number of connections occurring between classes appearing in different clusters.

Clusters also form the natural unit for the software development process. The "cluster model" of software development [Meyer 1990b] suggests an incremental development process relying on the principles of concurrent engineering, where various clusters are developed with partial overlapping, the order being from the more general clusters to the more specific and application-dependent ones. Several of the following chapters present a cluster-based architecture in some detail and discuss the problems of dividing a system into clusters and coordinating the development of the various clusters. You will find such discussions in particular in chapters 2 (temporal components), 3 (network surveillance), 6 (product modeling, using the term "domain" which, as the authors note on page 184, is a synonym for "cluster") and 7 (graphical animation).

1.1.4 Abstract data types and features

Classes are based on the idea of abstract data types, which implies that object types (as represented by classes) should be defined not through their implementation properties but through the applicable operations, or **features**. For example, the class *CALL* in the discussion of Broadband ISDN (chapter 4, see page 131) includes the following features:

- *make*: a command to initialize a call.
- *delete_connection*: a command to remove the connection for a given call.
- *connections*: a query returning the connections established by the call.
- *is_complete*: a boolean-valued query to determine if a call is finished.
- *wants_event*: a query returning the "basic call state machine" associated with the call.

As this example shows, features are of two kinds. A **command**, such as *make* and *delete_connection*, makes it possible to change objects. A **query**, such as all the other features listed above, makes it possible to access properties of objects.

The presence of both commands and queries explains why the word "features" is used rather than "operations", which would apply well to commands but less obviously to queries. The term "method" is also found in the literature, but it covers only a subset of features (routines, seen below); in addition, this use conflicts with the standard meaning of the word "method" in English.

1.1.5 Classes as modules

Object orientation is primarily an architectural technique: its major effect is on the modular structure of software systems.

The key role here is played by classes. A class is a modular unit of the software, which can be compiled on its own (assuming any other classes that it needs have already been compiled).

In the Eiffel approach, classes are the only modular construct. A system is simply an assembly of classes. (The notion of cluster, mentioned above, provides a convenient unit of project management, but clusters are not syntactical units of the software.)

There is no notion of main program. The method supports subprograms, called "routines"; routines may only appear as part of classes and do not exist as independent modular units. There is also no room for the "packages" of languages such as Ada.

1.1.6 Classes as types

A class is not only a module but also a type (or in the case of generic classes, as discussed below, a type pattern). This means that each class describes a set of objects (data structures) that may be created at run-time. These objects are called **instances** of the class. For example, the instances of class *CALL* in chapter 4 are objects representing individual calls.

The notion of class is powerful enough to avoid the need for any other typing mechanism. In particular, even the basic types *BOOLEAN*, *CHARACTER*, *INTEGER*, *REAL* and *DOUBLE* can be derived from classes, although such classes are built-in rather than defined anew by each developer. These basic classes are also known to the compiler, so as to reconcile the uniformity of the type system with the need to generate code whose efficiency is similar to what is produced by compilers for languages such as C, C++ or Pascal where the basic types are part of the language.

The type system directly supports the notion of subtype, through the inheritance mechanism discussed below.

1.1.7 Feature-based computation

In object-oriented computation, there is just one basic computational mechanism: given a certain object, which (in line with the previous discussion) is always an instance of some class, call a feature of that class on that object. The basic notation for such feature calls, known as dot notation is

> $t.f(a1, ...)$

where t, the target of the call, denotes the object to which the call applies; f is the feature of the call; and $a1$, ... are arguments. The argument part (in parentheses) is omitted if the feature has no argument. In the class *CALL* used above as example, some of the features have arguments and others have no argument; the class declaration appears as

> **class CALL creation**
>
> > *... See next section ...*
>
> **feature**
>
> > *make* ... See next section...
> >
> > *connections*: *CONNECTION*;
> > > -- The connections established by this call
> >
> > *delete_connection is*
> > > -- Delete the connection for this call.
> > > **do**
> > > > ... Implementation omitted ...
> > > **end**;

> *is_complete: BOOLEAN is*
> > -- Is the current call finished?
> > *do*
> > > ... Implementation omitted ...
> >
> > *end*;
>
> *wants_event (event: PROTOCOL_IPC_EVENT): BCSM is*
> > -- The associated BCSM if this call wants the current event;
> > -- Void otherwise.
> > *do*
> > > ... Implementation omitted ...
> >
> > *end*;

end -- class *CALL*

BCSM means Basic Call State Machine (chapter 4 has a glossary section: 4.9). If *new_call* denotes an object of type *CALL*, we can delete the connection through the call

> *new_call. delete_connection*

and to find out what state machine (BCSM) will be used by a call *new_call* to handle an event *some_event* we may execute the assignment

> *b := new_call. wants_event (some_event)*

In the above class feature *wants_event* has one argument, of type *PROTOCOL_IPC_EVENT* (another class of the system); the other features, except *make* discussed below, have no argument.

A class *C* which contains a call to a feature of a class *S* is said to be a **client** of *S*, and *S* a **supplier** of *C*.

The feature call mechanism is sometimes known as **message passing**; in this terminology, a call such as the last one above will be described as passing to *new_call* the message "tell me with what state machine you want to handle this event", with argument *some_event*.

The example also indicates further properties of the notion of feature. As noted above, a feature may be a command or a query. There are two ways of implementing a query:

- You may reserve a field in each instance of the class, representing the value of the query for that particular object. A query implemented in this way, similar to a component of a record in Pascal or a structure in C, is called an **attribute**. The above class text shows *connections* to be an attribute.

- Alternatively, you may define an algorithm which will compute the value of the query on any instance. The algorithm will appear in a clause of the form *is do* ... *end* as shown above. Such a query is called a **function**; the functions in the above class are *is_complete* and *wants_event*.

A query without arguments may be implemented as an attribute or as a function, but a query with arguments, such as *wants_event*, can only be a function.

A command, also known as a **procedure**, has an *is do* ... *end* part too; an example is *delete_connection* above. Procedures and functions provide the computations, and are together known as **routines**.

The feature call mechanism is the only computational facility available in the pure object-oriented form of computation. In particular, the use of infix and prefix operators, as in the following expressions appearing in class *BCSM*, also of chapter 4 (Broadband ISDN), pages 136-137:

Min_state_id >= 0

not has (st)

is viewed simply as syntactical convenience for function calls which, had the features been declared so as to use dot notation, could have been written more verbosely as

min_state_id. greater_than (0)

(has (st)). boolean_negation

1.1.8 The dynamic model

The object-oriented model of computation fits well with a highly dynamic approach to data structures. In Eiffel all objects are created dynamically. For example if *new_call* has been declared of type *CALL*, you may obtain at run time an instance of this class and attach it to *new_call* through a creation instruction, written

!! new_call. make (sp1, is_uni1, sc1)

where *sp1, is_uni1, sc1* are expressions whose types correspond to those of the arguments of the procedure *make* in the class (shown below). !! is the creation symbol.

The above creation instruction not only allocates a new object, but also initializes it through a call to the initialization procedure *make* with the arguments given. This form is necessary because the class appears as:

class CALL creation

   make

feature

   make (sp: SSP; is_uni: BOOLEAN; sc: SIG_CHANNEL) is
      do
             ... Implementation omitted ...
      end;

      ... See above for the other features of *CALL* ...

end -- class *CALL*

The *creation* clause indicates that any creation of an instance of the class must include an initialization call to one of the procedures listed – here the only one, *make*. Had there been no creation clause in the class, a creation instruction would have been written just

!! *new_call*

which will initialize all fields to language-defined default values (such as 0 for integers). By including a creation clause, the author of the class requires clients to call one among a set of designated initialization routines upon creation.

Before it has been the target of a creation instruction, *new_call* is not attached to any object and is said to be void. The tests

new_call = Void

new_call /= Void

will return ***true*** if and only if *new_call* is (respectively) void or attached to an object.

Note that procedure *make* is a normal procedure which, once *new_call* has been attached to an object, can be called on that object in the usual way:

new_call.make (sp1, is_uni1, sc1)

In contrast with the above creation instruction (using !!), this call does not create an object, but simply applies a feature to an existing object.

1.1.9 Assertions

Beyond their implementation, features have abstract properties which should be reflected in the corresponding classes.

Assertions play this role. They describe the effect of features on objects, independently of how the features have been implemented.

Assertions have three major applications: they help produce reliable software; they provide systematic documentation; and they are a central tool for performing testing, debugging and other forms of quality assurance on object-oriented software. People used to other approaches are sometimes skeptical as to the practical applicability of assertions, beyond academic examples, to production software; the examples of this book provide ample evidence that assertions are not just theoretically desirable but practically useful – and routinely used by Eiffel developers.

As our first example of assertion we may look class *PORT* from the Broadband ISDN discussion in chapter 4 (figure 4.12, page 131), whose procedure *deallocate_bw* (deallocate bandwidth) appears as follows:

deallocate_bw (peak_in, average_in, peak_out, average_out: INTEGER) is
              -- Deallocate the bandwidth specified
    require
           bw_is_allocated:
                   peak_in <= allocated_bandwidth_in **and**
                   peak_out <= allocated_bandwidth_out
    do
              ... Implementation of the procedure ...
    ensure
           bw_decreased:
                   old *allocated_bandwidth_in >= allocated_bandwidth_in* **and**
                   old *allocated_bandwidth_out >= allocated_bandwidth_out*

    end

This procedure includes two assertions: a precondition, introduced by **require**, and a postcondition, introduced by **ensure**. Each assertion is a boolean expression, preceded by an optional label (here *bw_is_allocated* for the precondition, *bw_decreased* for the postcondition).

The precondition states the conditions that any call to the procedure must satisfy to the correct. Here these conditions are consistency conditions on the arguments *peak_in* and *peak_out*.

The postcondition states the conditions that the procedure will ensure at the termination of any call. Here it uses the **old** notation, usable in postconditions only, which makes it possible to refer to the value of an expression as if it had been captured on entry to the procedure. The postcondition thus states that any call must decrease or keep the values of *allocated_bandwidth_in* and *allocated_bandwidth_out*.

Along with preconditions and postconditions, which are associated with individual routines (procedures and functions), assertions are used in **class invariants**, which characterize the general properties applicable to all instances of a class. For example class *PORT* has the following invariant (with labels omitted):

allocated_bandwidth_in >= 0;
allocated_bandwidth_out >= 0

This invariant states that the two attributes named must always remain non-negative. (The separating semicolon is equivalent to an **and**.)

The primary purpose of assertions is to help write correct software by encouraging developers state the correctness corrections explicitly. They also serve as tools for testing and debugging, since it is possible under the control of a compilation option to monitor assertions at run time at various levels (preconditions only, preconditions and postconditions, all assertions) to detect bugs which manifest themselves as inconsistencies between the instructions and the assertions. A run-time assertion violation will then cause an exception which (unless the software explicitly includes an explicit provision to recover from the exception through a Rescue clause as described below) will cause the execution to terminate and produce a detailed exception trace showing the assertion that failed and the sequence of calls that led to it.

Assertions also provide an important facility for documenting classes, in particular through the notion of short form discussed below.

The authors of chapter 7 (graphical animation, page 218) make the following comments about their use of assertions:

All the routines and the classes of our libraries are enriched with a set of preconditions, postconditions and invariants that specify their programming interface contract. We put some effort into defining these assertions, because we believe that they are a key element for promoting reusability. [...]

Another interesting fact we noted about assertions is that their use helps to produce efficient software: by clearly defining the responsibilities of each component, we can avoid using defensive programming techniques, and therefore obtain more readable and at the same time more efficient code.

Another good example of assertions is their use to express the formal properties of time intervals (chapter 2, page 44). In this example the assertion part of the language is used in a way that is strongly reminiscent of formal specification languages such as Z.

1.1.10 Information hiding

When writing a class, you will sometimes have to include features which the class needs for internal purposes only: features that are part of the implementation of the class, but not of its interface. It should not be possible for a client to call such a feature.

The mechanism which makes certain features unfit for clients' calls is called information hiding. It facilitates the smooth evolution of software systems by enabling the author of a class to change some of its properties without disturbing existing client classes.

The rule of information hiding states that features should only be exported to clients that absolutely need them. As a consequence, communication between classes is severely limited. In particular, Eiffel does not offer any notion of global variable; classes will exchange information exclusively through feature calls, and through the inheritance mechanism.

The notation for achieving information hiding is illustrated by this sketch of a graphical class (of which a more complete form appears on page 236) from the discussion of three-dimensional animation in chapter 7:

```
class FLIGHT_C ... feature

    target: NODE_3D;

    set_target (other: NODE_3D) is
        do
            target := other
        end
```

feature {*NONE*}

    handle_new_transform (*source*: *T_TRANSFORM*) **is**
        -- Handle the event using a flying vehicle metaphor
    require
        source /= *Void*;
    do
        if *target* /= *Void* **then**
            ... Details omitted ...
        end
    end

end -- class *FLIGHT_C*

The first two features, as all features seen in the previous examples, are exported to all clients; this means that the following extract is valid in any class:

fc: *FLIGHT_C*; *n3*: *NODE_3D*;

...

fc.*set_target* (*n3*)

Procedure *handle_new_transform*, however, appears in a feature clause labeled *feature* {*NONE*}. This means that its features are exported to no client, and can only be used (without dot notation) within the class itself. In other words, the following call would be invalid:

fc.*handle_new_transform* (*o*)

In practice, it is not enough for the information hiding mechanism to support exported features (available to all clients) and secret features (available to no client); class designers must also have the ability to export a feature selectively to a set of designated clients. This is achieved by declaring the feature in a clause which begins by *feature* {*A, B, C*...}, where *A, B, C* ... are the classes to which the features must be exported. (They will also be available to the descendants of these classes, in the inheritance sense discussed below.) This is known as selective export. The previous example of total hiding is in fact a special case of selective export; *NONE* is not a keyword but the name of a special library class, which has no descendants.

1.1.11 The short form of a class

To make information hiding practical, it is necessary to provide users of a class, most notably the authors of potential client classes, with a description containing only the elements of a class that matter to the outside world. This description, known as the short form of the class, includes the following elements for each exported feature:

- The **signature** of the feature: name, list of arguments and their types, type of the result for a query.

- The header comment (which, if present, comes right after the keyword *is* for a routine, or just after an attribute declaration).
- The precondition and postcondition of a routine, if any.

In addition, the short form retains the list of creation procedures and the class invariant. But it contains no mention of non-exported features, and no trace of the implementations (*do* clauses) of exported routines. In addition, for a query without arguments, the short form does not indicate whether the feature is a function or an attribute.

The short form of class *CALL* used above appears in chapter 4 as:

class interface CALL creation procedures

    make (sp: SSP; is_uni: BOOLEAN; sc: SIG_CHANNEL)
       require
           service_switching_point_supplied: sp /= Void;
           signalling_channel_supplied: sc /= Void

feature specification

    connections: CONNECTION;
           -- The connections established by this call
    delete_connection;
           -- Delete the connection for this call.
    ... etc. (see figure 4.13, page 131) ...

end -- class interface *CALL*

The short form uses special terms instead of the language keywords (for example **feature specification** rather than **feature** and **class interface** rather than **class**) so as to avoid any confusion with proper class texts: a short form is documentation, not executable software.

In the development environment, the short form may be generated from the class text by a tool of the environment – the **short** command. This is a useful tool for automatic documentation. Much of the detailed class descriptions in the library documentation is generated in this manner.

More generally, the short form plays a major role in software development since it provides a standard means of communication from developer to developer – and potentially from developer to manager and even users – based on the most important and abstract properties of the software modules, not on irrelevant implementation details. Several of the following chapters rely on short forms to describe the corresponding designs.

1.1.12 Design by contract

The combination of information hiding, feature-based computation and assertions yields a style of software analysis, design and implementation in which various components communicate on the basis of well-defined obligations and guarantees similar to contracts used in the collaboration between persons or between companies. A typical contract governing a routine of a class (the supplier) and a caller (the client) has the following form:

	Obligations	**Benefits**
Client	Ensure precondition before call.	Get the effect of the postcondition when call completes.
Supplier	Ensure postcondition on termination.	No need to deal with cases in which precondition is not satisfied.

This approach, known as Design by Contract [Meyer 1988, 1992a], favors the construction of bug-free systems where correctness is built-in. It has a number of important consequences on the exception mechanism (see next) and the proper use of inheritance.

1.1.13 Exception handling

Abnormal events may occur during the execution of a software system. In object-oriented computation, they often correspond to calls that cannot be executed properly, as a result of a hardware malfunction, of an unexpected impossibility (such as numerical overflow in an addition) or of some software bug.

To produce reliable systems, it is necessary to have the ability to recover from such situations. This is the purpose of an exception mechanism.

An exception is an event which prevents a routine from fulfilling its contract as planned. The routine may react in either of two ways:

- Trying again after changing some of the context. This is known as retry.
- Conceding failure, which means restoring the object's invariant and passing on the exception to the caller (or to the operating system if there is no more caller to be notified). This is known as failure (or "organized panic").

The exception handling mechanism is devised so as to satisfy these requirements. A routine may have a Rescue clause:

r (...) **is**
    require
        ...
    do
        ...
    ensure
        ...
    rescue
        One or more instructions
    end

The "One or more instructions" may include a *retry* instruction. Any exception occurring during the execution of *r* will trigger the Rescue clause. If the Rescue clause executes a *retry*, it will cause a new execution of the routine's normal body – the *do* clause. If it does not execute a *retry*, it will cause failure of the routine's execution, as defined above.

A routine with no Rescue clause is considered to have an empty one, so that any exception occurring during the execution of the routine will cause failure – and an exception in the caller which will then, through to its own Rescue clause if any, be faced with the same choice: retry or failure.

If this process is repeated and the failure is transmitted all the way to the first object that started execution, the execution as a whole fails; this is where, as mentioned above in the discussion of assertions, a precise assertion trace is generated so that the reasons for the failure may be analyzed and corrected.

1.1.14 Static typing

When the execution of a software system causes the call of a certain feature on a certain object, how do we know that this object will be able to handle the call?

To provide such a guarantee of correct execution, the language is statically typed. This means that it enforces a few compatibility rules; in particular:

- Every software entity (that is to say, every name used in the software text to refer to run-time objects, such as *new_call* in the above examples) is explicitly declared as being of a certain type, derived from a class. For example *new_call* was declared as being of type *CALL*, and the three arguments of procedure *make*, from class *CALL*, were declared with types *SSP*, *BOOLEAN* and *SIG_CHANNEL*.

- Feature calls on a certain entity only use features from the corresponding class.

- Assignment and argument passing are subject to **conformance rules**, based on inheritance, which require the source's type to be compatible with the target's type.

Thanks to these rules, it is possible to write a **static type checker** which will accept or reject software systems, guaranteeing that the systems it accepts will not cause any "feature not available on object" error at run time. The ISE Eiffel compiler includes such a static checker.

As pointed out by Paul Johnson in chapter 5, the 2.3 compiler missed some cases of type errors. The underlying problems are discussed in detail in chapter 22 of [Meyer 1992].

1.1.15 Genericity

For typing to be practical, it must be possible to define classes which are parameterized by types; such classes are called generic. For example, the graphical animation system described in chapter 7 needs a notion of history list. This is described (see page 222) by a generic class

HISTORY [*T*]

where T, the formal generic parameter, represents the type of the elements recorded in the history. Then a particular history list may be declared for example as

camera_hist: *HISTORY* [*CAMERA*]

where *CAMERA*, another class introduced in the chapter, describes the characteristics of the camera (including its position and its field of view) at a given instant. Each element in the list attached to *camera_hist* will be an instance of *CAMERA*. Here *CAMERA* is known as the actual generic parameter corresponding to T for the above generic derivation of *HISTORY*. Every practical use of *HISTORY* must specify an actual generic parameter, but the class text itself is shared by all such generic derivations; in that class text, any reference to the type of list elements will simply use the name T.

This form of genericity is called **unconstrained**. A companion facility described below, constrained genericity, involves inheritance.

Genericity is particularly useful for "container" classes which describe data structures containing various objects of compatible types: lists, sets, trees, arrays etc. Many classes of the data structure and algorithm library, EiffelBase, are generic.

1.1.16 Single inheritance

Software development involves a large number of classes; many are variants of others. To remain in control of the resulting potential complexity, we need a classification mechanism, known as inheritance. A class will be an heir of another if it incorporates the other's features in addition to its own. (A *descendant* is a direct or indirect heir; the reverse notion is *ancestor*.) The term "subclass" is also used in this book as a synonym for heir.

Examples of inheritance abound in the following chapters. A typical one appears in chapter 2. Class *ABSOLUTE_TIME* (see figure 2.8, page 42) inherits from *COMPARABLE*, a library class from EiffelBase describing objects on which an order relation exists; this is appropriate since it is possible to compare two absolute time instants (to determine which one occurs before the other). Another heir of *COMPARABLE* is *DURATION*; two durations can also be compared, although in this case the order relation is different (it determines which one of the durations is longer). These classes have their own heirs: for example *DATE* (see figure 2.11, page 48) is an heir of *ABSOLUTE_TIME*, and *YMD_DURATION*, which describes durations expressed in terms of years, months and days in the Gregorian calendar, is an heir of *DURATION*.

Another typical example of inheritance, used again below, appears in chapter 6 (see section 6.5.1, page 189). The code generated by the product modeling tool uses a class *GEO_OBJECT* describing geometric objects. Heirs of this class describe special kinds of geometric objects: *GEO_EDGE, GEO_VERTEX, GEO_FACE*.

The syntax for inheritance is straightforward; for example:

class *ABSOLUTE_TIME* **creation**

   ...

inherit

   COMPARABLE

feature

   ... Features specific to *ABSOLUTE_TIME* ...

end -- class *ABSOLUTE_TIME*

Inheritance is one of the central concepts of the object-oriented methods and has profound consequences on the software development process. Accordingly, many of the following chapters describe and justify in detail the inheritance structure used by the corresponding projects.

1.1.17 Multiple inheritance

It is often necessary to combine two or more abstractions. For example the animation system of chapter 7 uses a class *ANIM_V3D*. An instance of this class, as the name suggests, is a three-dimensional object (and hence should be described by class *VECTOR_3D*) which is also animatable (and hence should be described by class *ANIMATABLE*). As a result, *ANIM_3D* inherits from both *VECTOR_3D* and *HAS_TRACK*, itself an heir of *ANIMATABLE* (see the inheritance diagram of figure 7.3, page 222). Inheritance from two or more classes is called multiple inheritance.

Multiple inheritance is an essential tool for good object-oriented design, and is used heavily in EiffelBase to combine several views. (This approach is extended in chapter 5 by Paul Johnson through the notion of "fine-grained inheritance").

Multiple inheritance raises a few technical problems, in particular the resolution of *name clashes* (cases in which different features, inherited from different classes, have the same name). The language handles this problem in a simple way through a renaming scheme, which also serves to improve readability when an inherited feature can benefit from a new name better adapted to the context of the heir.

A typical example of renaming occurs for creation procedures. The recommended name for the basic creation procedure of a class is *make*. Again in the graphics discussion of chapter 7, class *VIEW* (page 231) has its own creation procedure *make*, but also needs to use the creation procedure inherited from its parent *GAP_LIST* (a generic class). To keep the name *make* for the local creation procedure, it renames the inherited version:

deferred class *VIEW* **inherit**

    GAP_LIST [*VIEWABLE_3D*]
        rename
            make as gap_make
      end

feature

    ... Rest of class omitted (see page 231) ...

end -- class *VIEW*

As a result, the text of *view* may refer to the inherited *make* under the name *gap_make*, with no name clash. (The keyword **deferred** appearing at the beginning of the class is explained below.)

1.1.18 Repeated inheritance

Multiple inheritance raises the possibility of *repeated* inheritance, the case in which a class inherits from another through two or more paths.

In such a case the language must provide precise rules as to what happens to features inherited repeatedly from the common ancestor. It may be desirable for a feature of the common ancestor to yield just one feature of the common descendant in some cases (*sharing*); but in others it should yield two (*replication*). Developers must have the possibility of prescribing either policy separately for each feature.

The rule is that a repeatedly inherited feature is shared if it is inherited under a single name, replicated if the different versions are inherited under different names. This gives developers the required flexibility.

1.1.19 Constrained genericity

The combination of genericity and inheritance gives rise to an important technique, constrained genericity, which makes it possible to specify a class with a generic parameter that represents not an arbitrary type as with the earlier (unconstrained) form of genericity, but a type that must be a descendant of a given class.

For example, the animation system of chapter 7, in its treatment of input (section 7.5.5, page 235), uses a generic class *EVENT* [*H*, *D*] with two formal generic parameters. The first, *H*, represents the type of event handlers. This means that a corresponding actual generic parameter may not be an arbitrary type any more, but must be a descendant of class *HANDLER*. As a result, the class is declared as

> **class** *EVENT* [*H* –> *HANDLER*, *D* –> *DYNAMIC*] *feature*
>
> ... Rest of class omitted
>
> **end** -- class *EVENT*

(The second parameter is also generically constrained.) Thanks to this declaration, any entity *x* declared of type *H* in the class text may be the target of calls to features of class *HANDLER*. Without constrained genericity, only features applicable to all classes (such as *copy* or *equal*, seen below) would be applicable to *x*.

1.1.20 Redefinition

As a class inherits from another, it may need to change the implementation or other properties of some of the inherited features.

For example, the text of class *GEO_EDGE*, which as mentioned above is generated by the product modeling tool of chapter 6, begins (see figure 6.6, page 190) with:

> **class** *GEO_EDGE creation*
>
> > *make*
>
> **inherit**
>
> > *GEO_OBJECT*
> > > **rename**
> > > > *make* **as** *geo_object_make*
> > >
> > > **redefine**
> > > > *boundary, class_parents, local_class_features, ...*
> > >
> > > **end**
>
> **feature**
>
> > ... Rest of class omitted ...
>
> **end** -- class *GEO_EDGE*

This means that the class will provide, in one of its *feature* clauses, a new declaration of the features listed after **redefine**: *boundary, class_parents, local_class_features, ...* For instances of *GEO_EDGE* rather than just *GEO_OBJECT*, the redefined versions override the versions inherited from *GEO_EDGE*.

Redefinition may affect the implementation of a feature, its signature (type of arguments and result), and its specification (assertions). It brings to object-oriented technology one of its key mechanisms for supporting reusability, by making it possible to adapt a reused class to a new context. Without redefinition, the developer who wishes to practice reusability would be forced to adopt an all-or-nothing attitude: reuse a module exactly as it is, or redo it. Thanks to redefinition, it is possible to reuse in part and redo in part.

1.1.21 Polymorphism

With inheritance brought into the picture, the static typing requirement listed above would be too restrictive if it was taken to imply that every entity declared of type C may only refer to objects whose type is exactly C. This would mean for example that an entity of type GEO_OBJECT could not be used to refer to an object of type GEO_EDGE or GEO_FACE, even though these classes simply denote variants of the general notion of geometric object.

Polymorphism is the ability for an entity to become attached to objects of various possible types.

To abide by the rules of static typing and guarantee type safety, polymorphism is strictly controlled by inheritance: for example, we should not allow our GEO_OBJECT entity to become attached to an object representing an object of type PM_OBJECT, a class of the same system which describes a different concept and thus does not inherit from GEO_OBJECT.

The rule is simple: an entity of a certain type X may be assigned a value of a type Y other than X, but only if Y is a descendant of X (that is to say, describes a special case of X, as GEO_FACE does for GEO_OBJECT). This applies both to assignment instructions and to the implicit assignment which occurs for arguments at the time of a routine call, when each actual argument is used to set the initial value of the corresponding formal argument.

The rule uses the inheritance structure to retain the reliability ensured by static typing while allowing the flexibility permitted by polymorphism.

1.1.22 Dynamic binding

The combination of the last two mechanisms mentioned, redefinition and polymorphism, immediately suggests the next one. Assume a call on a polymorphic entity, for example a call to the feature *boundary* on an entity of declared of type GEO_OBJECT. The various descendants of GEO_OBJECT may have redefined the feature in various ways, corresponding to the various algorithms available for computing the boundary of a geometric object. Clearly, there must be an automatic mechanism to guarantee that the version of *boundary* will always be the one deduced from the actual object's type, regardless of how the entity has been declared. This property is called dynamic binding.

In a call of the form

my_object.boundary

where *my_object* is declared of type *GEO_OBJECT*, but may dynamically, as a result of polymorphism, be attached to instances of *GEO_EDGE, GEO_VERTEX* or *GEO_FACE*, dynamic binding guarantees that the proper algorithm for computing the boundary will be applied in each case.

Dynamic binding has a major influence on the structure of object-oriented applications, as it enables developers to write simple calls (meaning, for example, "call feature *boundary* on entity *my_object*)" to denote what is actually several possible calls depending on the corresponding run-time situations. This avoids the need for many of the repeated tests ("Is this an edge? Is this a vertex?") which plague software written with more conventional approaches.

Several chapters emphasize the beneficial influence of this technique on the structure of the software. See for example the discussion of how the various redefinitions of a *render* routine make it possible to use a single, elegant algorithm for rendering a complete scene in graphical animation (chapter 7, page 230-231); a scene is a complex object with many components, but dynamic binding ensures that the appropriate operation is automatically called on each component. A similar technique is used by the simulated annealing system of chapter 5 to print information about the various components of a network (page 156); for each type of such component (node, link, process, channel) there is a different version of the *print_long* procedure. These applications are examples of the fruitful combination of inheritance with genericity, polymorphism and dynamic binding.

1.1.23 Run-time type interrogation

Object-oriented software developers soon develop a healthy hatred for any mechanism based on explicit choices between various types for an object. Polymorphism and dynamic binding provide a much preferable alternative. In some cases, however, an object comes from the outside, so that the software author has not way to predict its type with certainty. This occurs in particular if the object is retrieved from external storage or passed by another application.

The software then needs a mechanism to access the object in a safe way, without violating the constraints of static typing. Such a mechanism should be designed with care, so as not to cancel the benefits of polymorphism and dynamic binding.

The mechanism of **assignment attempt** introduced by Eiffel satisfies these requirements. An assignment attempt, which uses the symbol ?= (as opposed to := for the usual assignment) is a conditional operation: it tries to attach an object to an entity; if at execution time the object's type conforms to the type declared for the entity, the effect is that of a normal assignment; otherwise what is assigned is a special "void" value. For example, with the declarations *go: GEO_OBJECT; gv: GEO_VERTEX*

the assignment attempt

gv ?= go

will assign a non-void value to *gv* if and only if *go* is polymorphically attached to an object of type *GEO_VERTEX* (or a descendant); otherwise it will assign to *gv* a void value.

This important mechanism makes it possible to handle objects whose type is not known for sure, without violating the safety of the type system. Assignment attempt is particularly useful to retrieve objects from external storage, or from other systems, since in this case it is not possible from within the language to guarantee that a certain object will have the expected type.

1.1.24 Deferred features and classes

In some cases for which dynamic binding provides an elegant solution, obviating the need for explicit tests, there is no initial version of a feature meant to be redefined.

Take for example the EiffelBase class *COMPARABLE*, mentioned above. This class describes the general notion of comparable elements, with such features as "less than", which is actually declared as *infix "<"* to allow calls in infix notation as explained above. Class *COMPARABLE* is so general and abstract that it is not possible to provide a default implementation of this feature. This is in contrast with the above case in which *GEO_OBJECT* had a default implementation of *boundary* and other features.

In this case the "less than" feature is declared in *COMPARABLE* as being deferred. This means that the class only specifies the feature, but leaves the actual implementation to its descendants. The keyword *deferred* simply replaces the *do* clause which, for non-deferred features, provides the implementation. Any class such as *COMPARABLE* which has at least one deferred feature must itself be declared as deferred, as follows:

> *deferred class COMPARABLE feature*
>
> > *infix "<" (other: COMPARABLE) is*
> > -- Is current object less than *other*?
> > > *deferred*
> > > *end*;
> >
> > ... Other features omitted ...
> *end* -- class *COMPARABLE*

Thanks to dynamic binding, a call to "<" on an object of type *DATE* or *YMD_DURATION* (two descendants of *COMPARABLE* mentioned above) will trigger the appropriate version, as defined in the corresponding class. To avoid any run-time impossibility, it is not permitted to create an instance of a deferred class.

Deferred features and classes may still be equipped with assertions describing their abstract properties, but their implementation is postponed descendant classes.

Deferred classes (also called abstract classes) are particularly useful for object-oriented analysis and high-level design, as they make it possible to capture the essential aspects of a a system, while leaving details to a later stage. Assertions play an important role here, since they make it possible to attach precise semantic properties to the classes and features at the analysis and design level, without making any implementation commitment.

1.1.25 External routines

The reusability goal – and plain common sense – imply that object-oriented software must be able to communicate with software written in non-object-oriented languages. One approach to this problem, of which the best-known example is C++, is to use a hybrid language, combining a traditional language basis with object-oriented constructs. The Eiffel approach is different: for fear of compromising the consistency of the object-oriented approach at the language level, it provides explicit mechanisms for communication with software written in other languages.

The basic mechanism is simple: a routine may be declared as external. Instead of a body of the **do**... or **deferred** form, such a routine will have a body which is simply **external** *"language_name"*, where *language_name* is *C* or *Fortran* in the examples of this book but can be any language whose argument passing conventions are known to the Eiffel compiler. Almost all projects of this book have relied on such Eiffel encapsulation of external software. You will for example find on page 219 a description of how routines from the Fortran libraries BLAS (Basic Linear Algebra Subprograms) and LAPACK (Linear Algebra Package) were made available as external routines to the graphical animation package of chapter 7.

To the rest of the software, an external routine is just like a normal routine, which may have a precondition and a postcondition, and participate in all the object-oriented games. Only its implementation is special, having been entrusted to a different language.

The use of external routine highlights an important property of the object-oriented approach: its potential role as a packaging tool, which provides powerful structuring mechanisms – classes, assertions, information hiding, single and multiple inheritance, genericity – that can be used to organize existing non-OO software elements into a robust and extendible architecture. The "pure" approach to object-orientation embodied in Eiffel, which clearly separates the object-oriented and non-object-oriented aspects, helps rather than hinders this goal of supporting compatibility with older software and allowing it to be successfully re-engineered.

1.1.26 Further conventions

To understand the detail of the presentations in the following chapters, you need to know about four more simple properties of the approach. (The good news is that if you understand the above notions and these four properties, you essentially know all you need to understand the systems described.)

These four properties all appear in the following function generated by the product modeling tool (figure 6.10, page 194):

```
geo_edge_attributes: X_HASH_TABLE [PM_ATTRIBUTE, STRING] is
     local
                pm_attr: PM_ATTRIBUTE;
                ... Other local entity declarations ...
     once
                !! Result.make (100);
                parent_features := deep_clone (geo_object_attributes);
                Result.merge (parent_features);
                ... Rest of body omitted ...
     end
```

The first property is a simple convention for denoting the result of a function (query routine) within the text of the function itself. The predefined entity *Result* is used for that purpose. The result returned by the function is the value of *Result* on exit. So here the first instruction of the body (after *once*) creates an object; subsequent calls using *Result* as a target (such as the call to *merge* shown) modify this object. The function returns a reference to that object. Note that *Result*, like everything else, is initialized by default on routine entry, so that if no instruction affected *Result* the function would return a void value.

The second property is the use of "once" routines. If, as above, you use the keyword *once* instead of the usual *do* to introduce the instructions making up the body of a routine, the body in question will only be executed for the first call. Subsequent calls will do nothing; if the routine is a function, these subsequent calls will return the value computed by the first call. This is the case with the above function, which actually represents a shared object; the first call to *geo_edge_attributes*, regardless of where the call comes from, will create and initialize that object; later calls will simply return a reference to the same object. Once routines are particularly useful for taking care of initialization without disrupting the modular structure of a system, and for obtaining shared information without introducing global variables.

The third property is the presence of a few features which are available in all classes. Examples are features *clone*, which duplicates an object, *copy*, which copies the fields of an object onto those of an existing one, *equal*, which compares two objects field-by-field for equality, and *deep_clone*, used in the above function, which duplicates an entire structure recursively (not just a single object, as *clone* would do). These features are not part of the language in the strict sense, but come from the a general-purpose library class *ANY*, of which any developer-defined class is automatically a descendant; so any class can use them freely.

The final property is the possibility for a routine to have local entities, initialized anew for each call. The syntax, shown above for the declaration of *pm_attr*, is self-explanatory.

1.1.27 Memory management and garbage collection

The last point on our list of method and language properties may at first appear to belong more properly to the next category – implementation and environment. In fact it belongs to both. But the crucial requirements are those which apply to the language; the rest is simply a matter of good engineering of the implementation.

Object-oriented systems, even more than traditional programs (except in the Lisp world), tend to create many objects with sometimes complex interdependencies. Leaving developers in charge of managing the associated memory, especially when it comes to reclaiming the space occupied by objects that are no longer needed, would be a disaster both for the efficiency of the development process (as it would make software much more complicated and occupy a considerable part of the developers' time) and for the safety of the resulting systems (as it raises the risk of improper recycling of memory areas). For this reason most experts in the field agree that in a good object-oriented environment memory management should be automatic, under the control of a *garbage collector*, a component of the run-time system.

The reason this is a language issue as much as an implementation requirement is that a language that has not been explicitly designed for automatic memory management may make it impossible. This problem arises in particular for languages based on C, where a pointer to an object of a certain type may be temporarily converted, through "casts" (also called "coercions", for example by Paul Johnson on page 163), into a pointer of another type or even into an integer, making it difficult to write a safe a garbage collector. Languages such as Simula, Smalltalk and Eiffel were designed to make garbage collection possible.

The Eiffel environment provides an automatic garbage collector. The garbage collector is incremental (avoiding situations where the application would suddenly come to a halt to enable full collection), and a supporting library class, *MEMORY*, provides features for fine-tuning its operation. In particular the procedure *collection_off*, complemented by *collection_on*, makes it possible to disable the collector temporarily when appropriate, for example during the execution of a critical loop in a real-time system or another application with strict response time requirements.

1.2 IMPLEMENTATION AND ENVIRONMENT

We come now to the principal features of an environment supporting object-oriented software construction.

1.2.1 Compilation, portability and C generation

Although interpreted implementations of object-oriented languages have enjoyed some success, it is generally desirable to use compilation as the basic implementation scheme. Compilation is particularly interesting for the efficiency of the resulting code and for the improvement in reliability made possible by the various checks that a compiler performs – in particular, for a typed language, type consistency checks.

The compilation technique used by ISE implementations of Eiffel uses C as the target of the compiler. It then relies on a C compiler to generate the final code.

This use of C as portable assembly language has a number of advantages:

- It helps make the Eiffel compiler portable to many different platforms.

- It facilitates communication of object-oriented software with other software written in C, through the external routine mechanism mentioned above. All the developments described in this book used this possibility in some way or other.

- It makes it possible to use the compiler and environment for **cross-development**: from an Eiffel system, an option of the compiler generates a self-contained C package which can then be ported to a completely different platform.

1.2.2 Automatic update

More than by anything else, software development is characterized by change. Developers don't write thousands of lines at a time; they proceed by addition and modification, starting most of the time from a system that is already of substantial size.

When performing such an update, it is essential to have the guarantee that the resulting system will be consistent. For example, if you change a feature f of class C, you must be certain that every descendant of C which does not redefine f will be updated to have the new version of f, and that every call to f in a client of C or of a descendant of C will trigger the new version.

Most conventional approaches to this central problem of software development require developers to record all dependencies, and track their changes, using special mechanisms known as "make files" and "include files". This technique, still used in most implementations of C-based languages, is hard to accept in the object-oriented world where the dependencies between classes, resulting from the client and inheritance relations, are often complex, but may be deduced from a systematic examination of the software text.

With the ISE Eiffel compiler, the dependencies are processed automatically. After a change, the compiler determines what the changes have been, and what parts of the software must be recompiled as a result. This relieves software developers from a tedious and error-prone manual activity.

1.2.3 Fast update

In practice, the mechanism for updating the system after some changes should not only be automatic, it should be fast. More precisely, it should be proportional to the size of the changed parts, not to the size of the system as a whole. If this condition is not met, the method and environment may be applicable to small systems, but not to large ones.

The ISE Eiffel 2.3 implementation, used by the projects in this book, is criticized in chapter 5 as too slow for recompilations after changes to large systems, due in part to its use of a traditional linking phase.

The ISE Eiffel 3 implementation has addressed the problem by relying on a new approach known as the **Melting Ice technology**. The elements that have changed are usually not recompiled but interpreted, making the updating process significantly faster. As long as the changed elements are only a small part of the system, the impact of interpretation on overall system performance is small. When they become too big, the developers may start a recompilation process, which will take longer than a quick update but can be done off-line.

The name of this technology comes from the physical analogy used to describe it: a compiled system is similar to a frozen block of ice; the changed elements are "melted"; when too much has been melted, the developers will "re-freeze" the project. In both cases the analysis of what needs to be changed is, as with previous approaches, performed automatically by the environment (rather than manually by the developers).

The intent pursued by the Melting Ice technology is to combine the safety and efficiency of traditional compiled implementations with the speed of update which has made interpreted environments popular.

1.2.4 Persistence

Many applications, perhaps most, will need to conserve objects from one session to the next. The environment should provide a mechanism to do this in a simple way.

An object will often contain references to other objects; since the same may be true of these objects, this means that every object may have a large number of *dependent* objects, with a possibly complex dependency graph (which may involve cycles). It would make no sense to store or retrieve the object without all its dependents. A persistence mechanism which always stores an object's dependents along with the object is said to be **reference-complete**.

Some of the applications described in this book have relied on the reference-complete persistence mechanism offered by the environment through two library classes, *STORABLE* and *ENVIRONMENT*. If x is of type *STORABLE*, the procedure call

> x. *store* (*file*)

will store into *file* the entire data structure beginning with the object attached to x. A procedure *retrieve* then makes it possible to retrieve that structure from the file.

For some applications, mere persistence support is not sufficient; such applications will need full database support, either through interfaces to relational databases or by using an object-oriented database. None of the projects described in this book used an object-oriented database (which is perhaps a sign of the industry perception that the OODB field is still in its formative stage). The network surveillance system (chapter 3, see section 3.3.2, page 85) needed more than the above persistence mechanism, and used the external C routine facility to build an interface to a proprietary indexed file system.

ISE Eiffel 3 includes a new library, EiffelStore, which provides a unified persistence mechanism. EiffelStore offers interface to various persistence back-ends (relational databases such as Ingres and Oracle, object-oriented databases, *STORABLE*), shielding developers from the irrelevant details of any particular back-end.

1.2.5 Other tools

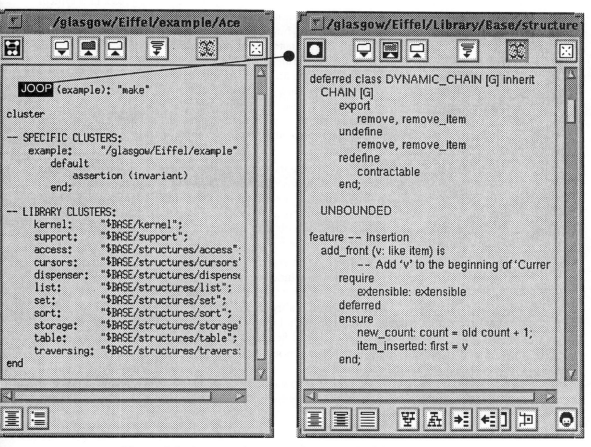

Figure 1.1: A screen from the ISE Eiffel 3 environment

An object-oriented method and language should be supported by an object-oriented environment. A proper definition of this notion should reflect the need to carry over the fundamental concepts of the object-oriented method – in particular abstraction and object-based decomposition – to the interface between the development environment and its users, the software developers. The following definition characterizes the properties of an object-oriented environment worthy of this name:

> A software development environment is object-oriented if it enables
> developers to produce software through the direct manipulation of
> visual elements representing abstracted objects.

Although the 2.3 environment offered some useful tools for browsing (exploring classes and their connections) and debugging, used by the projects described in this book, it fell short of this definition. ISE Eiffel 3, of which figure 1.1 above presents a typical snapshot, is a visual environment and was designed with the aim of meeting the definition. [Meyer 1993] describes the interaction principles that presided over its design. Developers work through visual abstractions representing the objects of software development: systems, classes, routines, run-time objects, explanations. To execute the various operations of software development, users of this environment manipulate the objects through their visual representations; the basic mechanism is **typed drag-and-drop,** whereby users drop "pebbles" associated with objects into the corresponding "holes". Just as the method and language rely on static typing, the pebbles and holes are typed; for example, a round pebble, representing a class, cannot be dragged into a cross-shaped pebble, representing a routine.

Traditional development environments (even when meant for object-oriented languages) are function-based, including such functional tools as a browser or a tester. In a truly object-oriented environment, as noted, the tools should be based on object abstractions; an activity such as browsing is achieved by manipulating the objects on the screen (for example picking the name of a class in the text of another class, and dragging it to a new class tool).

The environment also includes an interactive debugger based on the same general principles. The discussion of chapter 5 includes some complaints about the lack of such a debugger in the 2.3 version. As this chapter and others in this volume note, however, the debugging process in Eiffel is considerably aided by the presence of the assertion mechanism, which makes it possible to find many potential bugs early by checking the consistency of the software and its specification. In addition, several features of the method and language imply that some serious bugs that are common and damaging in other approaches occur here much less often, or not at all; this is true in particular of static typing, which allows the compiler to catch many potential errors, and of automatic garbage collection, which avoids dangling references, "memory leaks" and other dangers of manual memory management.

1.3 LIBRARIES

One of the major aspects of developing software in the object-oriented way is the ability to rely on existing libraries and to develop new ones.

The libraries form an important part of the environment used by the projects in this book. For further references on these topics, see [Meyer 1989], the library manual on which they relied, and [Meyer 1990], an article which describes the design concepts behind the libraries.

1.3.1 Basic libraries

The EiffelBase library, formerly known as just "the basic library", covers fundamental data structures of computing science – sets, lists, trees, stacks ... – and the associated algorithms – sorting, searching, traversing, pattern matching. The corresponding classes are constantly used by most developments, and often account for an important part of the final code. For example, the description of the network surveillance system in chapter 3 indicate (section 3.3.3, page 87) that along with the application-specific TRICS module which forms the core of the development a significant part of the final code comes from the general-purpose classes of EiffelBase.

1.3.2 Graphics and user interfaces

Many modern software systems are interactive and make use of convenient graphical mechanisms and other user interface techniques. This is one of the areas where the object-oriented model has proved most impressive and helpful. Developers should be able to build graphical applications quickly and effectively through the use of graphical and user interface libraries.

The 2.3 implementation included a graphics library covering basic windowing and graphical need. In ISE Eiffel 3 this has evolved into the EiffelVision library, a toolkit-independent library which provides many GUI (graphical user interface) abstractions, from scrolling windows and buttons to figures and events. Versions for several toolkits (such as Motif and OpenLook) are provided; developers can switch from one toolkit to another without change to the source code. The environment itself (see figure 1.1 above) was built using EiffelVision.

The EiffelBuild application development system provides an interactive framework for developing GUI applications, based on a context-event-behavior model. The output of EiffelBuild is a set of classes containing calls to the features of EiffelVision.

1.3.3 Other libraries

Other important libraries include:

- EiffelLex and EiffelParse, the lexical analysis and parsing libraries used by the simulated annealing project of chapter 5. EiffelParse, in particular, uses an object-oriented approach to the modeling of grammars and their analysis.
- EiffelStore, the persistence mechanism mentioned above.
- Other library components supplied by independent developers, and collectively known as the Eiffel Shelf.

It is clear that the library development effort is still in its early stages, and that much of the work in the coming years will be devoted to covering as many application areas as possible with high-quality reusable components.

1.3.4 Library evolution and indexing mechanisms

Developing high-quality libraries is a long and arduous task. It is impossible to guarantee that the design of library will be perfect the first time around. An important problem, then, is to enable library developers to update and modify their designs without wreaking havoc in existing systems that depend on the library. This important property belongs to the library category, but also to the method and language category.

This crucial long-term issue has been recognized in the language design through a mechanism which makes it possible to declare a feature or a class as *obsolete*, leaving it temporarily usable by existing clients, but preparing the migration to newer versions.

Another problem raised by libraries is the need for mechanisms to identify the classes addressing a certain need. This need affects all three categories: libraries, language (as there must be a way to enter indexing information within the text of each class) and tools (to process queries for classes satisfying certain conditions). The language supports it in the form of an *indexing* clause which developers may include in each class to provide information that advanced browsing tools can then exploit to facilitate index-based query and retrieval of reusable software components.

The Telstra (Telecom Australia) development provides a good example of how a project can use the *indexing* clause for systematic documentation of classes. See for example the clause which appears at the beginning of class *I_ACTIVE* on page 122. Each indexing line consists of an indexing keyword, such as *author* or *summary*, followed by a colon and one or more indexing values, for example *"David Giddy"* for the *author* line. The keywords and values are free, but may be standardized within a project or a company, as was clearly done at Telstra. One of the uses of indexing in this example is to provide a link with the configuration management tool, here SCCS (see the line having *sccsid* as its indexing keyword).

As the technology advances, and more sophisticated applications such as the ones of this book start yielding many reusable components, either as their main result or as side products, the need for such tools will grow. The method and the language stand ready to support this growth.

1.3.5 Bibliographical note

For book-length presentations of the issues discussed in this overview see [Meyer 1988], focusing on the method, and [Meyer 1992], focusing on the language. [Meyer 1990a] describes the 2.3 environment, used by the projects in this book, and [Meyer 1993] the principles behind the current ISE Eiffel 3 environment.

2

Temporal software components

Ted Lawson, Carmel Balthazaar and Alex Gray
University of Wales,
Cardiff (United Kingdom)

2.1 INTRODUCTION

In this chapter we describe a set of classes in the Eiffel object-oriented programming language [Meyer 1988, 1992] which act as "temporal" software components, offering useful services to specific application systems which need to process time-related information. Developing software components is considered to be a major application of object-oriented methods, and it is through such methods that a software engineering "component culture" may one day be established [Meyer 1990b]. Within such a culture, most software development effort would be spent on building software tools and reusable component libraries, rather than specific application systems. Current software engineering practices, which are labour intensive, would be replaced by a capital intensive approach, constituting, in effect, an industrial revolution in software development [Wegner 1984].

We were initially motivated to develop these classes through an interest we had in temporal services built into relational database management systems. Embodying various concepts of time in software has been a significant research activity in various areas of computing including artificial intelligence, office systems, distributed systems and database management systems. See in particular [Allen 1985, Barbic 1985, Clifford 1983, Gadia 1986, Hajnicz 1989, Hajnicz 1990, Jones 1980a, Lamport 1978, Snodgrass 1985]. Object-oriented DBMSs were starting to appear at the time and we were curious to see how these could be extended with temporal services, but we also realised that an embodiment of time in object-oriented software would be novel and useful in its own right.

The Eiffel classes described here are not yet "closed" in the sense that they are still being extended at the time of writing, and we are waiting to use them in their first non-trivial real-world application. Nevertheless, they provide an illustration of an Eiffel application – one that the reader should be able to assimilate easily because the application area should be familiar from everyday experience.

For many applications, especially scientific and engineering ones, the problem of embodying time in software is very straightforward because in these applications time can be treated simply as a number; it can be modelled using ordinary numerical arithmetic and processed by computer using ordinary numerical routines. This simple model has the advantage that it is independent of scale: the number 1, for example, can be used to represent any unit of time from say one picosecond to one millennium – whatever is appropriate to the application; and it can cover different definitions or concepts of time, such as time in the sense of the precise moment at which an event occurs, or time in the sense of the elapsed time between two events.

In applications more closely tied to human affairs, however, the problem is more difficult because time models are more elaborate and more varied. To begin with, time is usually represented not just as a single number but as a combination of different fixed-scale quanta or "granularities". The commonest ones, such as days and years, are closely linked to natural cyclic events which govern the lives of all human beings, such as the sun rising and the seasons changing. Others such as weeks and calendar months are based primarily on convention. More specialised granularities may arise in particular application areas. One example is the "working day", used in banking applications and some areas of business.

Anomalies between different granularities lead to complications. For instance, a commonly used temporal notion such as a "six month period" cannot be converted into a precise number of days without knowing which particular months the period covers. Further complications, which manifest themselves as, for example, leap years, time zones, and daylight saving, arise because of the peculiarities of the natural events on which some granularities are based. Yet more difficulties can occur because the conventions on which certain granularities are based may vary between nations or cultures. Textual representations of time also vary to a wide degree according to local custom and language.

On a more cerebral level, human beings can think about and specify time in different ways. The time at which a particular event occurs can be specified purely as, say, a date but, as many commentators have pointed out, it is much more common for humans to specify events by reference to other events, using relations such as "before", "during", and "after".

Clearly it is possible to model time in a rich variety of ways depending on the different temporal granularities, anomalies, conventions, concepts, relations and so on that the model covers. When it comes to embodying time in software, the designer of the software has to decide which model it should reflect.

The choice of model will affect the reusability of the software, i.e. its ability to offer useful services to a range of different applications. If the model is too general, the software may supply too little functionality and therefore be of relatively little value to an application programmer. If it is too specific then useful functionality may be available only to applications which fall within a narrow domain. If the model is too large, and attempts to incorporate, for example, many variations, then the software may not be cost-effective to develop or it may be too unwieldy for application programmers to understand and use.

This reflects a fundamental problem (perhaps the fundamental problem) that must be addressed when designing any set of reusable software components. The designer has to choose the degree of generality, functionality and practicality in the set, where these qualities are inversely related to one another.

It is thought that object-oriented languages, through their support for data abstraction, abstract data types, inheritance and dynamic binding, offer at least a partial solution because they allow a model to be embodied in software and then for the embodiment to be extended incrementally and in a controlled way in different directions as different potentially useful services are identified.

The Eiffel object-oriented language was designed particularly to address the problems associated with software component development and so we chose this language as the vehicle for embodying the temporal components.

At the time of writing, Eiffel is still in the process of becoming widely established as a programming language and Eiffel environments are not as readily available as those of some older object-oriented languages. So the potential reusability of our components is, at present, not as large as if we had chosen a more popular language. However, Eiffel code has a dimension of use which transcends the availability of Eiffel environments and which is not nearly so practicable in most other languages: Eiffel works well as a design and specification language. This is primarily because it enforces strong static polymorphic typing and because it provides a facility to embed executable assertions within classes. This means, for example, that the temporal classes described in this chapter can be used, not just as executable modules, but also as a semi-formal specification of the time model they embody. The model can be easily extracted from the code and implemented in another programming language. Therefore, possession of the components should allow an application programmer to exploit at least some of the analysis and design effort that was invested in their development.

In the rest of this chapter we describe how we went about developing the components, the temporal model we used, and the cluster of Eiffel classes which embody it. We then describe some extensions, in particular the implementation of time zones, daylight saving and "working days". We also look briefly at some future directions for extension, in particular the development of a general temporal event handler, capable of invoking actions at specific times, and the possibility of specifying the time of such events using temporal relations.

2.2 DEVELOPMENT METHOD

It is recognised that there is no truly systematic way to develop good software [Parnas 1986]; there is no well-defined sequence of steps that a developer can follow which will inexorably result in a high quality software system. Even if such a method did exist it would not necessarily be appropriate to the development of software components say, as opposed to specific applications, or to development using one particular tool, such as Eiffel. Absence of any mechanistic approach seems to characterise object-oriented development in particular [Booch 1991, page 188]; but there are a range of techniques associated with object-oriented development, the production of reusable software components and Eiffel programming that are recognised as being beneficial and worth pursuing. We consider the following activities to be particularly important:

- Domain analysis.
- System modelling.
- Generalisation
- Use of deferred classes.
- Use of a design notation.

Domain analysis [Neighbors 1984, Booch 1991] amounts to discovering the abstractions or concepts that are appropriate to a particular application area. For object-oriented analysis these will be abstract data types. Once discovered they can be organised into a model which can then be embodied in software. It is recognised [Standish 1984] that creating reusable components requires that the model they embody be stable and mature. It is difficult to develop generally useful components for application areas where there are no well-established abstractions.

Fortunately, much work had been done in the area of time modelling when we began this project, and a number of time models had become established. We investigated these and were able to select one as the starting point for our system. We chose the time model incorporated in the RUBIS relational database management system [Nobecourt 1988]. Several other temporal extensions to relational database systems exist [Jones 1980a, Sadeghi 1988, Sarada 1990, Snodgrass 1985, Snodgrass 1987] but we felt that the RUBIS model was the most complete of these. Searching out these models and assessing them took a significant amount of development effort. We also took note of the rather more restricted and ad-hoc time-related services provided by some well-established software systems including the UNIX libraries and several popular programmable spreadsheet systems.

We proceeded to embody the RUBIS time model in an initial cluster of Eiffel classes, details of which are given in [Balthazaar 1991]. We implemented them conscious always of the potential for exploiting existing software, primarily in the form of the ISE Eiffel library classes [Meyer 1989]. A number of these were ultimately used in the implementation, mainly ones from the Kernel and Structures clusters.

We tested our classes for correctness and then embarked on an exercise to see what useful extensions could be made to them. Two methods were used. One was simply to determine whether more aspects of the RUBIS model could be usefully embodied in the cluster. The other involved a paper and pencil exercise to see if the classes could be applied in a particular application area. The area chosen was banking. Various practices in a medium-sized banking organisation were analysed with temporal concepts particularly in mind. This exercise was intended to identify any shortcomings in the classes and any specialised temporal abstract data types which could potentially be embodied as new classes, inheriting perhaps from the primary `ones. We describe the main extensions in section 2.5.

The RUBIS system, and the time-related services in UNIX etc., are all "flat" in the sense that each temporal abstraction they reflect exists at just one level of generality. With object-orientation, of course, inheritance can be used to link classes together so that they reflect specialised and generalised versions of an abstract data type. Generalised classes can be derived from specialised ones in two ways:

- By identifying general aspects of a specialised class and abstracting them out.
- By factoring out the commonality between different specialised classes.

Such activities, typically carried out during "generalisation" phases of the development process, are considered to be very important for producing good software components [Meyer 1990b]. The most general classes created in this way are typically *deferred* classes (i.e. virtual or abstract ones). These will contain type information and quite possibly assertions, but some or all of their features will be unimplemented. They usually appear at the top of inheritance hierarchies and are used to prescribe the semantics of more specialised classes, which inherit from them. (For a fuller discussion see [Meyer 1990, Meyer 1992 pages 145-146].) Deferred classes are a way of embodying a model's abstract data types within a class cluster without tying them to any particular implementation.

We carried out a generalisation phase after the first set of classes had been implemented, driven to some extent by the results of the extension exercise. The existing class features were repartitioned into more, finer-grained classes. These new classes fell into two groups:

- Time-representation-independent-classes.
- Time-representation-dependent-classes.

Classes in the first group, two of which are deferred, embody temporal abstract data types that do not depend on representing time in any particular way, e.g. through any particular combination of granularities, such as days, years, etc. Classes in the second group, which inherit from the first, are more specialised and mainly reflect the semantics of the Gregorian calendar. Both groups are discussed in detail in the main body of this chapter.

Eiffel's suitability as a design language meant that we could use it at the design stage to specify a class's interface well before any of its implementation was produced; but we found that diagrams were needed too. These could be pitched at a more abstract level than the code and were better able to illustrate clusters of classes, class signatures, relations between classes and so on. Several different graphical notations have been devised recenlly for object-oriented design (e.g. [Booch 1991, Ackroyd 1991]) but none has yet emerged as a *de facto* standard. We therefore had to select a suitable notation. The one we chose has the advantage that it has been in use for some time. It was not originally intended for object-oriented design but we have been able to adapt it readily for that purpose. It is based on a diagram invented by the so-called "4ADJ group" of computer scientists who, in the 1970s, investigated the algebraic properties of abstract data types. ADJ diagrams have been used in a number of seminal works (e.g. [Goguen 1978, Jones 1980]) for illustrating the signatures of abstract data types. We used them throughout the development process and especially in the generalisation phase. Our version of the ADJ notation is described in the next section.

2.2.1 Extended ADJ diagrams

A traditional ADJ diagram depicts abstract data types as annotated circles (or ellipses or boxes); functions as annotated dots; and the signatures of each function (i.e. the type of the return value and the type of each argument) as arrowed lines running between the function and the data type of each element in the function's signature. Functions which share the same signature appear as different annotations on the same dot.

We use the diagrams to depict groups of Eiffel classes or types, and their interfaces. In our diagrams the large circles or ellipses represent classes or types (in Eiffel each class is associated with a type) and the dots represent class features, i.e. attributes (data fields) of the class's instances and operations (procedures and functions) which can be applied to those instances. In Eiffel, every operation has an implicit formal argument *Current*. This is always explicitly included in the diagrams as an arrowed line in the representation of the signature for the operation. In the diagrams, functions that take only the *Current* argument are indistinguishable from attributes, which is convenient since there is often no need to make the distinction at the design stage.

We have added four extensions to the original notation:

- An operation that alters the state of its *Current* object is indicated by a pair of opposing arrowheads on the line between the operation and the object's class. There is a convention in Eiffel that such operations are carried out only by procedures and never by functions, so this graphical device generally serves to distinguish procedures from functions.

- A deferred feature of a class, one that does not have an implementation, appears as an open dot (or small circle).

- The features belonging to a particular class are identified by a shaded area enclosing the class and the features;

- An "inherits from" relationship between classes is depicted as an uninterrupted arrow from the heir to the parent.

The extensions are illustrated in figure 2.1. This example depicts two classes from the ISE Eiffel structures library. The generic class *STACK* [*T*] is shown with five deferred features: two *BOOLEAN* functions, *empty* and *full*, a procedure, *put* which takes an argument of arbitrary type T, a function *item* which returns a result of type *T*, and a procedure *remove* which takes no arguments except, implicitly, a stack object. All these features are effected in the generic class *FIXED_STACK* [*T*] which inherits from *STACK* [*T*].

ADJ diagrams of course have their limitations. For example, they say little about

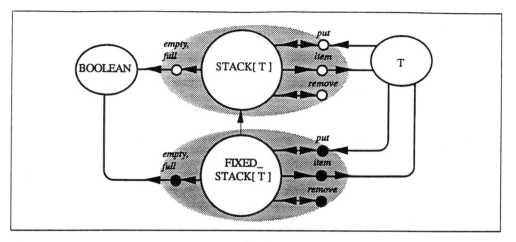

Figure 2.1: Extended ADJ diagram example

the semantics of individual features except what can be inferred from the names and signatures. Also, they show no distinction between value and reference semantics: a function in Eiffel can return either an object or just a reference to it but the diagrams do not indicate which. Relationships between objects can be depicted, but only in a round-about way, as operations (typically called *attach*, *detach* etc.) which establish or break the relationship. Systems where many different relationships may exist between objects are better described using more abstract means such as entity-relationship diagrams (see e.g. [Rumbaugh 1991, Coad 1989]).

Despite their limitations we have found ADJ diagrams to be helpful, and better in some ways than more recently developed notations. Firstly, they are economic – only a limited number of symbol types are used. This makes them easy to learn and very easy to sketch out by hand, which is particularly convenient when debating the merits of particular class and feature configurations in a software design group. Also, classes and their features are depicted separately. This is useful early in the design phase, and when features are being repartitioned during a generalisation phase, because, where a function is identified as having several arguments of different types, the class in which it should reside may not be immediately apparent. In an ADJ diagram one is not forced to make a commitment – functions can simply float between classes.

2.3 TIME-REPRESENTATION-INDEPENDENT CLASSES

In section 2.2 we said that the Eiffel temporal classes are divided into two groups according to whether or not they are dependent on a particular representation of time. We will shortly describe the classes in the first group – the representation-independent ones. Their representation-independence can be carried over to "client" classes – classes which use them. They also prescribe the general behaviour of classes in the second group, which inherit from them. First, though, we will discuss the representation- independent model of time that they embody.

2.3.1 Representation-independent model

This model is similar to the RUBIS one, but with the representation-dependent parts removed. Much of it may appear to be self-evident and almost not worth any discussion since it clearly follows everyone's common notion of time. However, we present it here mainly to distinguish clearly between representation dependence and independence. What has been left out of the model is perhaps more significant than what has been included.

We start with the notion of a time running on a "temporal axis", which is infinite in the past and future. From this we can identify three basic temporal abstract data types:

- Absolute Time.
- Time Interval.
- Duration.

An absolute time is a specific point on the axis. It corresponds to a particular moment in time such as

"the Big Bang",
"EInstein's birth",
"5.00 am on 18th April 1955",
"now",
"the end of the world".

All absolute time points, e.g. tp_1, tp_2, on the axis can be compared with one another and the comparison operations are transitive, as expected. These properties are specified formally in figure 2.2. We will consider some other operations appropriate to absolute times shortly.

The second type of time, the Time Interval, is a segment of the time axis between

$\forall$ $tp1$ $tp2$ $\in$ temporal axis	$\forall tp1$ $tp2$, $tp3$ $\in$ temporal axis
$tp1 = tp2$	if $tp1 < tp2$
or $tp1 < tp2$	and $tp2 < tp3$
or $tp1 > tp2$	then $tp1 < tp3$
comparative properties	transitive property

Figure 2.2: Comparative and transitive properties for absolute time points

two specific points. It is a kind of temporal "solid", just as a cube is a spatial solid; it has an inside and an outside. A huge range of common temporal concepts can be thought of as time intervals; for example:

"the Cretaceous period",
"Einstein's lifetime",
"August 1914",

"the summer of 1942",
"the last 3 minutes",
"tomorrow morning",
"the next TOOLS conference".

(Incidentally, the name "Time Interval" for this type is not particularly apt because the term is often used in everyday language to describe temporal objects which are not tied to any particular points on the time axis. It is, however, the name used in the RUBIS model and it does seem to have become fairly well-established in the literature.)

One way to define a time interval is as an ordered pair of absolutes: a start time and a finish time, where the start is less than the finish. The time interval "Einstein's lifetime", for example, can be defined as the pair of absolutes ["Einstein's birth", "Einstein's death"].

There are some operations which we can apply to intervals and absolutes. An absolute time can be compared with an interval to see if it occurs before or after it, or belongs inside it. Figure 2.3 illustrates these.

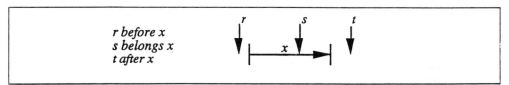

Figure 2.3: Comparison operations between intervals and absolutes

Time intervals can also be compared with one another. Figure 2.4 illustrates nine interval comparison operations.

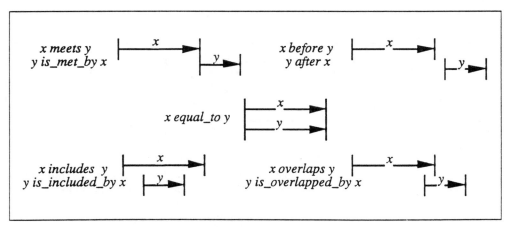

Figure 2.4: Comparison operations on time intervals

Two set-theoretic operations can be defined on time intervals: union and intersection. They are illustrated in figure 2.5. Union and intersection are only valid if there is at least one time point common to both intervals. In other words, one time interval should:

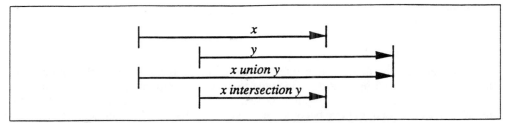

Figure 2.5: Union and intersection operations on time intervals

- meet the other

or   • include the other

or   • overlap the other

or   • be equal to the other.

The third time type in our model is the Duration. A duration is a length of time independent of any particular absolute time or time interval. Durations are purely relative times. They correspond to concepts such as

"a geological age",
"Einstein's age at death",
"a human generation",
"a 12-month guarantee",
"a 50-nanosecond delay".

Notice that a duration can be used to help specify a time interval. For example, we can define the time interval "Einstein's lifetime" using the duration "Einstein's age at death" along with either of the absolute times "Einstein's birth" or "Einstein's death" (figure 2.6).

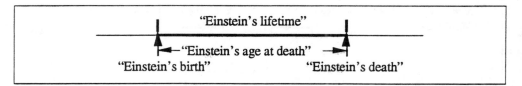

Figure 2.6: Specification of a time interval by a duration

Arithmetic operations connect absolute times and durations. Figure 2.7 illustrates these. One absolute time can be subtracted from another to give the elapsed time between them, which is a duration (example 1); and conversely, a duration can be added to or subtracted from an absolute time to give another absolute time (examples 2 and 3). However, it makes little sense to add two absolute times together: the result in example 4 has no obvious meaning. In fact, the arithmetic terms "add" and "subtract" are perhaps rather misleading here since, unlike their familiar numerical namesakes, the operations only make sense on absolute times when they are not closed, i.e. when they also involve durations. Nevertheless these are the terms used in the RUBIS model and we decided to stick with them.

1	"Einstein's death"	–	"Einstein's birth"	=	"Einstein's age at death"
2	"Einstein's birth"	+	"Einstein's age at death"	=	"Einstein's death"
3	"Einstein's death"	–	"Einstein's age at death"	=	"Einstein's birth"
4	"Einstein's birth"	+	"Einstein's death"	=	?

Figure 2.7: Arithmetic operations linking absolute times and durations

Durations, unlike absolutes times, behave much like ordinary numbers, and can sensibly be added to and subtracted from one another: the result of an operation such as "Einstein's age at death" + "a human generation" is clear. Furthermore, subtraction leads to an obvious notion of negative durations. However, multiplying one duration by another duration is not sensible (what is "a human generation" * "Einstein's age at death" ?), but multiplying a duration by an integer is ("a human generation" * 3 = "three human generations"). Division and modulus by integers also make sense.

That completes the model. Notice that it does not include any operation or property which depends on representing absolute times, durations or time intervals in any particular way. It is therefore very abstract and very general. We now look at three Eiffel classes, *ABSOLUTE TIME*, *DURATION* and *TIME_INTERVAL* corresponding to the three types described above, which together embody the model in software. Their main features are summarised in the ADJ diagram in figure 2.8.

2.3.2 Class *ABSOLUTE_TIME*

This class contains all the model's comparison operations involving absolute times, and the arithmetic operations involving absolutes and durations.

Comparison operations between two absolutes are inherited from the class *COMPARABLE* in the Eiffel Kernel Library [Meyer 1989], which contains the features

<, >, >=, <=

In *COMPARABLE*, the < operation is deferred and the other three operations are implemented in terms of it. The operation < must remain deferred in class *ABSOLUTE_TIME* because its implementation cannot be defined without knowing how absolute times are represented. This means that the whole class must be deferred.

A function *equal* is obtained from class *ANY*, which all Eiffel classes inherit by default. We will describe the other operations of *ABSOLUTE_TIME* in section 2.3.5, after introducing the other two classes.

2.3.3 Class *DURATION*

This class also inherits the comparison operators <, >, >= and <=from *COMPARABLE* and *equal* from *ANY*. Six arithmetic operations are introduced too:

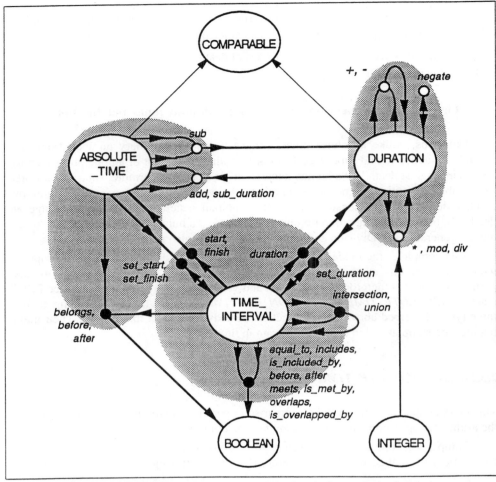

Figure 2.8: Signatures of representation independent classes

infix "+" (*other: like Current*): *like Current*
  deferred
infix "−" (*other: like Current*): *like Current*
  deferred
infix "*" (*other: INTECER*): *like Current*
  deferred
infix "div" (*other: INTEOER*): *like Current*
  deferred
infix "mod" (*other: INTEGER*): *like Current*
  deferred
negate
  deferred

The use of the *like* operator here avoids the need to redefine each function in any heirs of *DURATION*. The technique is fully explained in [Meyer 1988, pages 268-270].

The implementation and precise semantics of all of this class's features are heavily dependent on how durations are to be represented, and so they, and therefore the whole class, must be deferred.

2.3.4 Class *TIME_INTERVAL*

It happens that all the operations of this class can be implemented in terms of operations on absolutes and durations. So this class, unlike *ABSOLUTE_TIME* and *DURATION*, can be a fully implemented one rather than a deferred one.

An instance of class *TIME_INTERVAL* is represented by three attributes: its start time, its finish time and its duration. These are available via the exported features

> *start, finish: ABSOLUTE_TIME*

and

> *duration: DURATION.*

The attributes can be set by the operations

> *setstart* (*a: ABSOLUTE_TIME*)
> *setfinish* (*a: ABSOLUTE_TIME*)
> *set_duration* (*d: DURATION*)

A time interval can be defined by any two of the three attributes. So these operations are implemented in such a way that after any setting operation, the two most recently set attributes are used to update the remaining one. This ensures consistency within an instance's attribute values. Formally, we can say that all three operations maintain the class invariant

> **invariant**
> *equal* (duration, finish.sub (start)).

In our original pre-generalisation classes [Balthazaar 1991] this was not the case. Instead the *start* attribute was considered to be superior to the other two and could only be set via *set_start*. However, we subsequently realised that this was a rather arbitrary design decision. After all one might decide that a particular time interval, e.g. an event such as meeting or a concert, had to finish by a particular time and that it had to be of a certain duration. These would then determine its start time.

Consequently, we arranged that after any attribute setting operation, the two most recently set attributes are used to update the remaining one. Unfortunately there are complications. Specifically, the three attributes must be encapsulated so that they cannot be changed except via the setting operations in *TIME_INTERVAL*; otherwise it would be possible for a client of a time interval to obtain a reference to, say, its start time, and then to alter the start time, without causing either the finish time or the duration to be updated. The invariant would then be violated. We therefore implemented the exported features *start*, *finish* and *duration* as functions (rather than attributes), each of which clones and returns a copy of a corresponding non-exported (and therefore encapsulated) attribute. Likewise, each setting procedure clones its argument and assigns the corresponding non-exported attribute to the clone. In effect we have implemented a version of Eiffel's expanded type semantics [Meyer 1992, page 194], although our arrangement is actually more flexible, because use of expanded types incurs severe restrictions. In particular had we made *start*, *finish* and *duration* expanded type attributes they could not then be redefined if necessary in any heirs to *TIME_INTERVAL*.

The nine comparison operations on intervals that were illustrated in figure 2.4 are implemented. Declarations of three of them are shown below (the others, which are similar, are omitted for brevity).

> *equal_to* (*other*: **like** *Current*): *BOOLEAN*
> *includes* (*other*: **like** *Current*): *BOOLEAN*
>   **ensure** *Result* **implies** *other.start.belongs* (*Current*);
>   *Result* **implies** *other.finish.belongs* (*Current*)

> *before* (*other*: **like** *Current*): *BOOLEAN*
>   **ensure** *Result* **implies** *finish.before* (*other*)

The class also has the two set-theoretical operations that were illustrated in figured.

> *union* (*other*: **like** *Current*): **like** *Current*
>   **ensure** **not** (*overlap* (*other*) **or** *is_overlopped_by* (*other*)
>   **or** *includes* (*other*) **or** *is_included_by* (*other*)
>   **or** *meets* (*other*) **or** *is_met_by* (*other*)
>   **or** *equal_to* (*other*))
>   **implies** *Result* =*Void*
>   **or else** (*Result. start. equal* (*start.min* (*other start*))
>   **and** *Result.finish.equal* (*finish.max* (*other.finish*)))

> *intersection* (*other*: **like** *Current*): **like** *Current*
>   **ensure** **not** (*overlap* (*other*) **or** *is_overlapped_by* (*other*)
>   **or** *includes* (*other*) **or** *is_included_by* (*other*)
>   **or** *meets* (*other*) **or** *is_met_by* (*other*)
>   **or** *equal_to* (*other*))
>   **implies** *Result* =*Void*
>   **or else** (*Result. start. equal* (*start.max* (*other.start*))
>   **and** *Result.finish.equal* (*finish.min* (*other.finish*)))

The plethora of assertions here are mainly required to specify that a void reference is returned if one interval does not meet, overlap or include the other, or is not equal to it.

Uses of this class as a parent to more specialised heirs are described in sections 2.5.3 and 2.5.4.

2.3.5 Further operations in class *ABSOLUTE_TIME*

The *ABSOLUTE_TIME* class contains several operations which involve instances of the other two classes. There are three extra comparison operations involving time intervals that were illustrated in figure 2.3:

> *before (other:TIME_INTERVAL): BOOLEAN*
> *after (other:TIME_INTERVAL): BOOLEAN*
> *belongs (other:TIME_INTERVAL): BOOLEAN*

These are implemented by applying <, >, etc., to the attributes of TIME_INTERVAL.

The three arithmetic operations are included:

> *sub (other: **like** Current): DURATION*
>   **deferred**
> *add (other: DURATION): **like** Current*
>   **deferred**
> *sub_duration (other: DURATION): **like** Current*
>   **deferred**

but all must be deferred since their implementations will depend on how absolute times are represented. We used names rather than infix operators ("+","−") for these functions because Eiffel has no facility that would allow us to use the operator "−" for two features in the same class and no other operator was an obvious candidate for subtraction of a duration. We decided therefore to identify all three features by names.

The class also contains two special arithmetic operations (not shown in figure 2.8) whose purpose will be explained in section 2.4.4:

> *finesub (other: **like** Current): INTEGER*
>   **deferred**
>   **ensure** *Current = other.fine_add (Result)*
> *fine_add (other: INTEGER): **like** Current*
>   **deferred**
>   **ensure** *other = Result.fine_sub (Current)*

2.3.6 Textual representation

Despite these classes' representation independence, it is reasonable to assume that any representation of time has at least one textual form.

Consequently, the classes *ABSOLUTE_TIME* and *DURATION* each include two deferred features *as_string* and *set_from_string*. The *as_string* feature is a string representing the value of the absolute time or duration; and the *set_from_string* procedure sets the attributes of an absolute time or duration from a string argument. Their signatures are summarised in figure 2.9. A particular argument to *set_from_string* could of course be invalid and so the flag *was_set* is included to indicate the success or otherwise of the last *set_from_string* operation. This flag can be used as a convenient test in assertions.

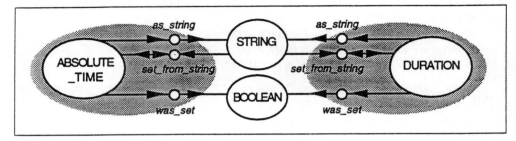

Figure 2.9: Deferred textual representation features

2.3.7 Representation-independent clients

Because *ABSOLUTE_TIME* and *DURATION* are deferred classes it is not possible to create instances of them, simply because without a full implementation, the behaviour of any instance is not fully defined. Nevertheless, it is possible to use them, for example, to specify the types of formal arguments to procedures, and then have the full behaviour defined by the actual argument when the procedure is called. In this way they can be used by client classes which process time to make them independent of any particular time representation.

Figure 2.10 shows a possible client class of *ABSOLUTE_TIME* and *DURATION*

```
class SOME CLIENT feature

    print_times (start: ABSOLUTE_TIME; period: DURATION; n: INTEGER) is
        local
                time: ABSOLUTE_TIME;
                dur: DURATION;
                count: INTEGER
        do
            from count := 0
            until count = n
            loop
                dur := period * count;
                time  : start.add (dur);
                io.putstring (time.as_string);
                io.new_line;
                count := count + 1
            end
        end
    ...
```

Figure 2.10: Use of representation independent classes

containing a procedure *print_times* which prints out a series of *n* absolute time points spaced at equal durations of length *period*, starting from a particular absolute time, *start*.

Unlike *ABSOLUTE_TIME* and *DURATION* this is not a deferred class – but it is independent of time representation. More specifically, the procedure *print_times* could, for example, print out a list of times of the day spaced 15 minutes apart, or dates spaced 18 months apart. Which one would depend entirely on the dynamic type of the arguments it is given at run time. The code is highly generic in this sense.

2.4 REPRESENTATION-DEPENDENT CLASSES

In this section we look at the second group of classes in the cluster – the representation-dependent ones. First, though, we will discuss some different ways of representing the three types of time identified in the representation independent model.

The simplest way to represent durations is as seconds or fractions of seconds, and absolute times as seconds from some chosen origin. Representation of time intervals then follows. This is typically the kind of time representation found in, for example, engineering disciplines and the physical sciences.

In natural sciences, absolute times are often stated in terms of the year and the Julian day – the day since the beginning of the year, with Julian day 1 corresponding to the 1st of January. In astronomy, where activities are heavily affected by the Earth's rotation and its motion round the sun, extremely precise granularities such as the sidereal day and the sidereal year are used.

In areas more closely tied to human affairs, such as business and finance, a duration is typically represented as a certain number of years, months and/or days, and an absolute time is represented as the year, month and day, according to some calendar scheme. Weeks, hours, minutes and seconds may also be involved.

Calendar schemes are dominated by the Gregorian calendar in Western culture, but there are alternatives such as the Chinese, Muslim and Hebrew calendars. These use a variety of origins and granularities; for example, a year in the Hebrew calendar contains 12 months of 29 or 30 days but an extra 30 day month is inserted in 7 selected years out of every 19. In the Muslim calendar, which is used widely in the Islamic world, a year consists of 12 months which are alternately 29 or 30 days long, although the last month sometimes contains an extra day [Britannica 1974].

Calendar schemes introduce anomalies. In the Gregorian calendar, month lengths vary throughout the year and in a leap year February contains 29 days instead of the more usual 28, and these cause complications, particularly in connection with durations. We discuss them in detail in sections 2.4.3 and 2.4.4. They do not, however, affect the representation independent model. More specifically, the model does not assume that any granularity used to represent time is regularly spaced when calibrated against another. So, for example,

- picoseconds,
- Gregorian calendar months,
- complicated periodic events such as eclipses of the moon

are all equally valid when representing durations, absolute times and time intervals (provided that, for absolute times and intervals, they can be numbered starting from some origin). Other, more esoteric granularities, based on geological epochs, for example, or coronations of UK monarchs, would be valid too but for the fact that they cannot represent all times on a time axis that is infinite in the past and future.

2.4.1 Gregorian classes

We now look at several classes which embody a particular representation of time. The two main ones are *DATE* and *YMD_DURATION*.These are heirs of *ABSOLUTE_TIME* and *DURATION* respectively and represent absolute times and durations in terms of years, months and days in the Gregorian calendar. The exported features they introduce, on top of the ones they inherit, are summarised in figure 2.11.

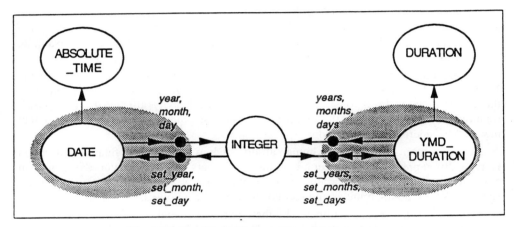

Figure 2.11: Main Gregorian calendar classes

2.4.2 Class *DATE*

An instance of class *DATE* corresponds to an absolute time represented as a combination of year, month and day. It has three exported attributes:

    year, *month*, *day*: *INTEGER*.

which can be set individually by the routines

    set_y ear (*y*: *INTEGER*)
      require *y* /= *0*
      ensure *year* /= *0*
    set_month (*m*: *INTEGER*)
      require *m* > *0*; *m* < *12*
      ensure *month* /= *0*
    set_day (*d*: *INTEGER*)

require *d > 0*; *d <= 31*
ensure *day /= 0*

A record is kept of the precision to which a date has been specified. So, for example, if only the year and the month are set, subsequent operations will ignore the day attribute. If the year and month remain unset after the day has been set then they are set automatically to the current year and month as indicated by the clock in the system in which the class is working.

The attributes can be set collectively by the operation

set_from_string (*s*: *STRING*)

inherited as deferred from *ABSOLUTE_TIME* and effected in this class. This procedure parses strings of the form

18th April 1955,
18 Apr 1955,
April 18 1955,
18/4/55,

and sets the attributes accordingly. It will interpret month names and their abbreviations provided they are in English. Possible future enhancements of this feature are discussed in section 2.6.

The function

infix "<" (*other*: **like** *Current*): *BOOLEAN*
ensure *Result* **implies not** (*Current >= other*)

inherited from *COMPARABLE* via *ABSOLUTE_TIME* is effected to return true if the current instance of the class is less than *other*. All the other comparison operations follow.

Although the *DATE* class is implemented with the semantics of the Gregorian calendar, the assertions on the setting operations do not prevent alternative calendars such as the Hebrew one, with its potential 13 month year, being implemented as heirs to *DATE*.

2.4.3 Class YMD_DURATION

An instance of class *YMD_DURATION* represents a duration in terms of Gregorian years, months and days. It has three exported attributes:

years, *months*, *days*: *INTEGER*

which are all initially set to zero on creation. The values can be set individually by the procedures

set_years (*ys*: *INTEGER*)
set_months (*ms*: *INTEGER*)
set_days (*ds*: *INTEGER*)

There are no preconditions on the arguments so the three attributes can take any values, positive or negative: months, for example, do not have to be in the range 1 to 12.

The attributes can be set collectively by the procedure *set_from_string*, inherited from *DURATION*. This is effected to parse arguments in a number of formats, e.g.

ly2m3d

123 months 456 days

The arithmetic functions, +, −, *, *div*, *mod*, inherited from *DURATION* are effected here. They treat the objects simply as tuples, adding or subtracting the corresponding attributes. Similarly the procedure *negate* negates all the attributes.

The class *YMD_DURATION* obtains the comparison function *equal* from class *ANY*, but it has to redefine it for reasons which we will now explain. As inherited the equal function compares the value of two objects of the same type, attribute by attribute [Meyer 1988, page 85]. For a pair of objects of type *YMD_DURATION*, such behaviour gives the correct answer only if they differ in just one of their three attribute pairs, *years*, *months*, *days* or if each attribute is identical to its partner. This situation is illustrated in figure 2.12 as rows 1 through 4 of the table.

	years	*months*	*days*	*equal*
1	=	=	=	*True*
2	=	=	≠	*False*
3	=	≠	=	*False*
4	≠	=	=	*False*
5	≠	≠	=	*months := months + years * 12;* *years := 0*
6	≠	=	≠	Years converted to days with margin of uncertainty.
7	=	≠	≠	Months converted to days with margin of uncertainty.
8	≠	≠	≠	Years and months converted to days with margin of uncertainty.

Figure 2.12: Comparison of ymd-durations

If, however, the durations differ in two or more attributes the result is less clear because, arguably, granularities are convertible. For example, a Gregorian duration of 1 year 0 months can quite reasonably be said to be equivalent to one of 0 years 12 months. To resolve such a case, the routine converts the years to months for each duration and then does the comparison again. Row 5 in the table shows the conversion needed to do this.

When the difference is in the years and the days (row 6) a similar conversion must he done – this time from years to days. Here there is a problem though: we have to take the leap year anomaly into account but we have no way of knowing whether a particular duration year includes any leap days or not – remember that a duration is independent of any particular point on the time axis. A one year duration could be as short as 365 days or as long as 366; a 5 year duration could be as short as 5*365 (if it included the year 1900 say) or as long as 3*365+2*366. A similar but more complicated problem arises when the difference is in months and days (row 7) or in all three attributes (row 8). Here months have to be converted into days and the irregular lengths of the Gregorian calendar months have somehow to be taken into account.

The *equal* function takes a generous approach. In the last three cases in figure 2.12, a margin of uncertainty is computed and the function returns a true value if the arguments *could* be equal within that margin. Some would say that this behaviour is too lax; a more rigorous implementation could, for example, raise an exception if there was any uncertainty about the equivalence. Consequently the behaviour is not specified in the function's assertions so that heirs to *YMD_DURATION* are free to redefine it. It is worth noting that other systems (including RUBIS), when faced with this problem, just apply arbitrary fixed conversion factors such as 30 days per month and 365 days per year.

Similar rules, where a margin of uncertainty is computed when appropriate, apply to the other comparison operation

> *infix "<" (other: DURATION): BOOLEAN*

which is inherited as a deferred feature from *DURATION* and effected in *YMD_DURATION*. They are also used in the feature

> *negative: BOOLEAN*

which indicates whether the overall value of the ymd-duration is negative.

2.4.4 Arithmetic operations in class *DATE*

The *DATE* class inherits the deferred arithmetic functions *sub*, *add* and *sub_duration* from *ABSOLUTE_TIME*, effects them and redefines their signatures as follows

> *sub (other:**like** Current): YMD_DURATION*
> *add (other: YMD_DURATION): **like** Current*
> *sub_duration (other: YMD_DURATION): **like** Current*

The *sub* function subtracts *other* from the current instance and returns a ymd-duration. If all the respective attributes of the *Current* date are greater than or equal to that of *other,* corresponding attributes are simply subtracted, as illustrated in figure 2.13 example 1. Otherwise granularity conversions are applied and the result is "normalised" so that the years, months and days of the duration are all within the ranges that one would expect of Gregorian calendar granularities, as in examples 2 and 3. Naturally, the anomalies associated with irregular month lengths and leap years are taken into account.

The *add* function adds a duration to a date by adding corresponding attributes and normalising the result so that the *year*, *month* and *day* attributes form a valid Gregorian date. Figure 2.14 examples 1 to 3 illustrate this operation. The *sub_duration* function subtracts a duration from an absolute time using much tbe same method.

Both provide a convenient way to add or subtract dates to or from coarsely grained

	x	y	x.sub(y)
1	18 April 1955	14 March 1879	76 years 1 month 4 days
2	18 April 1955	19 March 1955	30 days
3	18 April 1955	19 April 1954	11 months 30 days

Figure 2.13: Subtracting one date from another

durations involving months and years as well as days; but difficulties can arise in some
cases if the duration contains both months and days because the irregular lengths of the
Gregorian months can make the addition process non-associative. The result of the add
operation, for example, can depend on the order In which the different attributes of the
duration are added to the date. In figure 2.14 example 4, a duration of 1 month 31 days is
added to 1 January, but the result depens on whether the month is added to the date
before the days, or vice versa.

	years	months	days	+ 1 Jan 1955 =
1	0	0	1	2 Jan 1955
2	1	1	1	2 Feb 1956
3	0	0	31	1 Feb 1955
4	0	1	31	(1 Jan + 1 month) + 31days = 4 Mar 1955 (1 Jan + 31 days) + 1month = 1 Mar 1955
	years	months	days	+ 31 Jan 1955
5	0	1	0	31 Jan + 1month = 31 Feb 1955 (!) 31 Jan + 31 days = 3 Mar 1955 31 Jan + 28 days = 28 Feb 1955

Figure 2.14: Anomalies when adding ymd-durations to dates

In such cases our implementation adds the coarser granularity, i.e. months, first; but
the alternative strategy would, arguably, be just as valid. As with comparison of ymd-
durations, there is no correct solution, and alternatives could be implemented in heirs of
DATE. Perhaps the safest strategy would be to raise an exception when such a situation
arose.

Figure 2.14 example 5 illustrates a further complication. If we add 1 month to 31
January then the result is 31 February – which does not exist. To resolve this we have to
convert the month into a number of days; but do we convert it to 31 days (the number of
days in January) or 28 days (the number in February) ? Our implementation does the
former but the alternative could be just as valid. Again, for such special end-of-month
cases, heirs of *DATE* could do the alternative conversion, or raise an exception.

One consequence of these anomalies is that the assertion

$$a.add\ (d1 + d2) = (a.add\ (d1\ )\ ).add\ (d2)$$

is not always true if absolute *a* is a date and durations *d1* and *d2* are ymd-durations. A false result should occur only rarely but there will be situations where this kind of behaviour has to be avoided at all costs. This is the reason for introducing the two operations *fine_add* and *fine_sub* into *ABSOLUTE_TIME* (see section 2.3.5). These behave like *add* and *sub* but reduce everything to the finest level of granularity. In *DATE*, their implementations respectively accept and return an integer number of days rather than a mixed-granularity duration. This is less convenient, because we have lost the coarse granularities, but the operations are always associative and give perfect precision in all cases.

At the beginning of this section we mentioned that the argument of *add* and *sub_duration* and the result of *sub* were redefined in this class – from *DURATION* to *YMD_DURATION*. In the case of *add* it is necessary because adding a date to a duration is only possible if the duration is represented using Gregorian years, months and days. Likewise for *sub_duration*. This redefinition exploits the covariant policy of the Eiffel typing system [Meyer 1992, page 358], whereby a class is allowed to redefine the type of an argument of an inherited feature provided that the new type conforms to the type of the corresponding argument in the heir. Unfortunately this policy causes severe problems for any type checking system – problems that early Eiffel compilers did not address. They allowed run-time errors or incorrect behaviour to occur in certain situations, and consequently Eiffel's typing policy was criticised as being "unsafe" [Cook 1989]. It was argued that a contravariant policy should be adopted instead. The example here is a clear vindication of the original covariant policy.

Finally, the *add* feature illustrates a dilemma that Eiffel programmers sometimes have to face. We have defined it as a function returning a new instance of *DATE*. It could alternatively have been declared and implemented as a procedure, updating the existing date to which it was applied. We consider the first option to be preferable in this case because it makes the detailed semantics of the feature clearer and more elegant. The operation of adding a date to a duration becomes more analogous to addition on simple objects such as integers and, because it is a function, the feature can be used in expressions and assertions. When designing temporal class features we have tended to follow the first option where it seems appropriate.

That option has, however, a big disadvantage. Either the new object or the existing one will likely be discarded soon after the operation has heen called. It will then become garbage whose memory space must somehow be recycled. Fortunately, one of Eiffel's greatest assets is a garbage collection facility which will do this transparently, but it is well-known that garbage collection can be incompatible with applications which require operations to complete always within certain fixed time constraints. For such applications the second option would be better. We have noticed, incidentally, that much existing Eiffel software and most of the examples in the literature tend to follow the second option, though this may simply reflect the fact that garbage collection in early Eiffel implementations was known to be fairly inefficient.

Perhaps one way to resolve the dilemma would be to produce all components in two forms: one an elegant but wasteful variety which used functions wherever appropriate, and another "Mil-Spec" version in which all object-creating functions were replaced with object updating procedures to avoid generating garbage.

2.4.5 Class *YMDHMS_DURATION*

Class *YMDHMS_DURATION* is an heir of *YMD_DURATION* and represents durations in terms of years, months and days, and hours, minutes and seconds. It introduces three new exported attributes:

hours, *minutes*, *seconds*: *INTEGER*

and the corresponding procedures for setting them. The *set_from_string* procedure can successfully parse string arguments in a number of formats, e.g.:

1 year 2 months 3 days 4 hours 5 mins 6 seconds
5 hrs 6 secs
5000hrs

All the inherited features behave much as they do in *YMD_DURATION* but taking account of the finer granularities. No futher complications associated with comparison operations arise because of the regular relationship between days, hours, minutes and seconds.

2.4.6 Heirs of class *DATE*

Two important heirs of class *DATE* are included in the cluster. These are *DATE_AND_TIME* and *DATE_AND_WEEK*. Their signatures are summarised in figure 2.15.

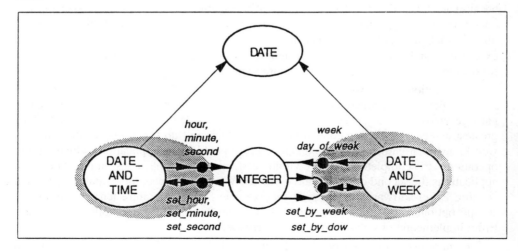

Figure 2.15: Heirs of class *DATE*

2.4.7 Class *DATE_AND_TIME*

This class just introduces a finer level of granularity on top of *DATE*, in the form of three new exported attributes:

hour, *minute*, *second*: *INTEGER*

which can be set individually by the routines

set_hour (*h*: *INTEGER*)
  require *h* >= *0*; *h* < 24
set_minute (*min*: *INTEGER*)
  require *min* >= *0*; *min* <60
set_second (*s*: *INTEGER*)
  require *s* >= *0*; *s* < 60

As in the class *DATE*, record is kept of the precision to which the date-and-time has been specified (see section 2.4.2). So, for example, if *second* and *minute* are not set, subsequent operations willl ignore those attributes. Similarly if any attributes of coarser granularity than one that has been set remain unset, they are set automatically to the current values as indicated by the clock in the system in which the class is working. So for example if the *year*, *month*, *day* and *hour* remain unset after *minute* has been set then they are set automatically to the system clock values.

The procedure *set_from_string* is redefined so that it can take a wider range of strings, e.g.:

18/4/5513:01:20,
1:01:20pm.

The comparison operations from *DATE* are redefined to take account of the extra level of granularity. The arithmetic functions *sub*, *add* and *sub_duration* are redefined and have their signatures changed to reflect the finer level of granularity:

sub (*other*: **like** *Current*): *YMDHMS_DURATION*
add (*other*: *YMDHMS_DURATION*): **like** *Current*
sub_duration (*other*: *YMDHMS_DURATION*): **like** *Current*

No new complications, of the kind described in section 2.4.4, arise because of the regular relationship between days, hours, minutes and seconds.

2.4.8 Class *DATE_AND_WEEK*

This class introduces several useful features involving weeks and weekdays. For example, the feature

day_of_week: *INTEGER*
  ensure *Result* > *0* **and** *Result* <= *7*

is the day of the week corresponding to the date. It is represented as an integer (Sunday = 1, etc.). Conversely, the procedure

set_from_dow (*dow n*: *INTEGER*)

> **require** *dow > 0*;
>   *dow <= 7*;
>   *n > 0*;
>   *year /= 0*;
>   *month /= 0*

sets the *day* part of the date to correspond to the *n*th day of the week in the month, as given by the arguments *n* and *dow*. So for example, *set_from_dow (3, 2)* sets the date to that of the second Tuesday in the month.

The feature

> *week*: *INTEGER*
>   **ensure** *Result >0*

is the number of the week in the year with *week* = 1 being the week that contains 1 January. Conversely, the procedure

> *set_from_week (dow, n*: *INTEGER)*
>   **require** *dow > 0*;
>   *dow <=7*;
>   *n > 0*;
>   *year /= 0*

sets the *day* and *month* attributes of the date to correspond to the *dowth* day of week *n* of the year. So for example, *set_from_week (3, 2)* sets the date to that of Tuesday in the second week of the year.

Features such as *as_string* are redefined to deal with day-of-the-week names in English, but the names are held in a table attached to each date and can be changed to accommodate different languages.

Weeks introduce a redundant level of granularity into dates. The features described here were separated into this class rather than included in *DATE* so that *DATE* could be seen as an *ABSOLUTE_TIME* that was represented in an uncluttered way by a non-redundant set of granularities.

2.5 EXTENSIONS

In section 2.2 we said that once we had developed our initial cluster of classes we embarked on an exercise to see what useful extensions could be made to it. We wanted to identify any shortcomings in the classes and any specialised temporal abstract data types which could potentially be embodied as new classes. We looked to see if further aspects of the RUBIS model could be usefully implemented and we carried out a paper and pencil exercise to see if the classes could be applied in a particular application area, specifically banking. Using these methods we identified need for the following extensions:

- Temporal sets.
- Time zones and daylight saving.
- Working days.
- Temporal events.

2.5.1 Temporal sets

The RUBIS system includes a facility for maintaining arbitrary sets of absolute times and intervals. These are called temporal sets and can be used to hold dates of meetings etc.

There seemed to be little point in making a specific extension to the Eiffel temporal classes to embody such a facility because the Eiffel structures library [Meyer 1989] provides a wealth of generic set and list classes. An application programmer only needs to derive any of these with *ABSOLUTE_TIME* or *TIME_INTERVAL* as an actual type parameter to create any kind of temporal container desired.

2.5.2 Time zones and daylight saving

Time zones and daylight saving are a response to the anomaly that the sun is observed to rise at different times of the day according to the time of year and the position of the observer on the Earth's surface. As a result, different local time regimes are followed in different jurisdictions. In the United Kingdom, for example, the local time is Greenwich Mean Time (GMT) from late October to late March, and British Summer Time, which is one hour ahead of GMT, for the rest of the year. Clearly it is important that the classes should be able to deal with these complications. Implementing a suitable extension turned out to be fairly straightforward.

To meet this requirement we introduced a class *GLOBAL_DATE_AND_TIME*, as an heir to *DATE_AND_TIME*. A global date-and-time incorporates representations of both the global time and the corresponding local time under a particular regime. The global time is represented in the inherited attributes *year*, *month*, *...*, *second*, while the local time is available in the feature

   local_time: *DATE_AND_TIME*

The *set_year*, *...*, *set_second* procedures are redefined so that they set the corresponding *local_time* too. Similarly both the global and local time can be set by the local time with the procedure

   set_by_local_time (*d*: *DATE_AND_TIME*)

Consistency between local and global times under a particular regime is maintained using conversion operations associated with a time zone object which is associated with every instance of *GLOBAL_DATE_AND_TIME*. This can be attached with the operation

   set_zone (*z*: *TIME_ZONE*)

The local time regime followed in a particular jurisdiction may be altered occasionally through legislation (this happened in the United Kingdom in the early 1970's), but, in general, regimes are stable and therefore it is worthwhile embodying them in reusable software. But there are of course a moderate number of regimes in use throughout the world and it would be uneconomic to implement conversion operations for all of them within the class *TIME_ZONE*. Instead, just the abstract notion of a time zone and daylight saving regime is captured in that class. This is done by giving

TIME_ZONE two deferred procedures

> *global_to_ global* (*l*: *GLOBAL_DATE_AND_TIME*)
>   **deferred**

and

> *local_to_ global* (*l*: *GLOBAL_DATE_AND_TIME*)
>   **deferred**

These are meant to be effected in heirs to *TIME_ZONE*, to be written by application programmers. The arrangement is illustrated in figure 2.16. The operations update their argument so that the local time and global tune are consistent under a particular regime.

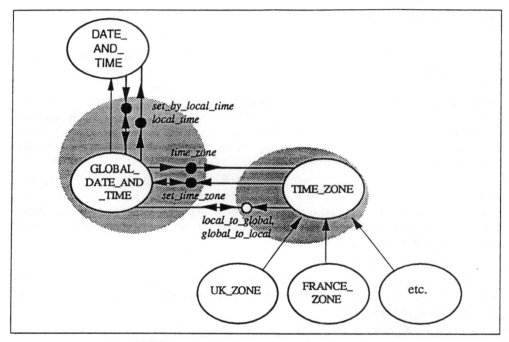

Figure 2.16: Time zone and daylight saving classes

With some regimes, the conversion to and from global time could be done algorithmically, depending on, for example, whether daylight saving follows clearly defined rules; in others it may be a case of looking up sets of temporal constants.

It is possible to translate a local time in one regime to that in another just by setting the *time_zone* attribute to a different zone. Also, because consistency is maintained between the global and local times, it is possible to find the duration between two local times, even if they are associated with different time zones or daylight saving regimes, just by applying *sub* to the instances of *GLOBAL_DATE_AND_TIME* of which they are part.

An alternative scheme would have dispensed with an explicit *TIME_ZONE* class and instead had different heirs to *DATE_AND_TIME* corresponding to different regimes, with the conversion rules incorporated in the *local_time* attribute. Fewer classes would be needed but all instances of these heirs would be tied permanently to particular regimes.

2.5.3 Working days

The notion of a period of "working days" arose in several places during our paper and pencil exercise in the banking domain. One of them was connected with the time taken for cheques to clear, and another with financial interest calculations. There was a clear need for the temporal classes to supply operations between working days and dates so that, for example, two dates could be subtracted to find the number of working days between them or a number of working days could be added to a date to find a date so many working days later.

From the point of view of extending the classes it was interesting that there was ambiguity over how best to incorporate working days into the embodied software. Specifically, a period of time specified as enclosing so many working days can be viewed in two ways: either as a kind of duration, or simply as an integer attribute of an interval.

A period of working days can be viewed as a duration because it can be specified independently of any particular absolute time. This, in fact, is why the concept is useful; we can say, for example, that a bank cheque takes three working days to clear without saying what the dates of those days are.

Initially therefore we considered extending the temporal classes by creating a *WORKING_DAY_DURATION* as an heir to *DURATION*. The most important features of it are summarised in Figure 2.17. The functionality of a working day duration is similar to that of an ordinary duration in that working day durations can be added to and subtracted from both each other and absolute times; but of course, with a working day duration the exact semantics of these operations will vary between nations and cultures, or more precisely, between different jurisdictions. In western countries, for example, working days are, by convention, all days except Saturdays, Sundays and public holidays. In many Islamic countries, however, Saturdays and Sundays are usually working days but Thursdays and Fridays are not. Public holidays in different jurisdictions add more diversity.

Obviously the number of potential jurisdictions is fairly large, and, as with time zones, we should defer the implementation of jurisdiction-dependent operations within the *WORKING_DAY_DURATION* and instead make arrangements for there to be a range of heirs of *WORKING_DAY_DURATION*, written by application programmers, in which the operations would be effected in the appropriate way. This arrangement has the advantage that any application software which uses the *WORKING_DAY_DURATION* class is independent of any particular jurisdiction. Porting such software across jurisdictions would simply be a matter of implementing and linking in the appropriate heir to *WORKING_DAY_DURATION*.

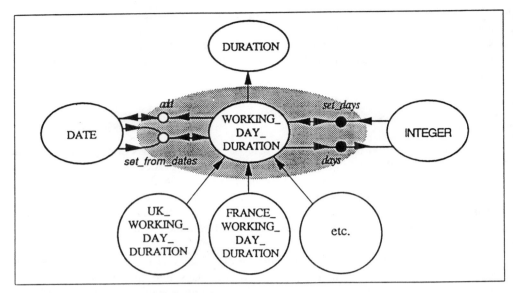

Figure 2.17: Working day duration

Our class *WORKING_DAY_DURATION* defines three temporal operations

set_from_dates (*a1*, *a2*: *DATE*)
   require *a1* >= *a2*

which sets the current instance to the number of working days between *a1* and *a2*; and

add (*a*: *DATE*)

which adds the current instance to a date changing it to the appropriate number of working days later.

The *add* operation could have been declared as a function rather than a procedure, returning a new date object instead of changing an existing one, but this would have hampered clients from using the operation with heirs of *DATE* such as a *DATE_AND_TIME*. As a function, *add* would have accepted date-and-time objects but to subsequently treat the result as anything more specialised than a date would require use of so-called "assignment attempt" [Meyer 1992, page 330] which has unusual semantics and perhaps should be avoided where possible.

The class also effects all the deferred routines that it inherits from *DURATION* and redefines the *equal* function. The problems associated with the comparison functions that arose with *YMD_DURATION* do not occur here because only one level of granularity is involved.

Although a working day duration can be specified independently of any absolute time its special semantics arise precisely because it is associated with a segment of the time axis between two absolutes – in other words it is associated with a time interval. Other than that it is nothing more than an integer. This observation leads to an alternative view of a working day duration, that is as simply an integer attribute of a special kind of time interval. Therefore an alternative way to extend the temporal classes to cope with working days is to define an heir to *TIME_INTERVAL*, called a *WORKING_DAY_TIME_INTERVAL* and illustrated in figure 2.18. A *WORKING_DAY_TIME_INTEVAL* contains two features:

   working_days: *INTEGER*

which is the number of working days covered by the interval, and

   set_working_days (*wd*: *INTEGER*)
       deferred

which updates the attributes of the interval so that it covers *wd* working days. The rules of deciding which attributes are updated are the same as those of *TIME_INTERVAL* (see section 2.3.4).

   Different jurisdictions are catered for by leaving the *set_working_days* feature deferred and effecting it in different heirs to *WORKING_DAY_TIME_INTERVAL* such as *UK_WD_TIME_INTERVAL* and *FRANCE_WD_TIME_INTERVAL* which provide algorithms and temporal sets relevant to the jurisdiction.

   Features such as *set_start*, *set_finish*, and *set_duration* inherited from *TIME_INTERVAL* have to be redefined so that they set *working_days* to the appropriate value in addition to their original actions. They can then be used, for example, to find the number of working days between any two absolute times.

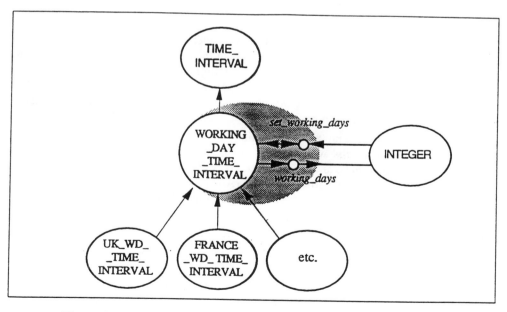

Figure 2.18: Working days as an attribute to *TIME_INTERVAL*

2.5.4 Temporal events

The RUBIS system, which we used as the starting point when designing our components, includes a temporal event handler, i.e. a mechanism that enables specific actions to be programmed to occur at specific absolute times. We have carried out some preliminary work which we hope will allow us to extend the temporal classes with a similar facility.

Our proposed extension consists of two classes *TIME_EVENT* and *EVENT_ CALENDAR*. A time event consists essentially of an action and an occurrence time – a time at which the action is to occur. An event calendar is a priority queue of time events sorted according to their occurrence time. A particular time event can be put in the queue by the procedure

> *attach* (*t*: *TIME_EVENT*)

in class *EVENT_CALENDAR*.

Specifying a particular type of event and its associated action is done by inheriting *TIME_EVENT* into an heir and effecting a deferred feature in *TIME_EVENT* called *action*. For example, if a bank statement had to be mailed out at a particular time we would implement a class *BANK_STATEMENT*:

> **class** *BANK_STATEMENT*
> **inherit** *TIME_EVENT*
> **feature**
>> *action* **is**
>>> -- code for mailing statement
>
> **end** -- class *BANK_STATEMENT*

When a time event is attached to an event calendar, the calendar puts it into its priority queue and calculates the duration between the current date and the time that the first event in the queue is to occur. An action-invoking procedure in the event calendar is then programmed to be "woken up" by a countdown timer after that duration has elapsed. On being woken it calls the *action* feature in the event at the front of the queue and then removes that event from the queue.

The arrangement does not allow the action of any particular type of time event to be changed dynamically If this were thought to be desirable then instead of a deferred action feature we could have an additional *ACTION* class and action objects which could be dynamically attached to a particular event. (A similar arrangement exists in the Eiffel user interface library [Meyer 1989] for attaching commands to menus.)

It may be desirable to make the invocation of an action dependent on the state of particular conditions prevailing at the occurrence time. To address this the *TIME_EVENT* class contains a feature

> *test*: *BOOLEAN*

which *EVENT_CALENDAR* requires to be true at the occurrence time if the action is to be invoked. In *TIME_EVENT* it is defined to return the value true. Any heir can redefine it to return a value which depends on arbitrary factors.

We will now discuss the nature of the occurrence time and how it can be specified. Firstly it is best to define the occurrence time not as an absolute time, i.e. as a single time point on the time axis, but as an interval. Justification for this is given in [Allen 1985]. One reason is that certain counter-intuitive semantics can arise if events are considered to happen instantaneously. It is better to think of them as occurring during a particular interval of time. In the RUBIS system this interval is called the occurrence domain. This suggests that the *TIME_EVENT* class should inherit from *TIME_INTERVAL*. We can therefore consider a time event as an interval with an associated action that should occur during that interval. The priority queue in *EVENT_CALENDAR* is ordered using the interval start time as the primary key and the finish time as secondary.

Figure 2.19 shows the configuration of classes for the event handler, and an example of an event class, in this case one associated with bank statements that had to be mailed out at specific times.

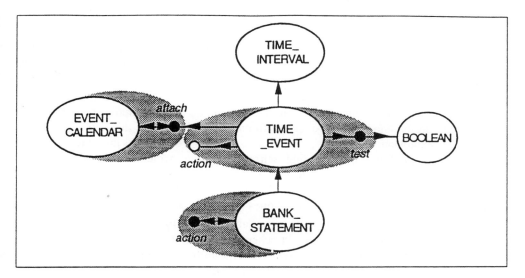

Figure 2.19: Time event example

We can envisage several possible ways of capturing the occurrence time. The simplest one, of course, is just to compel the creator of the event to set the start and finish times of its occurrence domain before attaching it to a calender. A more useful arrangement, however, is to let the creator specify the time by reference to absolutes or intervals, or to other events, using temporal relations such as *before*, *after*, *is_included_by*, etc. Such relations are counterparts of the Time Interval and Absolute Time comparison operations which were described in section 2.3.4.

To enable the occurrence domain to be specified in this way, the *TIME_EVENT* class has to incorporate what is, in essence, an inference engine. This must be invoked when the event is attached to an event calendar. We are currently investigating the practical extent and design of this engine.

We can envisage several interesting extensions. For example, a useful facility would be to have an inference engine which could operate even if the occurrence domains of some of the events that a particular event was related to were not specified at the time of attachment to an event calendar. This would require each event to maintain a list of the events it was related to, but it would free the application programmer from having to ensure that occurrence domains were always specified in order of dependence.

2.6 FURTHER TEMPORAL EXTENSIONS

There is considerable scope for further extension. Others facilities worthy of investigation are:
- Better conversion to and from strings.
- Alternative calendars.
- Periodic events.

Gregorian dates and times can take many textual forms. The *set_from_string* function in *DATE* and its heirs recognise some of these but not a complete set. A more comprehensive range of intelligent string conversion functions are currently being developed.

Different parsing arrangements could, of course, be implemented in heirs to *DATE* although given the enormous diversity of formats in common use this could lead to an undesirable explosion of classes. A better arrangement would be to introduce a *format* string attribute and its corresponding setting operation, which could indicate more precisely using a "little-language" to specify how time strings were to be parsed, and also generated by the *as_string* feature. The obvious little-language to use would be the one that UNIX string/time conversion routines interpret.

In section 2.4 we mentioned some alternatives to the Gregorian calendar. Conversion to and from these different schemes may be useful for certain specialised applications or within particular cultures. We hope to try to implement some classes to do this as heirs of either *ABSOLUTE_TIME* or *DATE*.

The RUBIS temporal model includes a type for encapsulating a set of absolutes which are spaced at regular intervals at a specific level of granularity (e.g. 1 month) along the time axis – in other words periodic events. A class embodying this type, in a representation-independent way, will be added to the temporal class set.

Finally, we mentioned in our introduction that for many applications the problem of embodying time in software is very straightforward – particularly science and engineering applications. This is true of course unless the application involves speeds or distances of relativistic proportions, in which case all kinds of temporal anomalies and complications may arise. Extending the classes to reflect the semantics of relativity is an exercise that we leave for the reader.

2.7 CONCLUSIONS

We have described a cluster of Eiffel classes offering useful services to specific application systems which need to process time-related information. Initially they were designed around the temporal model associated with the RUBIS relational database management system; but then we reconfigured them in the course of a generalisation phase to form two new groups of classes, one group independent of any representation of time, and the other tied mainly to the semantics of the Gregorian calendar. Classes in the first group are a software embodiment of a very general model of time. Their representation independence and generality can be carried over to classes which use them. They also prescribe the overall behaviour of classes in the second group, which inherit from them. These offer services based on specific Gregorian granularities and deal with the various anomalies that arise in this calendar scheme.

We have found the Eiffel language worthwhile as a development tool. The following features were especially valuable:

- Strong static polymorphic typing and assertions which, among other things, make deferred classes useful.

- The covariant typing policy which allows, for example, heirs of *ABSOLUTE_TIME* and *DURATION* to maintain their correct relationship as more and more representation dependence, in the form of finer and finer temporal granularities, is introduced.

- Garbage collection which allows, among other things, the relatively uninhibited use of functions returning complex objects, and cloning. The latter enabled us to maintain the correctness of the *TIME_INTERVAL* class by arranging that its three attributes to be cloned rather than dynamically aliased so preventing any violation of the invariant relationship between them.

At the time of writing the main classes in the cluster have been tested but they are not yet closed; their features are still being tuned. At the same time the cluster as a whole is being extended with time zone and daylight saving classes, working day classes and, potentially most useful of all, classes to handle temporal events. We hope to extend it further with classes embodying alternatives to the Gregorian calendar, more versatile handling of textual time representations, and periodic events. We hope also to be able to release the main classes for general use shortly and then follow, with interest, their application to real-world problems.

3

Engineering software with objects

**Gail C. Murphy, Paul Townsend,
Paulin Laberge and Mike Juzenas
MPR Teltech Ltd.
Vancouver (Canada)**

Few constants exist in the world of software. Each passing day, month and year bring new flavours of operating systems, new styles of user interfaces and new tools of the trade. It is within this ever-changing landscape that the industrial software developer is faced with the challenge of constructing increasingly complex software systems. The challenge here lies not only in providing the functionality of the system, but also in *engineering* its provision.

Object-oriented technology is a software technology that aids in the development of high-quality, complex systems. While the benefits of object-oriented technology have been discussed at length in the literature, little has been reported on the software process and management necessary to plan, effect and deliver solutions when applying the technology. This chapter describes our approach to object-oriented development as experienced in the construction of the distributed TRICS, the Trouble Reporting Integrator for Customer Surveillance, system. The objective of the TRICS software system is to improve the quality of service a telecommunications company may provide to large business customers by monitoring customer networks, identifying network problems prior to service degradation, and responding to discovered problems on a pro-active basis.

The development of the TRICS software system was not our first foray into object-oriented technology. We have been investigating and prototyping with the technology since 1988. As you will see, in the course of our technology adoption, we have enjoyed the thrill of victory, and although not quite the agony of defeat, there are aspects we would do differently in the future. Interspersed in this discussion you will find boxes encapsulating different viewpoints of object-oriented technology and the adoption process. We hope that this behind-the-scenes view will provide insights into the application of object-oriented technology in an industrial setting.

In any story, there must be characters. These characters interact in often unpredictable ways and contribute essential elements to the story. Ours is no different. We thought we had put together a script for developing object-oriented software that all the characters would follow. The characters had other ideas; they also wanted to write the script.

In this chapter, we will periodically let some of our characters speak. They will tell you about the script they wrote or wished they had written. They will let you in on secrets they kept hidden and insights they acquired while participating in our story. Through them, you might be able to learn how to write your own story.

I am the Voice of Management. In this story, I am trying to ensure that object-oriented technology goes from an art to a science that can be applied consistently to large projects. I am the one that tries to ensure that all the pieces are in place so that the company can enjoy the benefits of object-orientation. I wanted to write the script.

Of course, I let someone else do it. That is the Voice of Technology Transfer. In our story, Technology Transfer is asked to work out the details of making object-oriented technology practical. Technology Transfer is asked to find out what it feels like to be a voice in the wilderness.

The Voice of System Development will let you in on how practice differs from theory and reality differs from plan. They will talk about great ideas, and ideas that maybe were not so great after all. They will also let you in on how they will do it next time. We all will.

3.1 THE TRICS

Today, businesses operate in a very competitive global environment that requires sophisticated and reliable telecommunications networks. Because problems with these networks may radically affect a business' ability to function effectively and may cause lost revenue, businesses are demanding that the telecommunications supplier inform them of the status of their networks.

The telecommunications networks upon which businesses rely consist of hundreds of thousands of pieces of equipment supporting millions of voice and data connections. Multiple diverse monitoring systems are used by the telecommunications supplier to manage these complex networks. For the supplier, gauging the affect of a problem with the network on a specific business customer is a difficult challenge.

The TRICS system meets the demand for, and challenge of, a customer-oriented monitoring system through the use of object-oriented technology to express a model of the network and its use. Events reported from external monitoring systems are accepted by TRICS and are correlated against the object-oriented model of the network to determine the effect on customers (see Figure 3.1). Once the correlation is complete, the updated network status is displayed, through integrated textual and graphical presentations, to the supplier who may respond pro-actively to restore the service.

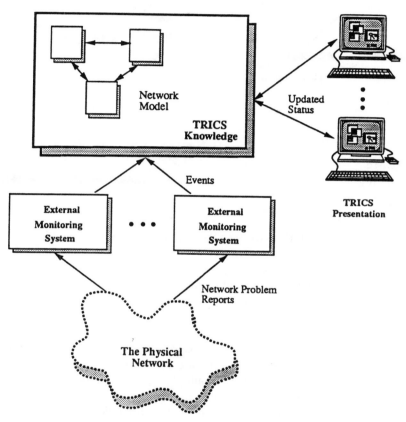

Figure 3.1: TRICS

3.1.1 The network model

TRICS creates an intuitive model of the network through the use of managed objects and a network topology. The managed objects in the system represent real world things like equipment, locations and circuits. Support for a topology representation of the connections between these managed objects is provided through three types of relations: composition, containment and association.

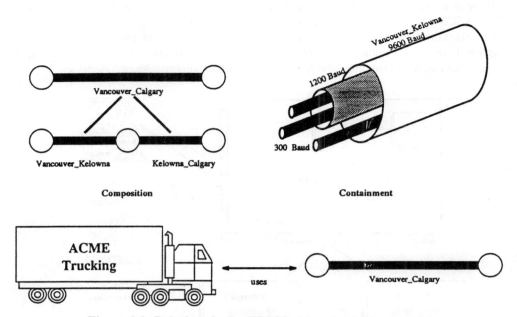

Figure 3.2: Relations in the TRICS network topology model

The composition relation permits the modelling of sequences of managed objects that logically constitute a higher-level, end-to-end, managed object. For example, Figure 3.2 illustrates how an end-to-end circuit, `Vancouver_Calgary`, is composed of circuits `Vancouver_Kelowna` and `Kelowna_ Calgary`.

The containment relation permits the modelling of parts and sub-parts. This type of relationship may be used to express how lower bandwidth circuits are contained within a higher bandwidth circuit. For example, in Figure 3.2, four 300 baud circuits may be carried on the 1200 baud circuit. Likewise, multiple 1200 baud circuits may be carried on the 9600 baud circuit. Association is a general relationship that may occur between various pairs of managed objects. For example, a customer object, `Acme Trucking`, *uses* a given circuit, a 9600 baud `Vancouver_Calgary` circuit, for data transmission.

Event information for any managed object within TRICS can arrive at any time from several different sources in the network. Based on information configured by the administrator of the TRICS system, these events will cause either the creation or destruction of alarm objects within TRICS. Alarm objects are associated with managed objects and it is from attached alarm objects that a managed object derives its status. A change in an alarm object may thus change the status of a managed object. TRICS propagates the status change in a managed object, using the topology relations, to all other affected managed objects. Status changes are reported by affected managed objects to any displays that have registered interest in those managed objects.

For example, consider the sequence of actions triggered by a backhoe cutting through the fiber optic cable carrying the `Vancouver_Kelowna` circuit. The event monitoring equipment may only monitor the 300 baud `Vancouver_Kelowna` circuits. The TRICS system will receive a series of events on the 300 baud `Vancouver_Kelowna` circuits causing the creation of alarm objects and the association of those alarm objects with the circuits. Using the topology relations, TRICS will propagate the alarms to the containing 1200 and 9600 baud `Vancouver_Kelowna` circuits. In turn, the `Vancouver_Kelowna` 9600 baud circuit will propagate the alarm to its composite circuit, the 9600 baud `Vancouver_Calgary` circuit. By traversing the uses association relation, the effect of the original outage on the `Acme Trucking` customer is determined and displayed on a graphical display. The telecommunications supplier can now respond pro-actively to restore service to the customer.

3.1.2 Complexity and capacity

TRICS is deployed within a distributed Unix environment. The system is capable of supporting up to 75 different workstations. Interfaces to six different types of external monitoring systems, and up to 255 simultaneous user interface sessions are supported. Processing delays are minimized with the total delay from the arrival of an external indicator of status change to display in a user interface being less than 5 seconds.

3.1.3 Processes

TRICS functionality is categorized into knowledge and presentation processes (see figure 3.3). The knowledge processes encapsulate the managed objects and the network topology; the presentation processes provide the integrated graphical and textual displays to visualize the effects of alarms on the network. Typically, the knowledge processes are grouped together and reside on servers. The presentation processes usually reside on workstations.

The knowledge processes include the Alarm Processing Engine (APE), the Object Correlation Engine (OCE), and the Object Topology Server (OTS). These processes propagate and correlate alarms, report the status of managed objects to the presentation processes, and administer the managed objects and the network topology. All knowledge processes are implemented in Eiffel.

The presentation processes are strictly involved with the display and manipulation of information supplied by the knowledge processes. Presentation displays include topology administration, event and status displays, and configurable pictorial displays of network status. The presentation processes do not have any knowledge of the application information presented. This was realized by having the presentation processes obtain display information from the knowledge processes. All of the presentation processes are based on the InterViews library [Linton 1989] and are thus written in C++.

Connections between the presentation processes and the knowledge processes are supported by the Network Message Router (NMR) processes. The NMR processes

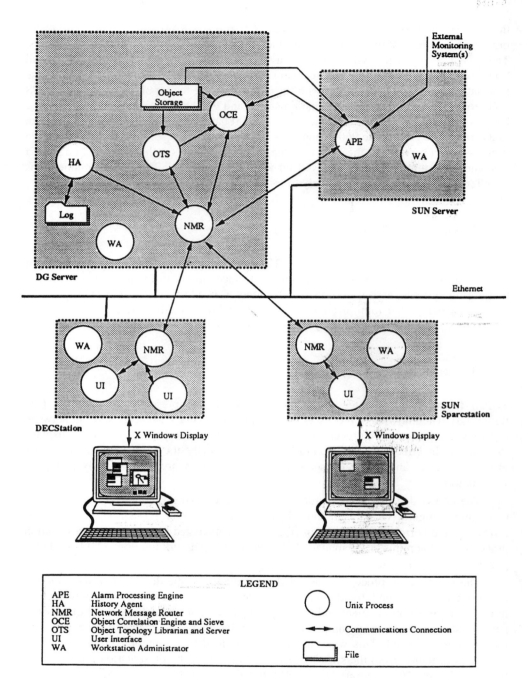

Figure 3.3: TRICS distributed environment

provide a message routing layer that enables TRICS processes to communicate regardless of their processor location. The Workstation Administrator (WA) processes support this location transparency by providing service name registration and service name resolution functionality for the NMR. Messages in the TRICS environment are ASCII based and message content is separate from the routing algorithms that are used to route messages. All TRICS communications occurs over Unix Internet socket and RPC connections.

3.2 THE METHODOLOGY

This section describes the methodology used to drive the requirements specification, analysis and design of TRICS. What is presented in not intended to be a prescription for a successful object-oriented development. Rather, it is a review of the steps taken on the path toward delivering a product to our client. Along the way we make comments on the major influences driving decisions, the aspects of the methodology that we felt were successful, and those aspects that did not turn out as hoped.

Technology Transfer: Before we begin to expose the trials and tribulations of the TRICS development, it is necessary to provide some context for our approach. We entered into the world of objects in 1988 because of the limitations of entity-relationship diagramming for expressing network management concepts. Our early attempts at applying object-oriented concepts were promising enough that we spent 1989 building a prototype of an object-oriented network management system, called POETS, in Eiffel. Many of the concepts first investigated in the POETS prototype (and even some of the classes) have since found their way into the TRICS system.

Although we were excited by the possibilities of object-oriented technology, we also knew that it was not something to be thrown at developers. As a result, we spent 1990 investigating those aspects of the technology that we felt required further understanding before embarking on a system development. This included: evaluating and choosing object-oriented analysis and design techniques; evaluating object-oriented database management systems; building a faceted classification mechanism for a software component library; understanding what distributed object technology was all about; and determining guidelines for multi-paradigm and multi-language development environments. These investigations were undertaken as part of the Foundations for Object-Oriented Developments (FOOD) project. The result of FOOD was a set of guidelines for developers and managers at MPR Teltech to use when applying object-oriented technology and encompassed development methodologies, storage mechanisms, languages, reuse and management approaches.

It was from within this context, with a previously developed prototype and guidelines for technology application, that the TRICS development was undertaken.

3.2.1 Prototyping

Much of the current literature regarding the development of object-oriented systems stresses the necessity of building a prototype prior to actual development. Although many agree that prototyping is desirable, it is seldom that the actual form of prototyping is described. Multiple forms of prototyping are available including: throw-away, mock-up, quick-and-dirty, exploratory and design-driven [Connell 1989]. Equally important as choosing to prototype is the determination of the kind of prototyping required for the particular system development being considered and the setting of objectives for the prototyping activity.

In the case of TRICS, prototyping was crucial as the end-result of prototyping was used to ensure funding of the development of the actual system. Thus, it was important to provide an *operational* prototype that supported the surveillance of actual network alarms with enough functionality to persuade the customer of the need for the system.

Based on the positive results of the POETS investigative prototyping activity, the TRICS prototypers decided that the climate and project were right for the application of object-oriented technology. As a first step, they were sent away for training in how to build object-oriented software with Eiffel. They returned from training as converts to the technology and enthusiastically set about to build the TRICS operational prototype using Eiffel, C++ (with the InterViews library) and some C sprinkled in for good measure. Based on a successful field trial of the operational prototype, the development of the actual TRICS system was undertaken. It is the development of the TRICS production system that is described in the rest of this chapter.

3.2.2 Analysis

The analysis phase had two closely related aspects: *requirements analysis* and *system analysis*.

In requirements analysis, a view of the needs of the end-users of the system was developed. This process involved a series of interviews where key systems concepts were identified, and key system features were discussed with the end-user. Between sessions, MPR analysts abstracted and documented the findings in a user-centered Requirements Specification which recorded the functional requirements of the system. This document was reviewed and approved by our client.

The requirements specification not only described the features that the system must deliver, but it also documented features that are desired, but that were not to be implemented in the current development. While the requirements that must be satisfied drove the implementation process, the importance of stated future requirements should not be underestimated. Such requirements set a long-term objective for the system and are important considerations when architecting a system to be extensible.

In system analysis, the problem domain was analyzed and a model of the system was constructed using the static portions of the Object-Oriented Analysis (OOA) technique developed by Coad and Yourdon [Coad 1991]. The model was based upon the requirements documented in the Requirements Specification.

The analysis model focused on the fundamental aspects of TRICS; the network topology and how alarms affect it. Figure 3.4 illustrates a portion of the managed object class hierarchy diagram documented in the analysis model. The analysis model did not contain the behavioural aspects nor the level of detail suggested by Coad and Yourdon and advocated by our internal technology transfer agent. A number of factors influenced this decision, including:

1. Time and resource limitations.

2. The lack of tools to support OOA.[1]

3. Designers did not, at the time, see the value in a comprehensive OOA model. In fact, there was an expectation that by keeping the model small, it would be easier to understand and review.

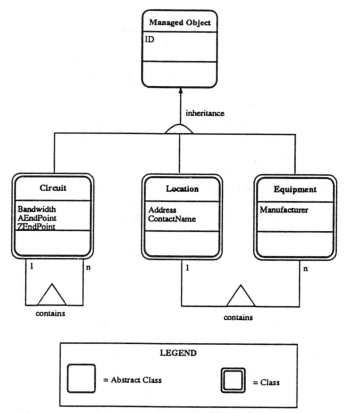

Figure 3.4: Portion of class hierarchy from OOA model

---

[1] At the time the TRICS development was undertaken, there were no commercially available tools to support OOA short of a drawing tool and a text editor.

Of course, hindsight is 20/20 and when one reviews past decisions one must resist the temptation to be blindly critical. In reflection, however, several drawbacks to this approach have been observed:

1. Despite our best intentions, the model was difficult to review. Without the behaviour, our client found it difficult to determine how the system was going to operate.

2. Only part of the system was modelled and none of the behaviour was included. The result was a lack of a common view of the system behaviour between developers of the system. Many decisions regarding functionality were thus left to the design and implementation stages causing domain classes like Circuit to be less reusable. Without the high-level specification of class interaction in the OOA model, we also have found it difficult to familiarize new developers with the existing system.

System Developers: The perhaps obvious conclusion is that, next time, we would prepare a more comprehensive object-oriented analysis model. However, we have also concluded that an object-oriented analysis model, no matter how detailed or complete, is still "static". In reviewing the model, it is difficult to determine the dynamics of the system. For example, what is the sequence of events when an alarm is created? What classes are involved? We eagerly await object-oriented analysis modelling technology that would permit the construction of an *executable* analysis model that would visually depict the processing of selected scenarios.

Management: Object-oriented analysis models reveal far more about a system than their structured analysis counterparts. Ours are more compact, provide more information per page, and are easier to read than the bulky tomes from the structured era. (Yes, you still need to look at three or four different diagrams at once to really understand it.) Until executable analysis models are available, build a quick prototype of the analysis model. It will help you understand the model and find problems you would otherwise miss.

3.2.3 Design

The design phase built on the abstractions prepared during analysis and developed two distinct, but interrelated views of the system: the *class design* view and the *process design* view. These two separate views are required as it is impossible to capture the details of a complex distributed system using a single view. The class design describes the classes and the relationships between them in order to specify the logical design of the system. The process design specifies how the system functionality is distributed amongst processes and how these processes can be arranged on processors.

The process design also describes process connectivity and the role of any external devices. This gives the physical design of the system and was crucial in order to ensure that the performance, capacity and reliability requirements of TRICS were met. The process design relates to the class design in that each process actually contains a network of cooperating objects. Each object is an instantiation of a class defined in the class design. Some of the classes are specific to the process, and some are shared between one or more processes. Classes are logically grouped into clusters. The relationship between classes, clusters, and processes is depicted in Figure 3.5. This figure shows a subset of the clusters developed for the TRICS system and how they depend on the Eiffel libraries.

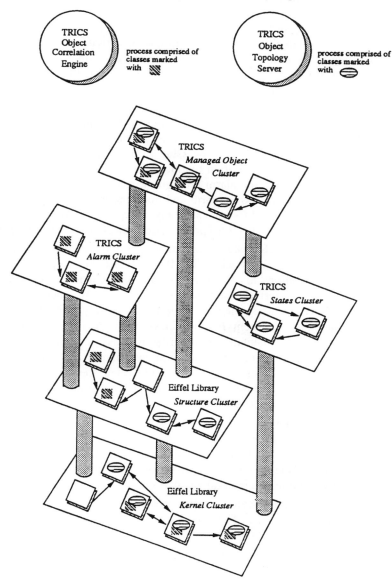

Figure 3.5: Eiffel clusters

The relationships between classes and two of the processes in the TRICS system, the Object Correlation Engine and the Object Topology Server, are also depicted.

The processes of TRICS were designed based on the experience gained from the development of the operational prototype. In the prototype, all of the TRICS knowledge processes were in one Unix process resulting in a performance bottleneck. For the production system, we wanted to take advantage of parallel processing opportunities by breaking the single Unix process into a number of cooperating processes. The opportunities for parallel processing were identified by grouping activities that occur in a typical event flow through the system. The groups of activities identified were then analyzed according to the kind of access required to objects within the grouped activity (i.e., read access, read/write access). Processes were then selected such that concurrency problems would be minimized.

For example, the typical flow in TRICS is for an event to enter the system and be processed into an alarm. The managed objects driven by that alarm are identified and the alarm is correlated against the network topology. Based on this flow of events, two Unix processes were partitioned: the Alarm Processing Engine (APE) that creates an alarm from an event; and the Object Correlation Engine (OCE) that associates an alarm with a managed object and propagates the alarm through the network topology. Each of these processes requires only read access to alarm and managed objects, so separation of the functionality into two processes does not cause any concurrency problems. Write access to the objects is controlled through a third process, the Object Topology Server (OTS).

The classes of the TRICS system were identified and designed by applying the Responsibility-Driven Design approach [Wirfs-Brock 1990]. This approach ensures the class fulfills its responsibilities to all three types of clients it may have: the external clients that use the class's interface; the subclass clients that will inherit from the class; and the class itself. In many cases, one class at design eventually expanded into a cluster of classes in the implemented system. For each class at design, a "stub" was created that contained enough of the implementation to describe the class. It is important to note that at this stage, the stub did not contain the actual implementation, but rather it: described the contracts and responsibilities of the class; identified the class's parent(s) and suppliers; and provided the signature of all externally visible features. These design stubs were legally formatted Eiffel and C++ classes.

An example of a partial stub for an Eiffel class at design time is shown in Figure 3.6. This class provides a generic class to support the thresholding of alarms. For example, a particular alarm object may only be created in TRICS if five specific events from the external monitoring system are seen within a 30 second interval. If less than five of the events occur within the interval, no alarm is created.

For Eiffel classes, features were described not only by signature, but also through preconditions and postconditions.[2] The specification of these assertions at design was

---

[2] Preconditions are used to specify the conditions that must exist before the feature is executed. Postconditions express the conditions that must exist at the completion of a feature's execution. Pre/post-conditions are, in essence, the expression of a contract between a class and its clients; they are important contributors to the production of reliable software [Meyer 1988].

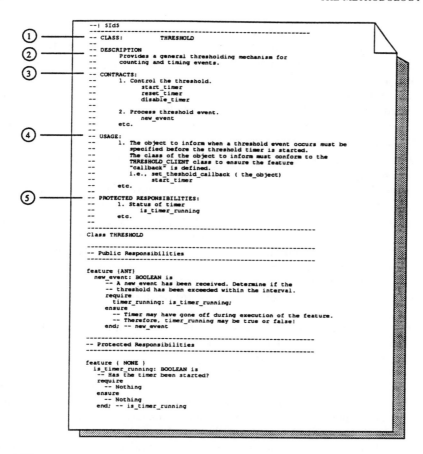

```
--| SIds
------------------------------------------------------------
-- CLASS:          THRESHOLD
--
-- DESCRIPTION
--     Provides a general thresholding mechanism for
--     counting and timing events.
--
-- CONTRACTS:
--     1. Control the threshold.
--            start_timer
--            reset_timer
--            disable_timer
--
--     2. Process threshold event.
--            new_event
--     etc.
--
-- USAGE:
--     1. The object to inform when a threshold event occurs must be
--        specified before the threshold timer is started.
--        The class of the object to inform must conform to the
--        THRESHOLD_CLIENT class to ensure the feature
--        "callback" is defined.
--        i.e., set_theshold_callback ( the_object)
--              start_timer
--     etc.
--
-- PROTECTED RESPONSIBILITIES:
--     1. Status of timer
--            is_timer_running
--     etc.
--
------------------------------------------------------------
Class THRESHOLD
------------------------------------------------------------
-- Public Responsibilities
------------------------------------------------------------

feature {ANY}
  new_event: BOOLEAN is
      -- A new event has been received. Determine if the
      -- threshold has been exceeded within the interval.
    require
      timer_running: is_timer_running;
    ensure
      -- Timer may have gone off during execution of the feature.
      -- Therefore, timer_running may be true or false!
    end; -- new_event

------------------------------------------------------------
-- Protected Responsibilities
------------------------------------------------------------

feature ( NONE )
  is_timer_running: BOOLEAN is
      -- Has the timer been started?
    require
      -- Nothing
    ensure
      -- Nothing
    end; -- is_timer_running
```

① The name of the class.

② A brief description.

③ A list of the contracts provided by the class to its clients or descendants. The features that encompass each contract are listed below it.

④ A description of how the class is used or other miscellaneous notes/warnings.

⑤ A list of the features that are available to the class and its descendants.

Figure 3.6: Eiffel header

integral to the development process as it forced many implicit assumptions about classes to be made explicit. For example, within a Multiplexor class, it was possible to assert a design assumption that a particular value would cause the multiplexor to block forever until an event occurred. Assertions also permitted a class designer to explicitly state the acceptable values of arguments passed on feature invocation. That is, a designer could specify that a string argument must not only be an initialized value, but that it must have a non-zero length. This defensive programming stance helped to decrease duplication in code that checked argument correctness.

The use of assertions was only possible because of the previous experience that the developers and designers had obtained through the development of the operational prototype. The reader may notice that we have not mentioned any use of invariants. This is because in our experience it takes approximately six months for developers to effectively use preconditions and postconditions, and about a year for effective use of invariants. At the time of the TRICS design, our developers had become comfortable with feature assertions, but not invariants. In our experience, once familiar with assertions, developers are loath to give them up.

Ideally, tools would be available to permit the specification of the object-oriented design in a highly interactive, graphical environment. Unfortunately, a survey of the market at the time TRICS design started yielded few prospects. Not to be dissuaded, object-oriented design proceeded using a more primitive, but still effective, approach. Diagrams depicting the inheritance and client-supplier relationships between classes were drawn either by hand or by using a drawing tool. These diagrams were depicted using Booch's object-oriented design notation [Booch 1991]. We had actually developed some in-house tools so that design specifications could be extracted from (or generated from) the stubs. The diagrams depicted the inheritance and client-supplier relationships between classes, and were accompanied by an abstract form of the class specifying the inheritance of the class, and an extraction of the signatures of exported features. These specifications were produced using the Eiffel "short" utility and a modified form of the C++ genman[3] utility. Unfortunately, these tools were too slow and cumbersome to be effective. Hence, they were rarely used.

System Developers: The design approach described was effective; it did permit a design to be proposed, reviewed, revised and ultimately implemented. Also, the preparation of the stubs during design provided a welcome "kick start" to the implementation phase since an outline of each class was already completed. However, since the headers replicate information found in the class body (e.g., the names of the features), some effort is required to ensure that the documentation headers are kept up to date. In the future, we will develop tools to aid in this endeavor.

Management: I am willing to overlook the lack of effective object-oriented design tools only because object-oriented designs build on object-oriented analysis models. Today's CASE tools do a great job in producing structured design models. The problem is that the transformation of a structured analysis model to a structured design model often results in two models that cannot even be compared, let alone traced. And forget about maintenance. The better object-oriented analysis and design methods solve some of these basic problems. Whatever you do, do not skip analysis and design when you build an object-oriented system (unless you really want to waste a lot of money.)

---

[3] genman is a public-domain utility developed by Bob Mastors for generating Unix style "man page" documentation about a C++ class.

3.2.4 Words of wisdom

What we did right:

- We educated the development team in object-oriented technology. Equally important as the formal education, the development team was able to apply the technology in a prototyping environment *before* undertaking the development of the system.
- We changed our methodological approach and did not apply structured analysis and design techniques. We treated the system in terms of objects from analysis through the logical and physical design stages.
- We designed classes in terms of their responsibilities and grouped those responsibilities into contracts. Assertions were used to specify the features of a class.

What we will do differently the next time:

- We will continue to use prototyping to clarify user requirements, but we will try not to build *operational* prototypes. Instead, we will combine prototyping of the analysis model with user interface prototyping to achieve the same result.
- We will apply *all* of object-oriented analysis including the specification of object behaviour.
- We will increase the focus on class design by requiring the specification of invariants. If it is difficult to specify an invariant for a class, the class abstraction will be questioned.

3.3 THE IMPLEMENTATION

An important factor in the TRICS development was an intent, from the start, to leverage as much power as possible in the form of improved productivity from the development environment. This brought two competing forces into focus. On one hand, productivity is improved if the developers have experience with the toolset. This implies that the existing toolset should not be drastically changed. On the other hand, improved productivity results from the use of more powerful languages, such as object-oriented languages, and more integrated environments than traditionally available in a C/Unix environment.

As you will see in this discussion, the TRICS development balanced these two competing forces by utilizing the more powerful object-oriented languages and their associated libraries in conjunction with existing Unix development environment tools.

3.3.1 Multi-language development

In the object-oriented world, productivity is leveraged through the use of libraries and frameworks.[4] For the operational prototype, we knew that we required both a strong object structuring library and a strong X-window graphical library. A review of the available tools led us to choose Eiffel for, in part, its object structuring capabilities, and C++, in conjunction with the InterViews library, for its graphical capabilities. These languages and libraries were chosen because they also provided us with strong support to access C. In our delivery environment, access to C is a necessity to interface to network protocols and external monitoring devices.

The end result of these choices was a multi-language development environment. For the most part, it was not necessary to integrate directly the languages we chose. As we described earlier, the partitioning of the system into multiple Unix processes permitted the implementation of most processes in only one of the two object-oriented languages. The knowledge processes were implemented in Eiffel, and the presentation processes in C++. When implementing the connectivity layer for communication between the knowledge and presentation processes, however, it was desirable to use Eiffel, the most productive language for us. Implementing the connectivity layer in Eiffel meant that it was necessary to have Eiffel and C++ co-exist within the same Unix process. This was accomplished through the use of the C-Package option of the Eiffel compiler[5] to generate a self-contained C library of the communications package. This C-Package provides a C callable programming interface to any Eiffel class that was designated at compile-time as *visible*.

The communications package consists of 25 Eiffel classes. These classes provide: access to the Unix socket facility; encapsulation of the multiple sockets necessary for a TRICS connection; and the management of message delivery through the virtual connections in the TRICS environment. Applications interface to the communications package through just two classes: `Network_Msg` and `Network_Router`. Eiffel processes interface to the communications package directly through these two classes. For the C++ processes, though, wrapper classes (in C++) that accessed the Eiffel classes through the generated C library were required. Figures 3.7 and 3.8 depict a portion of the Eiffel and C++ classes involved in this mapping.

In addition to the productivity improvements from using Eiffel to create this connectivity functionality, we also gained benefits from the use of the Eiffel garbage collection mechanism within the C++ processes. Although explicit destruction of objects created from the C++ `NetworkMsg` and `NetworkRouter` classes was still necessary, non-visible Eiffel objects within the communications package, including a significant

---

[4] A framework is a reusable design expressed as a set of abstract classes and the collaborations between those classes. By defining the appropriate subclasses, multiple applications may be derived from the framework.

[5] The Eiffel environment used in TRICS development was the environment from Interactive Software Engineering Inc (Version 2.3).

network_router.e file

```
--| $Id$
-------------------------------------------------------------
-- CLASS:          NETWORK_ROUTER
--
-- DESCRIPTION
--      This class permits messages to be exchanged between TRICS
--      processes. It interfaces to the transport layer.
--
-- CONTRACTS:
--      1. Initialize communications
--              init
--
--      2. Receive messages
--              get_message
--
-- etc.
-------------------------------------------------------------
Class NETWORK_ROUTER


-------------------------------------------------------------
-- Public Responsibilities
-------------------------------------------------------------

feature {ANY}
  init ( serv: STRING, pname: STRING) : BOOLEAN is
    -- Initialize the NETWORK_ROUTER
    require
      service_not_void: serv /= Void;
      process_name_not_void: pname /= Void;
    ensure
      -- Nothing
    end; -- init

  get_message ( wait_forever: BOOLEAN, timeout: INTEGER ): NETWORK_MSG is
    -- Get the next available message from one of the connected channels.
    require
      valid_timeout : timeout >= 0;
    ensure
      network_message_not_void: Result /= Void;
    end; -- get_message

etc.
```

nr_interface.e file

```
--| $Id$
-------------------------------------------------------------
-- CLASS:          NR_INTERFACE
--
-- DESCRIPTION
--      This class works around the garbage collector to permit
--      access to the Network_Router from C.
--
-- etc.
-------------------------------------------------------------
Class NR_INTERFACE

inherit
  NETWORK_ROUTER

-------------------------------------------------------------
-- Public Responsibilities
-------------------------------------------------------------

feature {ANY}

  nr_get_message ( wait_forever: BOOLEAN, timeout: INTEGER ): INTEGER is
    -- Get the next available message from one of the connected channels
    -- using the inherited get_message feature.  Return a reference to
    -- the NETWORK_MSG rather than the NETWORK_MSG itself.
    require
      valid_timeout : timeout >= 0;
    ensure
      network_message_not_void: Result > 0;
    end; -- nr_get_message

etc.
```

Figure 3.7: Eiffel interface

NetworkRouter.h file

```
class NetworkMsg;

class NetworkRouter{

  public:

    NetworkRouter();
    ~NetworkRouter();

    int          Init (char *, char *);
    NetworkMsg* GetMessage (int WaitFlag,
                            int Timeout);
}; // NetworkRouter
```

NetworkRouter.C file

```
#include <NetworkRouter.h>
#include <NetworkMsg.h>

extern "C" {
#include <_eiffel.h>                        // Eiffel Run-Time Definitions

void   nr_interface_eiffel_init();          // Initialize the Eiffel C-Package
OBJPTR nr_interface_create();               // For creating "visible" NR_INTERFACE Objects
DATUM  init_c (OBJPTR, char*, char*);       // C API to NR_INTERFACE "init"
int    get_message_c (OBJPTR, int, int);    // C API to NR_INTERFACE "nr_get_message".
                                            // The es system permits a new name to be
                                            // specified for the feature.

}

static OBJPTR eiffel_nr_interface;          // One and only one NR_INTERFACE per process.

// Constructor
NetworkRouter::NetworkRouter() {
   nr_interface_eiffel_init();              // Initialize the Eiffel Run-Time
   eiffel_nr_interface =                    // Create the NR_INTERFACE Eiffel
     nr_interface_create();                 // object.
}

int NetworkRouter::Init (char *ServiceName, char *ProcessName) {
   DATUM success;

   success = init_c ( eiffel_nr_interface, ServiceName, ProcessName);
   return ( BOOLDAT (success) );
}

int NetworkRouter::GetMessage (int WaitFlag, int Timeout) {
   OBJPTR eiffel_nm_interface;
   NetworkMsg *m;

   eiffel_nm_interface = (OBJPTR) INTDAT (get_message_c (eiffel_nr_interface,
                                                         BOOLDAT (WaitFlag),
                                                         INTDAT (Timeout)));

     // Copy Fields from returned Eiffel
     // Network_Msg object to C++ NetworkMsg
     // object.

     return m;
}
```

Figure 3.8: C++ wrappers to Eiffel

amount of routing information, were automatically reclaimed. The use of garbage collection within the generated library, however, was not without problems. For example, Eiffel objects created using the interface generated by designating an Eiffel class *visible* were not garbage-collected and there was no mechanism to cause the destruction of these objects. We worked around this limitation by creating a subclass to the `Network_Router` class, `NR_Interface`, that created the necessary Eiffel objects as though they were non-visible, and by providing features that returned references to those objects for use from C++. Care, though, had to be taken to ensure Eiffel objects referenced from C++ were not garbage-collected too early! Thus, while the ability to integrate Eiffel and C++ in this manner was beneficial, it was also clear that interfaces between language environments must be designed with mechanisms like garbage collection in mind.

System Developers: In an ideal world, it would have been preferable to develop the entire TRICS application using a single object-oriented language. This would have greatly simplified issues such as training, testing and configuration management. Reality, however, always casts a different light on a problem. To achieve the results desired in the most economical manner possible, we concluded that the multi-lingual approach made sense. In fact, it played an essential role in ensuring the success of the project by improving the productivity of the developers.

3.3.2 Object storage

The storing of objects was a point of contention from the earliest stages of development. Our experiences evaluating object-oriented database management system products in 1990 had not convinced us that they were ready for use in a network management system.

During the prototype development, we utilized the persistent storage facilities available in the Eiffel library. While sufficient for a single user prototype, this persistent store mechanism did not support the storage and retrieval of individual objects, and did not provide us with any support for concurrency control. For system development, we had to find another solution.

In the spirit of reuse, we pursued an option to use an existing proprietary indexed file mechanism. Through an Eiffel interface class, we were able to build upon this proprietary set of C modules to store the attributes of our objects as ASCII strings. The mechanism also provided us with simple object lookups using configurable keys and a locking mechanism. Again, the ability to interface to C was critical in permitting this development option.

As with tools to support analysis and design, we anxiously await industrial quality object-oriented database products that support the storage and exchange of objects created within a multi-lingual environment.

3.3.3 Metrics

What underlies the TRICS system? What really got built?

Table 3.1 summarizes measurements taken from the classes underlying the knowledge processes of the TRICS system. These processes were implemented primarily in Eiffel with a few dips into C, now and again, for access to the operating system, communication systems, and the like. The classes have been divided into four groups: classes specific to the TRICS application (TRICS); classes of a more general nature such as classes encapsulating Unix sockets (TRICS LIBRARY); classes from the Workstation Administrator that provide a distributed name server (WA); and the classes of the Eiffel Library (EIFFEL LIBRARY). The measurements on the Eiffel library include classes from the kernel cluster (*STRING, INTEGER* etc.), classes from the structure cluster (*LINKED_LIST, QUEUE* etc.) and classes from the support cluster (*STORABLE, ITERATOR* etc.). There are several interesting observations from these measurements:

- The incidence of multiple inheritance in Eiffel classes is high, particularly compared to the InterViews C++ code underlying the presentation processes which has a 0% incidence of multiple inheritance. Inheriting from multiple parents is particularly evident in the TRICS classes which tended to inherit to gain access to constant values and common utility methods like debugging statements. Multiple inheritance was also used to achieve mixin behaviour, for example inheriting the behaviour to store a class.

- The incidence of genericity is much higher in classes designated as reusable (i.e., library classes) than it is in application-specific classes.

- The number of source lines of code (not including comment and blank lines) is lower than we anticipated given the complexity of the system and the functionality delivered. A system built in-house that provided similar, but *substantially less complex*, functionality compared to the Eiffel knowledge processes, had required on the order of 35,000 source lines of C code and 10 person-years of effort. Estimates to add the alarm propagation capabilities of TRICS to that C-based system were astronomical. The 8 presentation processes developed in C++ (including a modified version of the InterViews Idraw editor) required approximately 143 classes and 34,145 source lines of code.

- The maximum number of statements per method for the TRICS and TRICS Library cluster are very high and indicate a further decomposition of methods in at least a few classes is necessary.

- Approximately half of the classes developed were designated as *library* classes suitable for use, possibly with some generalization required, in other system developments. As many of these classes provided functionality we would rather buy than build (e.g., classes to support time), this percentage of reusable class generation should be expected to decline significantly in future developments. The development of classes suitable for reuse directly from a development will *not* occur without an investment of effort!

- The incidence of deferred (i.e. abstract) classes is low. This is an expected result because there had been no explicit attention paid to the building of a framework. Once again, however, it is shown that reusable abstractions do not come for free with object-oriented technology.

Table 3.1: Metrics from Eiffel development

	TRICS	TRICS LIBRARY	WA	EIFFEL LIBRARY
# Classes	155	72	12	92
Source lines of code	11365	9010	2335	11872
% of Classes that inherit	83	72	83	64
% incidence of multiple inheritance	72	35	25	21
% incidence of genericity	3	24	0	49
Avg # of parents	2.7	1.8	1.8	1.3
Max # of parents	8	8	6	3
% of deferred classes	3.9	12.5	0	22.8
Avg # of features per class	5.5	9	14	12
% of features that are methods	65	66	56	68
% of features that are attributes	35	33	44	32
Avg # of instructions per method	13	10	8	2
Max # of instructions per method	670	120	53	35
Avg # of suppliers per class	5.9	4.7	5.9	2.6
Max # of suppliers per class	36	15	13	11

3.3.4 Multi-platform development

The end customer of TRICS was interested in the delivery of the TRICS system on a single platform. Early on, though, the development team formed the objective to develop the system such that it could run on most 32-bit Unix systems provided that Eiffel, InterViews and a suitable C++ compiler were available. The approach was not to develop the system on a single platform and then port it to the others, but rather to support multiple platforms simultaneously at all points in the development cycle. This parallel multi-platform development offers several benefits that are important to recognize:

1. It takes advantage of a heterogeneous (i.e. multi-vendor) workstation environment, making it unnecessary to completely re-tool a project team for each new development.

2. It produces more robust software since the system is exposed to multiple environments. On numerous occasions, bugs have gone undetected on a more "forgiving" platform only to be uncovered during testing on another.

3. It builds in vendor independence. The days are quickly disappearing where a software product can be tied to equipment from a specific vendor.

4. The reusable components produced have wider applicability.

These benefits, however, do not come for free. Invariably, when developing for multiple platforms, variations or differences between the platforms surface including: variations in system call signatures; variations in system call behaviour; system calls not supported on platforms; and occasionally application code that just plain does not work on one platform but works on another. As the development of TRICS progressed, it was not uncommon to hear "but it works on the Sun" uttered from a neighboring office. This observation will come as no great revelation to the experienced C/UNIX programmer.

In general, we have found Eiffel to be very transportable between platforms, and in most cases we have been able to move a process written in Eiffel to another platform simply through re-compilation. Why is this? One likely reason is that the source of many subtle bugs in a C or C++ program, namely memory management and pointer manipulation, is hidden from the Eiffel developer and is thus less likely to cause problems upon porting. This does not mean that all porting problems disappear. At times, typically when a call to an external C function was made from Eiffel, it was still necessary to account for platform variations.

One approach to supporting variations in Eiffel is to implement a class hierarchy to encapsulate operating system peculiarities. Another is to place #ifdef statements in Eiffel source files and pre-process them with cpp before running the Eiffel compiler. We did not pursue either of these solutions as they were felt to be clumsy and impractical. Instead, we encapsulated platform variations in a C module that itself contained #ifdef statements. As this approach does not address variations required in code other than at the C level, a preferable solution would be to extend the Eiffel language or environment with a mechanism to handle this situation.

Of course, the total development effort expended in a multi-platform development environment is higher than in a homogeneous environment due to the extra testing and re-work required to obtain correct operation on each platform. The total cost of testing components on multi-platforms *as they are developed*, though, is significantly lower than performing a bulk port and re-test later. Even considering the extra costs, it has been our experience that a parallel multi-platform development approach is cost-effective, and yields a more stable software product.

3.3.5 Configuration management challenges

A multi-paradigm, multi-language and multi-platform development presents some challenges for configuration management. Two of the more interesting are: revision control and load generation.

In revision control, we are interested in a systematic scheme to manage the evolution of software entities. Traditionally, the software configuration management unit (SCM) was the module. When developing object-oriented software, the basic SCM unit is the class. In TRICS, revisions to classes were tracked individually. Thus, it is somewhat surprising that the most convenient unit of access to the managed software entities in TRICS development has been the cluster. This is because modifications to the TRICS software generally involved changes to several classes within a cluster. The revision control tool we used, cvs,[6] supported both the tracking of revisions to individual classes and the retrieval of entire clusters. As cvs was independent of the programming language, we were able to use the same revision control system for software in the Eiffel, C++ and C languages.

The other side of configuration management, load generation, is concerned with the production of end products such as executables and libraries from the software entities in the SCM system. Unlike the revision control system, we were forced to use different load generation tools for the different languages. The es system was used to generate Eiffel loads, while common Unix utilities, namely make and makedepend, were used for C and C++ software entities. A common Makefile was developed to provide a transparent means of integrating the different load generation tools.

Different load generation challenges were faced in each of the language environments. For C++ entities, the technical challenge lay in the automatic maintenance of dependencies. We approached this challenge through the use of the `makedepend` utility, but found that the reliance of C++ on the `#include` mechanism to resolve inheritance and supplier dependencies complicated the process and was not for the faint of heart! While the es system relieved us of the `#include` nightmare, it was not without its own heartaches. es provides no help if you wish to build targets for more than one platform, an obvious requirement given our development environment. The difficulty arises because the Eiffel compiler creating a sub-directory in the directory where the class being compiled is located. Thus, if one attempts to compile the classes in a directory tree for another platform, a mixture of compiled objects from two or more platforms could be produced yielding very strange results! Our solution to this challenge was to construct, at the extremities of the source tree, sub-directories for each platform containing links to the Eiffel source classes in the parent directory. This required us to wrap the es command in a shell script that created the platform specific sub-directories and set up the links prior to running `es`.

The moral of the story is not to expect the challenges of configuration management to disappear with the use of object-oriented technology. Perhaps the situation will improve when object-oriented technology is applied to the particular challenges of configuration management.

---

[6] Concurrent Version System is a public-domain revision control tool built on top of RCS. CVS "extends the notion of revision control from a collection of files in a single directory to a hierarchical collection of directories consisting of revision controlled files" [Grune 1989].

3.3.6 Testing

TRICS testing was based on the premise of cluster layering. This means that cluster tests are the lowest denominator for official testing. The motivation behind choosing cluster testing over class testing was that without the support of other classes in its cluster, class testing was thought to be costly; both in time required to write code to support the class, and in time writing test plans.

The development and testing of clusters was ordered by dependency similar to the approach described in [Gindre 1989]. The least dependent cluster was developed first and was tested using specification-based testing techniques. Once tested, this least dependent cluster was used to supply a support environment for the testing of the next cluster. Each additional cluster tested thus supplied additional functionality to the overall process(es) being built. This technique helped to eliminate integration testing, since by adding clusters layer by layer, an integration process was implicitly occurring.

Informal system testing took place throughout the development cycle as developers used partially implemented and tested processes to develop and test new functionality. The system itself, then, essentially provided its own test bench. Formal system testing was also conducted based on conventional specification-based techniques.

Based on our experience with this testing strategy, it was identified that some form of class testing is required in conjunction with cluster testing. Too many classes were being lumped into one cluster test with the result that boundary conditions on the class and cluster were not tested adequately. Defects that could have been caught early in the development cycle slipped through to system testing. To address these problems, we are currently investigating several of the issues surrounding the testing of object-oriented software, like strategies for regression testing of classes given changes to the inheritance hierarchy, with the goal of developing a methodology for use in future object-oriented software construction activities.

Management: I feel that I may have been lured into a false sense of security about the "inherent" reliability of object-oriented systems. I had assumed that by their nature object-oriented systems were more reliable than non-object-oriented systems. By reusing components and inheriting from other classes, I thought it was OK to have a more relaxed attitude to testing. I am rapidly changing my mind. I now see that a comprehensive testing strategy will be required if we want to produce robust systems. The dilemma is how to accomplish this without unduly affecting development productivity and innovation. Clearly, automated support will be required. Another feature for an object-oriented CASE environment anyone?

3.3.7 Words of wisdom

What we did right:

- We chose the right tools for the job even though it meant pursuing development in multiple languages. The extra effort required to integrate languages and tools has been more than compensated by the productivity improvements resulting from the use of the most appropriate tool to fulfill a TRICS requirement.
- Using object-oriented technology we were able to develop a complex, highly functional system with fewer lines of code and less effort than we had experienced building similar systems in C. Frameworks and reusable classes will not be generated automatically from using the technology, but require investment and foresight.

What we will do differently next time:

- We will adopt a testing methodology that includes testing at the system, cluster and class levels.

3.4 THE MANAGEMENT

Software system development, whether object-oriented or conventional, requires appropriate management strategies to control the process. Although we have made changes to our software project management approach to reflect the needs of object-oriented technology, we do not yet have all the answers. This section describes our experience in several aspects of object-oriented project management, and discusses how we plan to improve our approach in the future.

3.4.1 Iteration

A common message emanating from many of the experts in object-oriented technology has been the need to develop object-oriented systems iteratively. The motivation for and content of an iteration, however, varies between the experts from a view of evolving clusters [Meyer 1990] to rounds of analyze a little, design a little, implement a little, and test a little [Berard 1990].

Our previous experiences with the inflexibility of the waterfall approach had led us to experiment with the iterative spiral model [Boehm 1988] in our early investigations into object-oriented technology. Although we found the spiral model provided a strong basis for the development of research prototypes, we did not feel it provided adequate closure for operational prototyping or system development. Instead, we approached the development of the TRICS system according to a process similar to the recursive/parallel model [Berard 1990a]. Figure 3.9 illustrates the TRICS development approach as well as additions we plan to make in future developments.

The tasks performed during the Requirements Analysis, System Analysis, Process

Design, Class Design, Implement, Test and System Test activities have been described earlier in this discussion. Figure 3.9 provides the missing link in this discussion by showing the flow between the activities. Those flows shown as solid arrows indicate the paths taken between activities in TRICS development. Based on the Requirements Analysis, the System Analysis and Process Design were undertaken. Based on a rough completion of the Process Design, three initial parallel development streams for classes in the system were identified: the knowledge classes and processes development stream; the presentation classes and processes development stream; and the connectivity classes development stream. Development progressed in parallel along these streams through Class Design, Implementation and Test. Just in case it appears that the sheer number of activities will never cause development to complete, we must stress that each activity is lightweight when compared to its counterpart in a more traditional structured approach.

Sometimes, the result of a stream development uncovered aspects missed at Process Design. For example, the Process Design activity included the definition of the protocol between knowledge and presentation classes. If a single development stream required changes to the protocol, it was necessary to revisit the Process Design and iterate back through the Class Design, Implement and Test activities for each stream affected (see the flow labelled 1 in Figure 3.9).

Iterations of Class Design, Implement and Test were also planned for the individual development streams. We refer to this as the development of towers of features. Iterations through streams to develop a "feature tower" were planned to ensure the presence of a stable base system for each stream to test against (see the flow labelled 2 in Figure 3.9).

Finally, iterations through the streams also resulted from the System Test stage when the system did not conform to the requirements (see the flow labelled 3 in Figure 3.9). Obviously, it is desirable to minimize iterations resulting from this flow.

This process model provided three main advantages during the TRICS development. Firstly, it permitted a planned approach to parallel development activities. Secondly, it partitioned the development effort permitting the development of the more risky and the more reusable classes early in the project's life. Finally, it permitted the addition of parallel development streams in a controlled manner without adversely affecting the planned activities. For example, an additional stream of development was added late in the development phase of the project to implement additional historical logging capabilities that were unforeseen at the System Analysis stage.

Reviews were generally held between each activity. For example, a review was held between the Requirements Analysis and System Analysis activities, and between the Class Design and Implementation activities. When iterating, however, reviews were not generally held as it was felt that the modifications were not significant. In the future, we intend to institute stronger guidelines for reviewing upon iteration.

The reader may notice that the operational prototyping step described early in our methodology does not appear in Figure 3.9. While in the case of TRICS this form of prototyping was required to ensuring funding for the development, it is not a necessary activity in our development approach. We view prototyping during development as occurring in parallel to the activities shown. Within each activity, the responsible

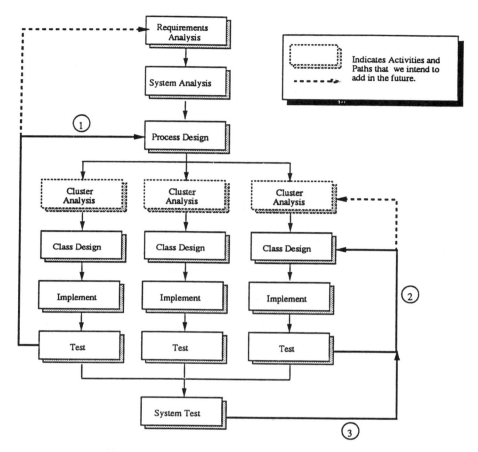

Figure 3.9: Software process model applied in TRICS development

developers are encouraged to apply any one of a number of forms of prototyping, such as mocking up a user interface or prototyping a cluster design, to manage development risks.

Technology Transfer: As shown in Figure 3.9, the software process applied in the TRICS development did not apply analysis iteratively for each independent stream. In the future, we plan to integrate in analysis activities on the cluster(s) of classes of a stream. This analysis will focus on the specific *tower of features* to be provided by the stream and will update, as required, the Systems Analysis model. The Cluster Analysis activity will permit the object-oriented analysis model to remain up-to-date with the development and thus improve the traceability from analysis through implementation.

3.4.2 Project structure

The development of the TRICS system through to field test at the customer site, and including the effort expended in the development of the operational prototype, required almost 8 person-years of effort. Figure 3.10 illustrates where that effort occurred. It is interesting to note in this comparison that:

- Extensive investigation of the needs of the user were conducted prior to the development of the operational prototype. This is evident in the high effort associated with the Requirements Analysis activity for the operational prototype. This investment paid off in a lower effort for Requirements Analysis prior to the actual system development.

- The operational prototype was developed without any System Analysis. Although a significant effort was expended in System Analysis for the TRICS development, we expect this to grow in future developments as we more fully exploit the capabilities of object-oriented analysis.

- The building of the operational prototype lowered the effort required for Process Design in the TRICS development.

- Although much of the implementation for the presentation processes (in C++ and InterViews) was reused from the operational prototype, a significant effort was still required in the TRICS development. The effort expended for the knowledge class and process development in Eiffel was expected because of the increased functionality in the TRICS production system. The TRICS system development minimized C development and encapsulated all existing C code from the prototype within Eiffel and C++ classes, hence the zero effort expended in C development.

- The Software Maintenance effort captures changes to the system required prior to release to the customer and will rise over the lifetime of the system.

- The effort categorized as "Other" includes time expended for giving demonstrations of the system, developing user documentation, configuring the user's workstations and workstation environments, etc. As always in a project, the effort required for "Other" should not be underestimated!

It is important to stress that although we were able to reuse some portions of the design and some individual classes between the prototype and the system development, we are not pursuing an evolutionary prototyping and development approach. Nor do we believe that an evolutionary approach is viable. We see prototyping as the activity where we, as developers, have a chance to "build a system to throw away" [Brooks 1982].

3.4.3 Team structure

The TRICS development team was comprised, primarily, of two senior designers, two intermediate designers and one junior designer. With the exception of the junior designer, all personnel had participated in the development of the operational prototype.

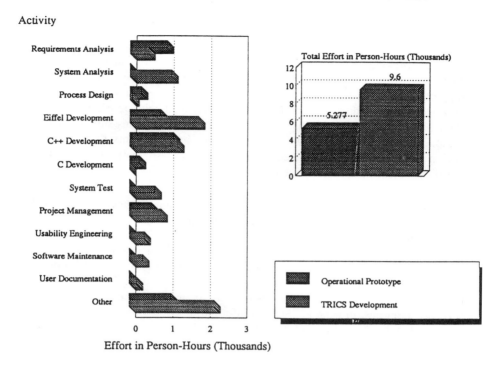

Figure 3.10: Comparison of effort

The structure of the team was flexible and reflected the process model described above. In general, one team member was primarily responsible for each of the independent development streams with one or more other designers collaborating on that development. As necessary, however, it was possible for a given designer to work on one or more independent streams.

Management: Although it works and is satisfying for the developers, I fear that assigning personnel to projects from cradle to grave is no longer feasible or desirable. Projects such as TRICS consist of many complex components each requiring specialized skills to produce. Today's projects resemble an operating room with many specialists working somewhat autonomously under the direction of the surgeon. Object-oriented technology does not remove the need for specialists. It only provides a sharper scalpel, or a better anesthetic. It does not provide the talent nor the skills to do every job that must be done. The TRICS project could probably have benefited by having more specialists such as domain experts, analysts, framers, librarians, graphic user interface designers, usability engineers etc., applied to the project rather than have a small group of individuals do it all themselves.

3.4.4 Reuse

Reuse of software assets is a desirable, but elusive goal. From our perspective, one of the most interesting reasons to pursue object-oriented technology has been its ability to support reuse. Even with our first prototyping experience using Eiffel, we were able to experience the productivity improvements associated with reusing object structuring classes like linked lists and hash tables from the basic libraries supplied with the Eiffel compiler. Equally important as the productivity improvements that resulted from not having to write yet another linked list was the increased creativity and ability to create complex object structuring and containment without having to drudge through the creation of those containers.

To date, most of the prototyping and development we have pursued in Eiffel has been in the domain of network surveillance. Because the domain has stayed constant, we have been able to reuse the basic design of classes. This design has not yet been formalized into a framework, but it does support the general mechanism of correlating environmental events to managed objects and manipulating the managed objects. Reuse of operating system encapsulations, like socket classes, and miscellaneous helper classes, like a tokenizer for strings, has also occurred and is more widespread. Reusing a software asset has, in general, been an informal three step process that involves at least two developers: the reuser and the class owner. The three steps involved in this process are: scrounge, modify, and abstract. A typical scenario of reuse involving these steps is summarized in Figure 3.11.

Scrounge	The reuser is charged with a task to add new functionality to the system. To provide the desired functionality, the reuser determines that he will need a `tokenizer` class to break a string into substrings based on a defined delimiter character. Through informal mechanisms like hallway conversations, the reuser determines that such a class already exists. The reuser obtains a copy of the class from the class owner. It is important to recognize that the class owner is not always aware this reuse is occurring.
Modify	The reuser analyzes the `tokenizer` class and decides it does not perform all of the functionality he desires or does not perform the existing functionality adequately. The reuser modifies the class to his liking.
Abstract	Through informal means, the class owner finds out that the `tokenizer` class has been "reused", that is, it has been modified. The class owner analyzes the changes and is aghast at the mutilation of the original intention of the class. In an important step (which does not always happen), the class owner approaches the reuser and together, they refine the class and determine an abstraction that provides the features required while retaining the abstraction originally desired. This refinement and abstraction process may result in the creation of new classes.

Figure 3.11: The steps of reuse

We have found that most of the classes we consider reusable have had this reuse process applied to them multiple times. Each time, the abstraction gets incrementally better, and hence, the class more reusable. Some of our classes have gone through four major reuse processes. For example, the classes underlying our connectivity and communication layer which are based on Unix sockets have been re-visited four times. Because many of our developments have been prototype efforts, we have only had to experience the re-integration of an improved abstraction once or twice. The evolution of our socket and interface[7] classes is provided in Figure 3.12. The evolution of these classes has been marked by:

- An increase in the level of abstraction. This has become evident in a simpler, cleaner interface with fewer methods providing more functionality, and an ability to easily specify invariants.

- A movement of much of the functionality from C code into Eiffel code.

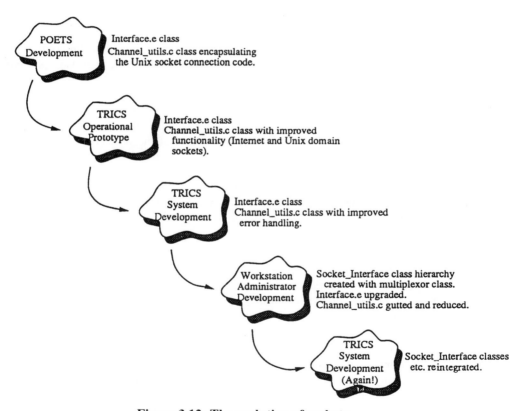

Figure 3.12: The evolution of sockets

---

[7] An interface encapsulates the multiple socket connections required between a client and server Unix process in our environment.

Technology Transfer: Obviously, the reuse process described above is insufficient to support reuse throughout an organization. As a result, we have been pursuing, in parallel, more formal approaches to software asset libraries. Our work has centered on the development of a combined browser and library that uses faceted classification [Prieto-Diaz 1987] to organize components. The use of a centralized asset library should permit the three step process to move from scrounging assets to locating assets. By ensuring each class has an owner that must be involved in any modification and abstraction process, we hope to maintain asset consistency and reduce the introduction of problems into existing systems resulting from class modifications. While these activities will help to support the reuse process, a corporate reuse strategy and change in culture are required to instigate the process in the first place!

3.4.5 Maintenance

A benefit often cited in the literature of adopting object-oriented technology is an expected improvement in the maintainability of the constructed software system. Although the TRICS system has yet to enter into its later stages of life where it will experience maintenance modifications, we have had a glimpse into some of the difficulties to expect based on the experience of personnel who joined the project as it progressed.

In general, one expects that the maintenance phase of the project will suffer from personnel having problems understanding how the system was constructed. Without an understanding of the system, it is impossible to determine where the modification should be made. The bad news is that we have only found this to be worse with systems constructed using object-oriented techniques! Although modifications to an object-oriented system do tend to be encapsulated, finding the correct place to make the modification is complicated by:

- The lack of a road map to the system.
- The lack of direct traceability between classes in the system. That is, the difficulty in determining the particular class implementing an inherited or supplied feature. The very aspects of the technology such as polymorphism that are a strength during specification and design become a curse to the system maintainers.

The good news, however, is that these difficulties could largely be alleviated by an appropriately tooled development environment that provides: graphical views of significant portions of the inheritance hierarchy (not just a given class's parents and children); an ability to focus in on a class in the hierarchy and view its source code; inspection of classes by selecting methods and requesting the implementing class; etc. Similar tools are available in some object-oriented environments like Smalltalk, but are just now appearing in industrial-strength form for object-oriented systems written in Eiffel and C++. In the long run, these implementation level tools must be integrated with the tools supporting analysis and design. It is important to remember that object-oriented technology is not magic and requires sophisticated CASE support.

3.4.6 Words of wisdom

What we did right:

- We applied an iterative software process model to development. This iterative software process model enabled us to respond effectively and quickly to problems, to pursue reuse and to provide a stable base of software on which to build the system incrementally.
- As abstraction and generalization of classes has occurred, we have re-introduced those classes back into the existing system to reduce the number of versions of a class that exist at any one time.

What we will do differently next time:

- We will integrate analysis activities into each parallel stream of development to improve traceability.
- We will define the roles involved in developing object-oriented software. Personnel will be assigned to perform their specialized role within multiple projects.
- We will continue to formalize our reuse process through improved mechanisms to locate classes. Class owners will be formally involved in any reuse process.
- We will acquire more tools to facilitate personnel in gaining an understanding of an existing software base.

3.5 THE FUTURE

Is object-oriented technology worth the effort? The answer is a resounding YES. Can software be engineered using object-oriented technology? The answer is a qualified yes.

The Software Engineering Institute (SEI) has defined five levels of process maturity based on the standards, procedures, tools and methods an organization uses in building or maintaining software [Paulk 1991]. The five levels of maturity are: an *initial* chaotic state where there are no formal procedures; a *repeatable* state where software development is dependent upon the individuals involved; a *defined* state where the software process is institutionalized; a *managed* state where the process is measured; and an *optimizing* state where improvement is fed back into the process.

Over the last few years, we have matured in our adoption and application of object-oriented technology moving from an initial chaotic state towards an increasingly repeatable and defined object-oriented software construction process. Today, we feel that we are hovering in between the second and third levels on the SEI maturity chart. Achievement of the characteristics of a fully definable process and beyond will require improvements in the traceability of development artifacts within the iterative process, stabilized and tooled development environments, and an integration of software quality techniques, to name but a few enhancements.

Based on our positive experiences building the TRICS software system, we will certainly continue in our efforts to exploit object-oriented technology for all it is worth. In particular, we plan to improve our application of object-oriented development methodologies, begin the development of frameworks, and integrate expert system technology into our object-oriented systems. Our story of object-oriented development is not finished, but will continue to unfold as our characters describe...

System Developers: A new and promising technology is seductive, and objects are no exception.

During the initial prototype, the motivation to use objects was mostly due to a fascination with the technology, and our object-orientation was limited to the implementation level. We enjoyed considerable success at this level, and were amazed at how quickly we could put together software using objects. Rather naively (in retrospect) we proceeded forward to develop a production system. We did not fully understand the degree to which objects were going to affect the way in which we developed software. We were frustrated by the lack of a proven and established object-oriented methodology. We were stymied by a lack of tools. However, we endured, produced a complex and reliable commercial application, and learned a lot along the way. Just wait until next time!

Technology Transfer: The wilderness is getting a little less lonely every day. Now that we have developers experienced with object-oriented technology, we can continue a push towards a time and place where systems will be constructed from reusable components and objects will be able to migrate through a distributed heterogeneous environment. For new object-oriented technology advocates, I have three bits of advice:

1. Before embarking on technology transfer, have a strong sense of the benefits of the technology and where it can take you. Define a few necessary terms, such as framework, and make sure everyone you deal with understands the same definitions.

2. Be pro-active. Try to keep the technology on the right path by participating in the system analysis and attending design reviews.

3. Realize that a dash of tormenting is necessary to reinforce the mentoring.

Management: Two years from start to finish. That's a long time. Enough time for the users to change, for their needs to change, for object-oriented technology to change. It took less code to do a lot more, but it still took a long time.

We knew a lot before we started, and learned a lot more along the way. The technology was (and still is) immature. There were not (and still are not) very good tools. We did not (and still do not) know very much about reuse.

Would I advise you to do it? Would I do it again? ABSOLUTELY! Once you know how to use it, object-oriented technology lets you build systems you could only dream about in the past. It's not easy. It certainly is not the silver bullet, the silver lining or the pot of gold at the end of the rainbow, but when it comes to building complex systems, it is better than anything else I have seen so far.

What is my advice? Simple. Teach your people about object-oriented technology. Plan to use the technology in projects. Let your people apply what they were taught. And, start small.

Now about that next script...

ACKNOWLEDGMENTS

The authors are indebted to the talented and dedicated members of the TRICS development team: Leslia Chow, Randy Chapman, August Wehrmann, Kevin Wittkopf, and Richard Loo. The authors also thank Ron Westfall for his valuable suggestions on the content and format of this chapter.

4

Development of control software for an experimental broadband ISDN switch

David Giddy
Telstra Corporation[1]
Melbourne (Australia)

4.1 INTRODUCTION TO THE EXPERIMENTAL B-ISDN NETWORK PROJECT

This chapter describes the ongoing development of the control software for an experimental Broadband Integrated Services Digital Network (B-ISDN) switch. Those unfamiliar with telecommunications technology should find that the introduction to switching, signalling and B-ISDN in the next section provides sufficient background to understand the remainder of the chapter (a more detailed introduction to B-ISDN may be found in [Delisle 1991]).

The software for this project is being jointly developed by Telecom Australia Research Laboratories (now Telstra) and the Electronics Research Laboratory of the Defence Science and Technology Organization (DSTO). DSTO is an Australian government body providing scientific expertise and leadership to the Department of Defence.

The aim of building an experimental B-ISDN network is to provide a vehicle with which to study a number of aspects of the technology. These studies are aimed at improving our understanding of the issues involved in B-ISDN and also providing a basis from which to contribute to the standardization of B-ISDN through the CCITT (the

---

[1] At the time the project developed in this chapter was being started, Telstra Corporation was called Telecom Research Laboratories and was part of Telecom Australia.

CCITT is an organ of the United Nations responsible for recommending international standards for telecommunications).

The chapter concentrates on the control software for a switch in the experimental network. It is a real-time control system responsible for carrying out the operations necessary to establish, monitor and release calls passing through the switch. These actions are carried out in response to stimuli such as a customer lifting the handset from a telephone and dialing a number. Although it is a real-time system, the performance of the experimental system is not a major development priority as it will never have to handle large quantities of traffic. It is sufficient that the system complete a single call establishment within a few seconds.

4.1.1 Why choose an object-oriented approach?

This project is experimental in nature and hence apart from correctness the most important criteria in developing this software is modifiability. Many of the elements involved in the software are current research topics and are not yet specified by CCITT or other standards bodies. It is essential therefore to allow the final product to be easily modified and adapted to conform to standards as they emerge and to allow experimentation with protocols, and control strategies, many of which have yet to be devised.

By capturing data and the associated code in a single class, each module is easier to understand. This also ensures that changes can be localised and modifications made without fear of breaking dozens of other parts of the system. Careful modeling produces a system which is relatively straightforward to extend.

In light of the above, the implementation language for the major processes in the system was a choice between C++ and Eiffel (other languages were considered not general purpose enough or were incapable of being interfaced to portions of the code that had to be developed in C).

It was felt that C++ was an unnecessarily complex hybrid language which could lead to difficulties in a multi-programmer team. In addition, as most of the team had little experience in object-oriented programming, a pure language would better facilitate the process of mentally shifting from a structured to an object-oriented paradigm.

A final consideration was the experimental (as opposed to prototype or production) nature of the project. This allowed us to take a risk in specifying a relatively new language.

The following sections provide an introduction to telecommunications and give an overview of the environment in which the software must execute. Later sections briefly describe the overall software system and they provide some detail of the more interesting portions of one subsystem of a single process.

4.2 INTRODUCTION TO SWITCHING, SIGNALLING AND B-ISDN

Out of necessity, this chapter includes a number of telecommunications terms which will not be familiar to many readers. The terms are defined where they are first used, and there is a glossary in section 4.9 providing additional explanations which the reader may find helpful.

4.2.1 Telecommunications circa 1993

The telecommunications network is a vast infrastructure spanning the globe and theoretically capable of connecting any two telephones, modems, facsimile machines or other devices anywhere on the planet. Like most large systems, its complexity is due to extensive replication of a small set of functional components. Figure 4.1a illustrates the major components (exchanges, transmission and signalling equipment) of the basic telephone network as it exists in 1993. A subscriber is connected to a local exchange by an analogue subscriber loop. At the exchange, the voice signal is digitized and then switched to the appropriate destination exchange. The digital signal is transmitted to the local exchange of another subscriber on an inter-exchange trunk circuit. At the end exchange, the signal is converted back to analogue and transmitted down the subscriber loop to the receivers telephone.

This simplified description of how a voice signal is carried over the telephone network neglects one very important aspect: signalling. Telecommunications signalling refers to the communications required to establish, maintain and release calls. There is signalling between the subscriber and the local exchange, and between exchanges. The signalling between a subscriber and their local exchange will be familiar to most people,

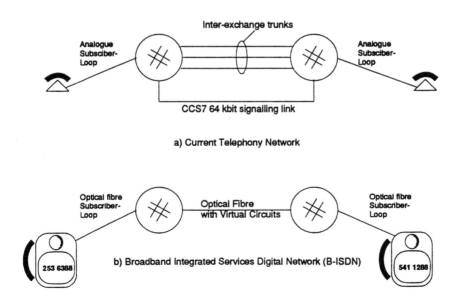

Figure 4.1: Telecommunications networks

although they probably don't think of it in these terms. When you lift the handset from the telephone, you 'signal' the local exchange that you either wish to make a call, or wish to answer a call, depending on whether the phone is ringing at the time. Similarly, replacing the handset in its cradle signals the local exchange that you wish to break the connection to the other party. Another type of signalling occurs when you dial a phone number; in this case, signalling to the local exchange the destination of the call.

The signalling on an analogue subscriber loop is carried by changes in impedance and audio tones. In contrast, the signalling between modern exchanges consists of digital messages carried on a separate data network. This system is known as Common Channel Signalling System No. 7. A single signalling link may carry the signalling messages for many individual calls.

By way of example, we will examine what happens in establishing the call described above. First, subscriber A lifts the handset, signalling to the local exchange (the 'originating' exchange) that she wishes to make a call. Next, she dials the number of the subscriber (subscriber B) with whom she desires to communicate. The local exchange decodes the tones produced by her telephone and examines the dialed number (known as the 'called party number'). It determines the route to the called party's exchange (an adjacent exchange in this case, but may involve many intermediate 'transit' exchanges) and seizes a trunk circuit between the two. The originating exchange then sends a 'setup' message to the called party's exchange (the 'terminating' exchange) via the signalling link. This setup message includes information such as the called number and the trunk circuit number so that the terminating exchange knows that a call is arriving on that circuit and is destined for a particular subscriber. The terminating exchange will then check whether the called subscriber is free (not already using the telephone) and if so, signal the called subscriber that it wishes to establish a call (it rings the telephone). When the called subscriber picks up the handset, the terminating exchange connects the incoming trunk circuit to the subscriber loop and thus completes the connection.

The signalling system has been described as the nervous system of the telephone network. It is a packet switched data network carried over 64 kbit/s links with sophisticated congestion control and re-routing capabilities. It is designed to be highly reliable and fault-tolerant. The signalling network carries much more than simple call control messages, it is the basis on which today's advanced services (such as credit card calling, cellular mobile phones, 800 numbers, etc.) and those coming in the future (such as universal personal telecommunications where phone numbers are associated with people rather than telephone instruments) are built.

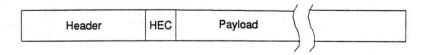

Figure 4.2: An ATM cell

4.2.2 Telecommunications after 2000

So much for today's telecommunication network. The project described by this chapter addresses the telecommunications network of the future – the Broadband Integrated Services Digital Network (B-ISDN). This technology will likely first appear in the network around 1994-95 and will not be in common use until after the year 2000.

Figure 4.1b illustrates a scenario similar to figure 4.1a as it might be implemented in the B-ISDN. The basic elements are the same; there are originating and terminating exchanges, subscriber loops, inter-exchange trunks and terminal equipment. The differences lie in the available bandwidth, the manner in which the signals are carried and hence the range of services which may be supported.

The subscriber loops will be optical fibres and offer up to 622 Mbit/s of transmission capacity. This is sufficient to allow transmission of many full colour high definition video channels in addition to voice and data.

The B-ISDN is based on a switching technique known as asynchronous transfer mode (ATM). It consists of high speed packet switching using fixed length packets known as 'cells'. The switching is done entirely in hardware. An ATM cell is depicted in Figure 4.2. It consists of a header of 4 bytes, which carries information identifying the cells belonging to a particular connection. The Header Error Check (HEC) is an 8 bit Cyclic Redundancy Check over the header to detect corruption of header information. The payload consists of 48 bytes of information representing the transmitted signal. This may be digitized voice or video samples, or computer data. There is no error check on this field as it is not needed for all types of signal. The B-ISDN guarantees cell sequence integrity across a connection, but does not guarantee delivery of cells (if required, delivery must be guaranteed by higher level protocols).

One of the key features of the B-ISDN is that multiple logical connections (known as 'Virtual Channels') of arbitrary bandwidth may be carried over a single physical interface. One of the fields in the cell header is a Virtual Channel Identifier (VCI) which identifies a cell as belonging to a particular virtual channel. This allows a user to request an amount of bandwidth exactly matching their requirements. It also allows calls consisting of multiple connections such as a videophone call which has a video connection and a voice connection.

The signalling in the B-ISDN will be similar to that in the existing network, with the addition that the signalling between the subscriber and the local exchange will also be in the form of digital messages carried on a virtual channel.

4.3 SYSTEM LEVEL DESIGN

The system under development will consist of up to 100,000 lines of code by the time it is completed. Thus I will focus on one fairly fundamental module after presenting an overview of the entire system.

4.3.1 Hardware configuration

The experimental network consists of a number of switches connected together by trunks and servicing many subscriber loops. All the communication links are optical and operate at 50 Mbit/s.

The architecture of an ATM switch is far removed from conventional switches. A switch (also referred to as a node) consists of three main sub-systems: a self-routing switch fabric, port controllers and a Node Controller (see figure 4.3). In the experimental system under development, the switch fabric is implemented in VLSI and switches cells which have had a routing header prepended. The routing header provides the port number of the port through which the cell is to leave the switch. The fabric is self-routing and contains no intelligence of its own. The routing header is obtained from a table within the port controller and is indexed by the VCI in the cell header.

The Node Controller is responsible for setting up and modifying routing tables in, the port controllers, hence controlling a cell's route through the node. To perform this function, the Node Controller must also handle the signalling on the subscriber loops and on the signalling links connected to the node. All the signalling is carried on the same trunks as the data being switched, but within separate virtual channels.

The Node Controller is interfaced to the port controllers through a switch port itself. It sends special control cells which are recognized by the port controllers, decoded, and

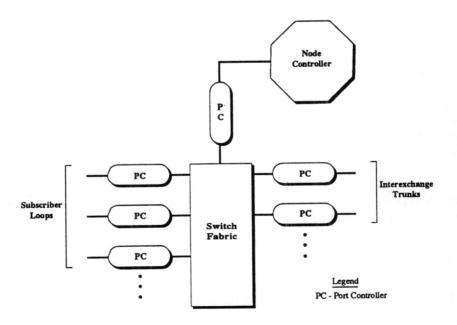

Figure 4.3: A switch node

the information contained within them used to update the routing tables instead of being sent out on a trunk.

The Node Controller is implemented on a Sun 4 workstation with an optical fibre link to a switch port. The use of a common workstation as the controller for the switch allows the software to be developed and debugged in an environment supporting a full range of development tools without the need to port the code to another environment for testing. The limitation this entails is the potential call handling capacity of the Node Controller. A modern telephone switch processor can handle more than 1 million call attempts per hour; our switch will be lucky to handle 500 call attempts per hour. This trade-off is acceptable due to the experimental nature of the network.

4.3.2 Constraints on the design

The design of this system has a number of constraints which have influenced decisions during the development. Firstly, this is a joint project with the software being designed and written at two separate sites (800 km apart) with only electronic mail and telephone for communication between them.

Another constraint was the desire to use existing protocol specifications written in CCITT SDL (see section 4.5.2.) This led to the separation of protocol modules from the higher control functions with the intention of automatically coding them using an SDL to C translator called Melba [Cheng 1989][Jackson 1989]. It also influenced the design of the control structure of the highest level process and this is detailed in section 4.5.2.

4.3.3 Software process structure

The Node Controller consists of a number of UNIX processes communicating using Internet domain sockets (Internet domain sockets were used to allow the processes to be distributed over a number of processors if necessary) and are illustrated in Figure 4.4. The distribution of tasks among processes was arrived at for practical reasons of facilitating independent development and to simplify the use of automatically generated protocol processing code. The following paragraphs briefly describe the processes. The descriptions are simplified and only include the details necessary to the understanding of later sections.

ATM driver

The ATM Driver process interfaces between the optical link interface and the rest of the software. The interface is a VME bus device plugged into the backplane of the workstation and is accessed through a standard SunOS VME bus driver. The driver sends and receives cells and transfers them to and from the ATM/AAL process.

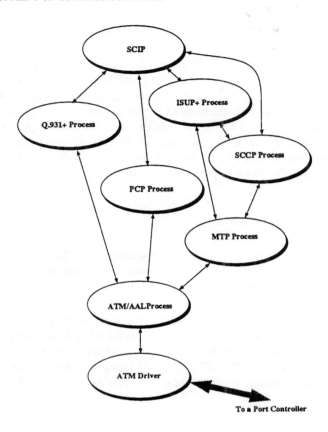

Figure 4.4: Process structure

ATM/AAL process

The ATM layer of the protocols is concerned with the contents of the cell headers only
and simply passes the payload of the cell up to the next layer, the ATM Adaptation Layer
(AAL).

The AAL is responsible for adapting the signal data to the fixed length cell format.
It thus performs segmentation and reassembly of larger messages and can provide error
detection if required.

The ATM/AAL process performs the functions associated with the ATM and AAL
layers of the protocol stack.

PCP process

This process implements the protocol used to communicate with the switch port
controllers. It is a simple request-response protocol with timers to detect lack of

response. The primitives instruct the switch hardware how to connect virtual channels to appropriate outputs.

MTP process

The network signalling system is made up of a number of separate protocols which share common lower layers. The common layers are known as the Message Transfer Part (MTP) and contain most of the functionality of the OSI data link and network layers. The MTP process implements these layers.

SCCP process

The Signalling Connection Control Part (SCCP) is a protocol layer which sits just above the MTP and provides a true OSI network layer service. This layer is used by some application layer protocols while others simply use the MTP services directly. The SCCP Process implements the SCCP protocol.

ISUP+ process

The ISDN User Part (ISUP) is an application layer protocol in the network signalling system. It is responsible for conveying information about calls between exchanges. This protocol is currently being extensively modified to suit B-ISDN and is likely to be replaced in the longer term by the B-ISDN Application Part. For this project we have modified the protocol to support our experimental work and renamed it ISUP+. The ISUP+ process implements this protocol.

Q.931+ process

The Q.931 protocol provides the network layer service on the subscriber loop in the current narrowband ISDN. This protocol is also being actively modified to support B-ISDN by CCITT. Again, we have defined a modified version of this protocol to support the needs of the experimental network and named it Q.931+. The Q.931+ Process implements this modified protocol.

Switch, call and interface processor (SCIP)

The SCIP is the overall controlling process which handles the call control aspects of the user and network signalling protocols. It also handles the user interactions associated with network management functions such as switch configuration and monitoring.

The SCIP process is the only process written in Eiffel; however it contains most of the code in the system and thus represents the major development effort. It is expected that the final process will have around 50,000 lines of Eiffel code. It is this process that will be discussed in the rest of this chapter.

4.3.4 A short trip through the process structure

The previous sections outlined the purpose of each of the processes in figure 4.4. To help put these into context, I will describe briefly how a call establishment is handled by these processes.

While reading this description, please refer to figure 4.3 and figure 4.4. Figure 4.4 may be best put into context by picturing it inside the octogon marked "Node Controller" in figure 4.3.

When a user first signals their desire to make a call, a message is sent from their telephone (note: here we are talking about a telephone for simplicity, but it would actually be a B-ISDN terminal which will be considerably more complex than today's telephones) to the switch. As this is a signalling message, it will be directed to the Node Controller and will enter the process structure of figure 4.4 through the ATM driver. This process will pass the message up to the ATM/AAL process where its header will be examined. It will be recognised as a message from the user's telephone and passed to the Q.931+ process (as it is a message from this protocol). The Q.931+ process will decode the message and pass it to the SCIP process. Here, the real work begins. The dialed number is examined and a call is created. Assuming that this call is to a subscriber at a remote exchange, a request to set up a call is sent to the remote exchange. This involves sending an appropriate message to the remote exchange via the ISUP+ protocol. Hence, the message is created in the ISUP+ process, transmitted through the MTP process and ATM/AAL process finally to pass through the ATM driver and on to the switch hardware where it is transmitted on an optical fibre to the remote switch. Simultaneous to this message being transmitted, the SCIP process sends another message through the PCP process to set up the route through the local switch. The PCP message also passes through the ATM/AAL process and the ATM driver, but is intercepted by the local switch hardware rather than being transmitted to any other switch.

After an acknowledgement is received from the remote switch (following the path: switch –> ATM/AAL process –> MTP process –> ISUP+ process –> SCIP), a confirmation is sent to the subscriber's telephone (following the path: SCIP –> Q.931+ process –> ATM/AAL process –> ATM driver –> switch) and the call is said to be active. A similar process is involved in terminating a call.

Naturally, the description above is highly simplified and deals with only a simple telephone call. The B-ISDN will need to support much more complex scenarios involving multiple connections and parties.

The only process not mentioned above is the SCCP process. This is used in more complex calls such as credit card calls and 800 number calls.

4.4 SCIP STRUCTURE

The SCIP is a single Unix process which is being developed at two separate sites. The first step in designing this process was to divide it into eight subsystems (clusters of classes) with broadly specified responsibilities as shown in figure 4.5. The figure also indicates the main interactions between subsystems. The subsystems were divided between the two sites for detailed design and implementation and are briefly described in the following sections.

4.4.1 User interface subsystem

This subsystem is responsible for providing the complete interface to the user. In this context, the 'user' would be an exchange technician. It includes a number of different interface windows for controlling various aspects of the system. The subsystem also receives and dispatches all external events received by the process. User interface events are processed by the subsystem while inter-process communication events are passed to the IPC subsystem.

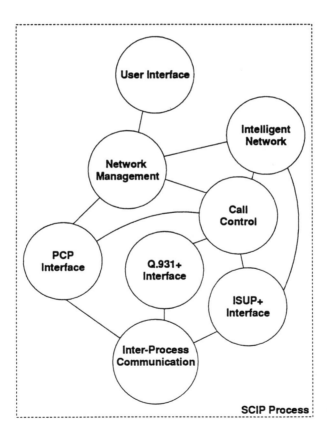

Figure 4.5: SCIP subsystems

4.4.2 Network management subsystem

The Network Management subsystem is responsible for initialising the Port Controllers, the Q.931 protocol and ISUP protocol, and anything else that requires initialization.

This subsystem provides facilities to initiate testing of the switch. It carries out both autonomous tests on a regular basis and provides facilities for the User Interface to initiate such tests.

The subsystem is responsible for maintaining fault records for all fault/alarm type protocol messages received by the SCIP. In addition, fault management provides an information presentation service which presents fault data for the use of the user interface.

The Network Management subsystem also provides facilities to update various entities within the SCIP. These services are mainly for the use of the configuration management window of the user interface. Typical examples of entities requiring such update are the routing tables and the Intelligent Network (IN) trigger tables (see below).

A final responsibility of the Network Management subsystem is to collect and record statistics about traffic through the switch.

In the future, the Network Management subsystem may be extended to allow remote control of the entire Node Controller.

4.4.3 Call control subsystem

The Call Control subsystem implements the call control logic associated with processing a call. The modeling of the call is consistent with the IN Basic Call State Model (BCSM) to provide for implementation of Intelligent Network services in the future (see below).

The Call Control Subsystem is, in addition, responsible for establishment and clear down of virtual channel links.

This subsystem is examined in more detail in section 4.4.5.

4.4.4 Intelligent network subsystem

The Intelligent Network is a new architecture (currently being standardized by CCITT) for providing advanced services such as credit card calling, 800 numbers, and time-of-day dependent routing. It is based on the concept of locating service processing logic in remote databases and providing generic 'functional components' at the local exchange or 'service switching point'. The call processing logic at the local exchange detects certain 'triggers' (such as the first three dialed digits being '800') and queries the Service Control Point (SCP) for instructions on how to provide the service. The aim of the architecture is to allow easy creation and rapid deployment of new services.

The Intelligent Network subsystem is responsible for interfacing to a remote SCP to provide Intelligent Network services.

4.4.5 PCP, Q.931+ and ISUP+ interface subsystems

These subsystems have similar responsibilities and perform very similar functions. Each is responsible for coding and decoding the primitives which are exchanged between the SCIP process and the processes implementing the protocols. The external primitive format is a union of all the possible fields that may appear in all the defined primitives. It is coded as a C structure to allow flexibility in the definition of the external processes (some of which are coded in C).

Within the SCIP, the primitives are objects containing the fields relevant to particular primitive together with routines to manipulate them. Heavy use is made of inheritance to capture the common elements of the primitives and substantial reuse across the three subsystems has been achieved.

4.4.6 Inter-process communication subsystem

The IPC subsystem has responsibility for reading and writing datagrams to and from sockets of other processes.

It contains the code to distribute a received message to the subsystems that need to know about it. For example, a fault message from a Port Controller would need to be seen by the Call Control subsystem as well as the Network Management subsystem for logging purposes.

Typical classes in this subsystem are used to represent entities such as datagrams, IPC channels and various I/O specific events.

4.5 DETAILED DESIGN OF ONE SUB-SYSTEM: CALL CONTROL

The call control subsystem is the one which deals most directly with the objects modeling the real-world telecommunications objects. It is here that concepts such as a call, a virtual channel connection, a switch port and a signalling channel are represented.

This subsystem therefore provides an interesting example of object oriented modelling and in particular how the state machine world of telecommunications protocols maps to an object oriented implementation.

The class interfaces of all the classes mentioned in this section are included in the appendix to this chapter (pages 128–139) and are worth examining to gain a better appreciation of the system.

4.5.1 Design methodology

In designing the call control model, we did not follow a specific methodology, but used a combination of techniques that achieved the desired end.

We began the design by 'brainstorming' every concept we could think of related to B-ISDN and ATM switching with the 'domain experts' (our project team). The author and another experienced designer then sifted through the list of candidate objects and came up with a list of what we considered to be the fundamental objects. These objects were transferred to Class, Responsibility, Collaborators (CRC) cards [Wirfs-Brock 1990] as candidate classes and their responsibilities were examined. We refined the cards by performing 'walkthroughs' of typical execution scenarios and identified new classes and responsibilities.

The cards spread out on a table proved to be an excellent aid to discussing the system and examining what happened under various input conditions. An important side effect of this process was to help the designers understand the way other members of the team thought about the problem and greatly aided mutual understanding. It would seem that this technique would be of great use in teaching new staff how to design systems.

Once the major classes of the subsystem had been established, skeleton classes to implement them were written. It would be pleasing to say at this point that the next step involved careful definition of class features complete with pre and post conditions and gradual refinement – it did not. The reality has been that the classes were developed in an ad hoc manner, and although they still have approximately the same responsibilities, the implementations have been distorted somewhat from the original specifications. We have found that during the coding, new responsibilities have been identified and in particular the structure of references to objects has altered substantially. Much of this has been due to our lack of experience with object-oriented design.

Despite the difficulties, the experience has not been unpleasant as we have found that restructuring and making radical changes during the coding has been straight forward and the result is a reasonably clean system. This would not have been so easy in a traditional structured design.

We have found that in the process of writing code, assertions, particularly invariants tend to be left out due to the fact that invariants appear at the bottom of an Eiffel class and are easily forgotten. It is not difficult to add the assertions at a later stage. This is a worthwhile exercise since the assumptions made during the original coding can be re-examined.

Our slightly less than rigorous approach to design and coding could probably not be tolerated in a larger project, or one where the application was more critical. We have typically had only two or three people working on the same process at one time and only one on a particular sub-system. Due to the experimental nature of the project, complete specification down to the last carriage return was not possible nor desirable. We need to be free to experiment and try out new ideas. The object-oriented paradigm and Eiffel in particular have given us the freedom to do this while maintaining some semblance of order in the code.

If we had to start from scratch again, the main change to this methodology that would be of benefit would be to define the interfaces between subsystems more clearly so that it was easier for programmers working on different subsystems to understand how to make use of their colleagues work.

4.5.2 Call control subsystem in detail

The call control subsystem consists of two conceptual entities: a hierarchy of classes representing telecommunications objects; and a set of classes to model the specifications of the call control logic. A high level representation of these classes is illustrated in figure 4.6 using the notation of Nerson [Nerson 1991]. All the classes illustrated exist in the system. The real situation is a little more complex; for example, the *LEG* class models a section of a connection and may be either the section from the user to the exchange or the section from this exchange to another exchange. There are a number of differences in these types of legs, so inheritance is used to define two sub-classes (*UNI_LEG* and *NNI_LEG*) to represent actual legs. The class *LEG* is deferred and hence never instantiated.

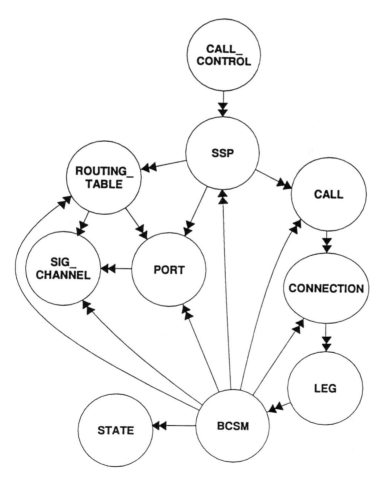

Figure 4.6: Major telecommunications objects

The call control subsystem has a root class called simply *CALL_CONTROL*. This provides the features that the rest of the SCIP needs to know about. At present this interface is extremely simple consisting of only a creation feature and a feature called *respond_to* which processes a received event. In the future, features will be added to allow other portions of the SCIP system to alter the routing table and other dynamically configurable data within the call control subsystem. The aim is to have the *CALL_CONTROL* class provide a single interface to the subsystem and thus reduce the dependencies within the whole system.

Modeling telecommunications objects

The objects representing telecommunications objects map quite naturally from the problem domain.

Referring to figure 4.6, the following classes directly model real-world tele-communications entities: *SSP, CALL, CONNECTION, LEG, ROUTING_TABLE, PORT* and *SIG_CHANNEL*.

The SSP (Service Switching Point) models the concept of the whole switching node and is thus a container class for the other major objects such as *ROUTING_TABLE, PORT* and *CALL*. These entities have significance for the whole node. In addition, the SSP is responsible for managing the allocation of call reference numbers to calls (these must be unique within the node).

There is only one *ROUTING_TABLE* for the node and this provides functions to map telephone numbers to outgoing ports and a variety of similar mappings. These mappings return references to signalling channel objects as each subscriber loop and inter-exchange trunk has a signalling channel associated with it.

The *PORT* class represents a physical switch port and thus has features which allow virtual channels to be established and manipulated through the port. It also has the responsibility of allocating bandwidth to new connections through the port as this function must be performed with reference to all connections through the port. The port also has references to one or more signalling channels as it is possible to connect a number of physical terminals to a single subscriber loop.

It may seem that a *CALL* is related to a port and should therefore be a supplier to *PORT*; however the concept of a call in the B-ISDN is extended to allow for multiple connections and multiple parties (such as a conference call). This could involve a number of physical ports, so it was necessary to define calls as entities independent of ports. The model of a call used in this design allows for multiple *CONNECTIONs* (an example would be a videophone call involving both a voice and a video connection). It also permits multi-party calls by defining a connection in terms of *LEGs*, where a *LEG* is a section of a call entering or leaving the node. A normal two-party call (such as described in section 4.2.1) would have just a single *CONNECTION* object and two *LEG* objects describing it at each exchange node.

The *CONNECTION* class describes a single connection with two or more legs. At present, the software is limited to just two legs, an originating leg and a terminating leg.

In the future, this can be easily upgraded to allow multiple legs. Note that it is in this object that the called number and the bandwidth attributes are stored as they are attributes of a connection as a whole rather than of the individual legs.

There are two types of *LEGs*, those representing subscriber loops (user-network interface – *UNI*) and those representing inter-exchange trunks (network-network interface – *NNI*). While there are a number of common attributes, the protocols used on each leg are quite different and have different methods of call identification and so two different types are defined: a *UNI_LEG* and a *NNI_LEG* class. Naturally these both inherit from a common parent: *LEG*. A LEG also has a reference to a Basic Call State Machine (*BCSM*), which is described below. Each leg of a connection within a node has a BCSM as each may be in any state at a given time.

The final major telecommunications object is the *SIG_CHANNEL* class representing a generic signalling channel. This too has descendents, called *UNI_SIG_CHANNEL* and *NNI_SIG_CHANNEL*, capturing the differences between signalling at the user-network interface and at the network-network interface. This class has a feature to implement the sending of each of the possible protocol primitives for that protocol.

The classes described above capture the essence of telecommunications in a very natural manner and are the core of the call control subsystem. The other major classes illustrated in figure 4.6 are associated with the coding of the call control logic and are described in the next section.

Coding telecommunications specifications

The CCITT uses the Specification and Description Language (SDL) to specify the protocols it defines and the logic associated with call control. In order to reduce the chance of logical errors in coding the call control logic, we have attempted to model the SDL specification as closely as possible. First a brief introduction to SDL.

SDL diagrams

SDL is a complete specification language based on the notion of processes sending signals to each other. Each process contains an extended finite state machine to define its behaviour. For the purposes of this chapter, we will look only at the definition of a single process and concentrate on the finite state machine description.

Figure 4.7 illustrates a simple SDL state diagram. This is an extract from the description of the call control portion of the ISUP+ protocol.

The rectangles with rounded end represent states and are given symbolic labels such as ISUP_ACTIVE. The rectangles with concave bites (called 'input symbols') represent possible inputs to the state machine and the rectangles with right-pointing arrows (called 'output symbols') represent signals sent from the state machine to other processes. A plain rectangle is used to represent an operation.

Figure 4.7 may be explained by assuming first that the finite state machine (FSM) is in the state ISUP_ACTIVE at the top of the diagram. The FSM will remain in this state

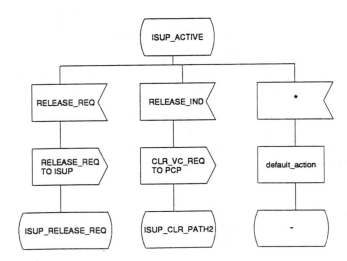

Figure 4.7: SDL diagram for the ISUP active state

until it receives an input which matches one of the input symbols. In this case the possible input symbols are a RELEASE_REQ message, a RELEASE_IND message or '*' which is a wildcard meaning 'any input not already defined for this state'. When an input matching one of the input symbols is received, the diagram is followed down the line of the received symbol to determine the actions. If we assume a RELEASE_REQ message is received, then the SDL diagram tells us that a RELEASE_REQ message must be sent to the process called ISUP. After this is sent, the SDL diagram indicates that the state machine is to change to the state ISUP_RELEASE_REQ. Similarly, if the FSM had received a RELEASE_IND message, then the SDL diagram requires the CLR_VC_REQ message be sent to the process called PCP and then to change to state ISUP_CLR_PATH2. Finally, if any other input is received, then the 'default_action' must be carried out and the state of the FSM left in the same state it was before the input was received (indicated by the '-').

Note that the SDL diagrams contain no information about the parameters of the messages. In formal SDL specification, these may be defined, but most CCITT recommendations do not include this detail. The aim of the diagrams is to define the logic behind call processing and define what happens in all possible input cases. We have used them as an aid to coding the call control logic rather than a complete specification.

Implementing SDL processes
The obvious method of modeling an SDL process is to define an abstraction of a finite state machine. However, this is not as simple as it first appears. The problem with finite state machines is that a transition is dependent on both an input and the current state. Using polymorphism, it is possible to select the correct routine automatically based on a single input variable. It is also possible to use polymorphism to select on the second

variable, but at the expense of creating a huge number of tiny classes. The solution we have implemented is to use polymorphism to select the current state and then use 'case' type code to select the correct routine for the given input. This also seemed the simplest approach given that there were four distinctly different input event types to deal with. Another advantage of this modeling technique is that it matches the SDL diagrams well. A single page of SDL typically defines all the transitions for a given state; in our implementation, all the code for this page appears in a single class, improving the readability.

Figure 4.8 shows the class structure implementing the finite state machine to execute the SDL processes. The top two classes (*FSM* and *FSM_STATE*) are generic enough that they have been included in a project library. The *BCSM* (Basic Call State Machine) class provides the data storage and specialization of the *FSM* class to provide the environment in which to execute the specifications. It may be seen (in the appendix) that this class has references to most of the other major classes in the subsystem. This is necessary as the code described by the SDL diagrams manipulates all these objects.

The *LEG_STATE_CONSTANTS* class defines symbolic names for the states. These are used within the code implementing each state to return a value indicating the next state that the BCSM should move to. The *LEG_STATE* class is the parent of all the specific classes defining individual states. It provides default code to handle input not recognised by the individual states. The actual state classes (*ISUP_ACTIVE_STATE* and around 20 others) contain only the code to implement the contents of the SDL diagram

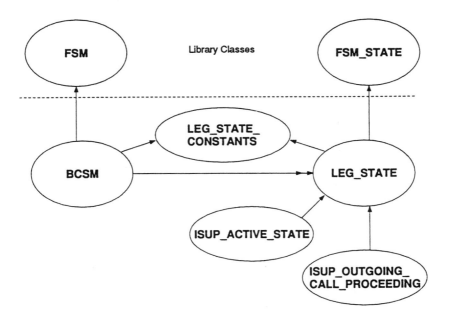

Figure 4.8: State machine classes and example states

and are not cluttered with code not directly related to the SDL diagrams. This makes them quite readable.

Finally, the SDL diagram discussed above and illustrated in figure 4.7 is implemented in the class *I_ACTIVE* (figure 4.9). The code can be fairly easily related to the SDL diagram - an important aim in our modelling.

```
indexing
    sccsid: "%W% %E% %U%";
    summary: "Models the Isup active state";
    cluster: "leg_states";
    author: "David Giddy";
    organisation: "Telecom Research Labs";
    orig_date: "27/9/91";
    description: "Models the Isup active state";
class I_ACTIVE creation
    make
inherit
    LEG_STATE
        rename Isup_Active as id
        redefine process_internal_event, process_isup_event end
feature {NONE}
    state_name: STRING is "Isup_Active";
    make (fsm: BCSM) is
            -- Create a new state belonging to fsm
        do
            Create_state (fsm);
        end
feature
    process_internal_event (release_req: INTERNAL_PROTOCOL_EVENT): INTEGER is
            -- Release the local end of a call
        local
            isup_sig_channel: NNI_SIG_CHANNEL;
            nni_leg: NNI_LEG;
            causes: ISUP_CAUSE_LIST
        do
            if release_req.type = release_req.Release_req then
                !! causes;
                nni_leg ?= my_bcsm.the_leg;
                check
                        right_leg_type: nni_leg /= Void
                end;
```

```
            -- Send RELEASE_REQ to ISUP

            isup_sig_channel ?= my_bcsm.the_sig_chan;
            check
                 sig_channel_right_type: isup_sig_channel /= Void;
            end;
            isup_sig_channel.release_req (nni_leg.spc,
                        nni_leg.sequence, causes.Normal_Clearing);

            -- Return next state

            Result := Isup_Release_Req
        else
            Result := default_action (release_req)
        end

    end;

process_isup_event (isup_event: ISUP_IPC_EVENT):INTEGER is
        -- Perform actions to release the remote end of a call
    do

        if isup_event.primitive.primitive_id.str_value.equal ("RELEASE_IND") then

            --Send CLR_VC_REQ to PCP

            my_bcsm.the_port.clr_vc (my_bcsm, 0, my_bcsm.the_leg.vcci.vci_in);

            -- Return next state

            Result := Isup_Clr_Path2
        else
            Result := default_action (isup_event)
        end
    end
end -- class I_ACTIVE
```

Figure 4.9: Code for I_ACTIVE class

Execution flow through the call control subsystem

Following the SDL model requires that execution flow be driven by inputs to the BCSM's. These inputs can be primitives arriving from another process, internal signals generated by states, or timer expiries. There are potentially large numbers of BCSM's active simultaneously within the SCIP and the problem is then to determine which BCSM a particular input is destined for.

When an input is received, it is passed to the call control subsystem via the *respond_to* feature of the *CALL_CONTROL* class (refer to figure 4.6). This immediately passes it to the corresponding feature of the *SSP* class. It is one of the responsibilities of the *SSP* class to determine the correct *BCSM* for the input. It does this by examining the type of the incoming event and then sequentially asking each of the *CALL* objects whether they want this particular event. If a call wants the input, it will return a reference to the appropriate *BCSM*. The call determines whether it wants the object by asking each of its *CONNECTIONs* which, in turn, ask each of their *LEGs*. If no existing call wants the input, and the primitive is a setup primitive, then it is assumed that this is a new call and a new *CALL* object is created. The *CALL* object creates a new *CONNECTION* which in turn creates a new *LEG* and a new *BCSM*. The *SSP* class then sends the setup primitive to the newly created *BCSM* for processing.

4.6 REVISION CONTROL

An important aspect of any multi-programmer project is that of access and revision control. In our case we have had the extra challenge of managing change control across two sites.

We have achieved a satisfactory level of change control through a number of mechanisms. Firstly, individual programmers have been given responsibility for a subsystem and only that programmer may make alterations to it. Between sites we use 'change requests' exchanged by electronic mail to request an alteration. The altered code is then sent back by email. At our site, all the system source code is stored in a central directory hierarchy under the control of the Unix Source Code Control System (SCCS). The aim of the central directory is to maintain a compilable copy of the code at all times. If programmers were allowed to modify the source code arbitrarily in situ the system would become uncompilable, preventing other programmers from testing their changes.

In order to provide the ability to modify a source file whilst simultaneously retaining a compilable version for other programmers, a system of command scripts have been created to maintain a duplicate copy of the central directory structure in each programmers private directory tree. When first set up, the duplicate structure contains no actual files, but directories full of symbolic links to their corresponding central files. When a programmer wishes to edit a source file, they 'check out' the file. This results in a copy of the file replacing the symbolic link in their private directory and the file being checked out for editing in their name within the SCCS system. The result of this is that all other programmers still 'see' the last checked in (and presumably compilable) version of the file. When a programmer has completed their modifications and tested them, they 'check in' the new version which makes it available to all the other team members.

The system is setup so that all the Eiffel-compiler-generated files reside in the programmer's private directory; including those of files which are checked in. This leads to a requirement for quite a substantial amount of disk space for each programmer (presently around 20 Mbytes). It would seem sensible to keep the compiler-generated files for checked in files in the central directory; however this leads to large amounts of unnecessary recompilation due to the compiler recognizing that a file has been moved and hence causing recompilation of its clients. It is also not clear what will happen if two programmers happen to trigger compilations of the same central class simultaneously. Both of these problems are avoided in the scheme we have implemented.

Having a development team split across two sites is not the ideal way to manage a project. In our case it has worked, but at the cost of missed opportunities for reuse within the system and some unnecessary complexity. These costs have come about mainly through insufficient communication between the teams (enforced by the high cost of a team meeting due to travel expenses).

4.7 CONCLUSIONS

The software described in this chapter is still under active development and is likely to be further extended for the next year or more. It is expected that the object-oriented approach used to develop the basic system will enable easy extension and also aid comprehensibility to those joining the project in the months to come.

Further work on the system will be dictated by the requirements for enhanced demonstrations and for the support of experiments. There are no plans to advance the switch to production stage.

The modelling of telecommunications systems fits well with the object-oriented paradigm and the results are easy to understand and modify.

The Eiffel language has provided us with a powerful tool with which to implement the system by combining support for the important elements of the object oriented paradigm with features to support software engineering. There is no reason why Eiffel could not be used as the implementation language for switching system software in the production environment provided there were efficient compilers available for the target machine architecture.

4.8 ACKNOWLEDGMENTS

The author would like to thank his fellow team members for their insights and skill in the design and implementation of this project. The author would also like to thank Dr. Rob Palmer, the project leader, for his encouragement and helpful advice in the preparation of this chapter.

The permission of the Director, Telecom Research Laboratories, to publish the above material is hereby acknowledged.

4.9 GLOSSARY

AAL - ATM Adaptation Layer - The protocol layer responsible for adapting data to fit into fixed length ATM cells.

ATM - Asynchronous Transfer Mode - Describes the transfer of data in cells with no timing relationship between successive cells. Commonly known as packet switching.

ATM cell - A 53 byte data packet used to transport all forms of data in the B-ISDN.

B-ISDN - Broadband Integrated Services Digital Network - The network that will gradually replace the current ISDN (known as the Narrowband ISDN). It will be based on ATM.

BCSM - Basic Call State Machine - The finite state machine used to describe a leg of a telephone call.

CCITT - International Telephone and Telegraph Consultative Committee - One of the committees of the International Telecommunications Union, an organ of the United Nations. The CCITT is responsible for standards associated with telecommunications.

CCS No.7 - Common Channel Signalling System No. 7. This is the signalling system used to control modern telecommunications networks. It consists of many different protocols and has many different functions. It is based on the concept of sending all the signalling information for several different trunks on a single signalling channel (or group of channels).

CRC cards - Class, Responsibilities, Collaborators cards. This is an OO design technique advocated by Wirfs-Brock et al. [Wirfs-Brock 1990].

Call - A call in telecommunications terms is any communication between two or more telecommunications users.

Cell - The term used in standards for the 53 byte packet of data used to carry all information in the B-ISDN.

Connection - A connection is a communication between two users used to carry information. Usually, only one type of information is carried on a single connection.

FSM - Finite State Machine

HEC - Header Error Check - The byte at the end of the header of every ATM cell containing an 8 bit CRC calculated across the other four header bytes.

IN - Intelligent Network. This term refers to a new network architecture currently being standardised which allows fast implementation of new advanced services. Typical IN services include 800 numbers and credit card calling.

ISDN - Integrated Services Digital Network. This refers to the network currently existing which provides 64 kbit/s digital links to the user with full switching capability.

ISUP - Integrated Services User Part. This is the application layer protocol used to control ISDN calls. It is a protocol that is part of the CCS No. 7 system.

Leg - A Leg is a part of a connection. A typical connection might contain a leg from the originating subscriber to their local exchange, from the originating exchange to the destination exchange and from the destination exchange to the destination subscriber.

Local exchange - The exchange to which a subscriber is directly connected.

MTP - Message Transfer Part. This is a protocol in the CCS No. 7 system. It provides the layer 2 and 3 of the OSI model for this system.

NNI - Network-Node Interface. This refers to the interface connecting one exchange with another.

Node controller - The hardware and software used to control a switch. This term is specific to this project.

Originating exchange - The exchange where a call was initiated.

Port - An input/output to a switch. Trunks and subscriber loops connect to switch ports.

Port controller - The hardware and software combination which interfaces a subsciber loop or a trunk to the switch fabric.

Q.931 - The protocol implementing the network layer of the OSI model for the ISDN. It operates between the users terminal and the local exchange.

Routing table - The table in the exchange which indicates which trunk or subscriber loop a call must be connected to in order to reach the dialed number.

SCCP - Signalling Connection Control Part. This is a protocol in the CCS No. 7 system. It is used to control more advanced signalling connections. It becomes important in the provision of IN services.

SCCS - Source Code Control System. This is a Unix utility used to provide revision history and access control to software system source code.

SCIP - Switch, Call and Interface Process. This is the name given to the main controlling process in our Node Controller. It is specific to this project.

SCP - Service Control Point. This is a special network element which controls the provision of IN services.

SDL - Specification and Description Language. A formal specification language defined by the CCITT and used in specifying telecommunications protocols.

SSP - Service Switching Point. Within the IN standards, this is an exchange where services are connected to subscribers wanting them. This will often be the subscribers local exchange.

Signalling channel - A connection to either a subscribers terminal or another exchange which is used to carry messages of various signalling protocols.

Subscriber loop - The physical connection between a subscriber and their local exchange.

Switch fabric - The hardware that actually performs switching of the ATM cells to route them to the correct output port.

Terminating exchange - The exchange to which a called subscriber is connected. Also called the destination exchange.

Transit exchange - A transit exchange is one which a connection passes through on its way to the destination. It connects to neither subscriber directly.

Trunk - The physical connection between two exchanges.

UNI - User Network Interface. Refers to the interface between a subscriber and the local exchange.

VCI - Virtual channel identifier. The number contained within an ATM cell header which identifies which virtual channel a cell belongs to.

Virtual channel - A logical transmission path between two users in the B-ISDN.

APPENDIX – CLASS INTERFACES

This appendix contains the class interfaces to all the major classes mentioned in the body of the chapter. Some features have been removed to aid clarity.

---

class interface SSP *feature specification*
    active_calls: *LINKED_LIST* [*CALL*]
           -- The currently active calls.

    allocate_cr: *INTEGER*
           -- Allocate a unique call reference number for a Q931 call

    deallocate_cr (*v*: *INTEGER*)
           -- Deallocate call reference *v*

    respond_to (*event*: *EVENT*)
           -- Process events relevant to the call_control subsystem
           -- Ignore any event which is not destined for this subsystem
           -- Also delivers any internal event generated.
    require
        event_not_void: *event* /= *Void*

    the_routing_table: *ROUTING_TABLE*
           -- The system routing table
end interface -- class *SSP*

Figure 4.10: Class interface for *SSP*

class interface ROUTING_TABLE *feature specification*

  is_local (*number*: *STRING*): *BOOLEAN*
            -- Is the dialed number supplied a number local to this node ?
    require
            number_supplied: *number* /= *Void* **and not** *number.empty*;
            number_right_length: *number.count* = 7;
            -- number must contain only digits.

  port_id_to_port (*i*: *INTEGER*): *PORT*
            -- Map a port_id to a port

  sci_to_port (*n*: *INTEGER*): *PORT*
            -- Map a sci value to a port.
    require
            -- sci value exists

  sci_to_sig_chan (*s*: *INTEGER*): *SIG_CHANNEL*
            -- Map a sci value to a signalling channel.
    require
            -- sci value exists
    ensure
            valid_result: *Result* /= *Void* ;

  translate_local (*number*: *STRING*): *UNI_SIG_CHANNEL*
            -- Translate a local number to a signalling channel reference.
            -- Returns a void reference if number cannot be translated.
    require
            number_supplied: *number* /= *Void* ;
            local_number: *is_local* (*number*);
            number_right_length: *number.count* = 7;
            -- *number* must contain only digits.

  translate_remote (*number*: *STRING*): *NNI_SIG_CHANNEL*
            -- translate a remote number to a signalling channel reference.
            -- Returns a void reference if number cannot be translated.
    require
            number_supplied: *number* /= *Void* ;
            non_local_number: **not** *is_local* (*number*);
            number_right_length: *number.count* = 7;
            -- Number must contain only digits.

end interface -- class ROUTING_TABLE

Figure 4.11: Class interface for *ROUTING_TABLE*

class interface PORT feature specification

> *allocate_bw (peak_in, average_in, peak_out, average_out: INTEGER):*
>   *BOOLEAN*
>   -- Allocate bandwidth for a new connection if possible.
>   **ensure**
>   *result_correct: Result = ((peak_in + allocated_bandwidth_in*
>   *< scip.max_link_bw)* **and**
>   *(peak_out + allocated_bandwidth_out <*
>   *scip.max_link_bw));*
>   *bw_increased:* **old** *allocated_bandwidth_in <=*
>   *allocated_bandwidth_in*
>   **and old** *allocated_bandwidth_out <=*
>   *allocated_bandwidth_out*

> *allocate_vci: INTEGER*
>   -- Allocate a unique virtual channel identifier for an ISUP call
>   **ensure**
>   *valid_vci: Result >= 0* **and** *Result <= scip.max_vci*

> *allocated_bandwidth_in: INTEGER*
> *allocated_bandwidth_out: INTEGER*
>   -- The currently allocated bandwidth for this port.

> *clr_vc (reply_to: BCSM; vci_in: INTEGER)*
>   -- Clear a Virtual Channel
>   **require**
>   *reply_to_known: reply_to /= Void ;*
>   *vci_in_ok: vci_in >= 0* **and** *vci_in <= scip.max_vci*

> *deallocate_bw (peak_in, average_in, peak_out, average_out: INTEGER)*
>   -- Deallocate the bandwidth specified.
>   **require**
>   *bw_is_allocated: peak_in <= allocated_bandwidth_in* **and**
>   *peak_out <= allocated_bandwidth_out*
>   **ensure**
>   *bw_decreased:* **old** *allocated_bandwidth_in >= allocated_bandwidth_in*
>   **and old** *allocated_bandwidth_out >= allocated_bandwidth_out*

> *deallocate_vci (v: INTEGER)*
>   -- Deallocate virtual channel identifier *v*

> *est_vc (reply_to: BCSM; vci_out, port_out: INTEGER)*
>   -- Establish a Virtual Channel

require
   reply_to_known: *reply_to* /= *Void* ;
   vci_out_ok: *vci_out* >= 0 **and** *vci_out* <= *scip.max_vci*;
   port_out_ok: *port_out* >= 0 and *port_out* <= *scip.max_ports* – 1;

is_uni: *BOOLEAN*
   -- True if this port is a UNI port.

my_sig_chans: *LINKED_LIST* [*SIG_CHANNEL*]
   -- The signalling channels associated with this port.

port_id: *INTEGER*
   -- The port identifier known to the rest of the system

invariant

allocated_bandwidth_in_positive: *allocated_bandwidth_in* >= 0;
allocated_bandwidth_out_positive: *allocated_bandwidth_out* >= 0;

end interface -- class *PORT*

Figure 4.12: Class interface for PORT

class interface *CALL* **creation procedures**

make(*sp*: *SSP*; *is_uni*: *BOOLEAN*; *sc*: *SIG_CHANNEL*)
   require
      service_switching_point_supplied: *sp* /= *Void* ;
      signalling_channel_supplied: *sc* /= *Void*

feature specification

connections: *CONNECTION*
      -- Only one allowed at present.
      -- The connections established by this call
delete_connection
      -- Delete the connection for this call

is_complete: *BOOLEAN*
      -- Is the current call finished with?

wants_event (*event*: *PROTOCOL_IPC_EVENT*): *BCSM*
      -- The associated BCSM if this call wants the current event
      -- Void otherwise
   require
      event_not_void: *event* /= *Void*

end interface -- class *CALL*

Figure 4.13: Class interface for *CALL*

class interface CONNECTION feature specification

bw_params: *BW*
-- Parameters describing a connections bandwidth

called_number: *STRING*
-- The called number

Create (*cl*: *CALL*; *sp*: *SSP*; *is_uni*: *BOOLEAN*; *sc*: *SIG_CHANNEL*)
    require
        ssp_supplied: *sp* /= *Void* ;
        call_supplied: *cl* /= *Void* ;
        signalling_channel_supplied: *sc* /= *Void*

create_term_leg (*cl*: *CALL*; *sp*: *SSP*; *is_uni*: *BOOLEAN*; *sc*:*SIG_CHANNEL*)
        -- Create a terminating leg and assign it to the term_leg
        -- reference
    require
        ssp_supplied: *sp* /= *Void* ;
        call_supplied: *cl* /= *Void*

orig_leg: *LEG*
        -- The originating leg of this connection

set_bw_params (*p*: *BW*)
        -- Set the bandwidth parameters for this connection.
    require
        bw_supplied: *p* /= *Void*

set_called_number (*n*: *STRING*)
        -- Set the called number for this connection
    require
        number_supplied: *n* /= *Void*

term_leg: *LEG*
        -- The terminating leg of this connection

wants_event (*event*: *PROTOCOL_IPC_EVENT*): *BCSM*
        -- Process event for this connection
    require
        event_not_void: *event* /= *Void*

invariant

   called_number_ok: *called_number.= Void **or** called_number.count = 7*;
   variables_set: (*orig_leg.the_bcsm.current_state.id =*
                    *orig_leg.the_bcsm.q931_active **or***
                    orig_leg.the_bcsm.current_state.id =
                    orig_leg.the_bcsm.isup_active) ***implies***
                    (*bw_params /= Void **and** called_number /= Void*
                    ***and** term_leg /= Void **and** orig_leg.parameters_set*
                    ***and** term_leg.parameters_set*)

end interface -- class *CONNECTION*

Figure 4.14: Class interface for *CONNECTION*

*class interface UNI_LEG **creation procedures***

   make (*cn*: *CONNECTION*; *cl*: *CALL*; *sp*: *SSP*; *orig*: *BOOLEAN*;
         sc: *SIG_CHANNEL*)
         -- Create a UNI leg.
   require
         service_switching_point_supplied: *sp /= Void* ;
         call_supplied: *cl /= Void* ;
         connection_supplied: *cn /= Void* ;
         signalling_channel_supplied: *sc /= Void*

feature specification

   call_ref: *INTEGER*
         -- The call reference associated with this leg.

   i_assigned_cr: *BOOLEAN*
         -- True if the Node Controller assigned this call_reference value.

   is_originating: *BOOLEAN*
         -- True if this leg is an originating leg
         -- (from *LEG*)

   parameters_set: *BOOLEAN*
         -- Are all this leg's parameters set ?

   scip: *SCIP_PARAMS*
         -- SCIP wide parameters
         -- (from *LEG*)

set_call_ref (cr: INTEGER)
          -- Set call reference value for this leg.

the_bcsm: BCSM
          -- The Basic Call State Machine controlling this leg
          -- (from *LEG*)

Undefined: INTEGER is − 1
          -- Constant representing an undefined value for an attribute
          -- (from *LEG*)

vcci: VCCI
          -- Virtual channel connection identifiers associated with this leg
          -- (from *LEG*)

wants_event (event: PROTOCOL_IPC_EVENT): BCSM
          -- If this leg wants this event, then BCSM reference;
          -- otherwise Void.
     require
          -- *event_supplied: event /= Void*

invariant

     *call_ref_ok: call_ref = undefined **or** (call_ref >= 0 **and***
                              call_ref <= scip.max_call_ref);

end interface -- class *UNI_LEG*

Figure 4.15: Class interface for *UNI_LEG*

---

class interface UNI_SIG_CHANNEL **creation procedures**

     make(s: INTEGER; ipc: IPC)
          -- Create the signalling channel and associate a
          -- signalling channel identifier and inter process
          -- communication object with it.
     require
          valid_signalling_channel_identifier: s >= scip.min_sci
                              ***and** s <= scip.max_sci;*
          inter_process_communication_object_exists: ipc /= Void;

feature specification

> *alerting_req* (*cr*: *INTEGER*)
> -- Terminal should begin alerting
> **require**
> *call_reference_ok*: *cr* >= *0* **and** *cr* <= *scip.max_call_ref*;

> *disconnect_req* (*cr*: *INTEGER*)
> -- Request that the terminal disconnect
> **require**
> *call_reference_ok*: *cr* >= *0* **and** *cr* <= *scip.max_call_ref*;

> *release_req* (*cr, cause*: *INTEGER*)
> -- Request terminal to release a call
> **require**
> *call_reference_ok*: *cr* >= *0* **and** *cr* <= *scip.max_call_ref*;
> *cause_ok*: *cause* >= *0* **and** *cause* <= *scip.max_q931_cause*

> *sci*: *INTEGER*
> -- The signalling channel identifier.
> -- (from *SIG_CHANNEL*)

> *scip*: *SCIP_PARAMS*
> -- System wide constants

> *setup_req* (*cr*: *INTEGER*; *bw*: *BW*)
> -- Request a call setup to the terminal
> **require**
> *call_reference_ok*: *cr* >= *0* and *cr* <= *scip.max_call_ref*;
> *bandwidth_supplied*: *bw* /= *Void*

> *setup_resp* (*cr*: *INTEGER*; *vcci*: *VCCI*)
> -- Respond to a call setup to the terminal
> **require**
> *call_reference_ok*: *cr* >= *0* **and** *cr* <= *scip.max_call_ref*;
> *vcci_supplied*: *vcci* /= *Void*;
> *vcci_all_defined*: *vcci.all_defined*

invariant

> *valid_signalling_channel_identifier*: *sci* >= *scip.min_sci* **and**
> *sci* <= *scip.max_sci*;

end interface -- class *UNI_SIG_CHANNEL*

Figure 4.16: Class interface for *UNI_SIG_CHANNEL*

class interface BCSM *creation procedures*

 make (*st*: *INTEGER*; *lg*: *LEG*; *sc*: *SIG_CHANNEL*; *cn*: *CONNECTION*;
   cl: *CALL*; *ss*: *SSP*; *pt*: *PORT*)
  require
   leg_supplied: *lg* /= *Void* ;
   signalling_channel_supplied: *sc* /= *oid* ;
   connection_supplied: *cn* /= *Void* ;
   call_supplied: *cl* /= *Void* ;
   service_switching_point_supplied: *ss* /= *Void* ;
   port_supplied: *pt* /= *Void* ;

feature specification

 current_state: *LEG_STATE*
   -- The BCSM's current state

 define_state (*st*: **like** *current_state*)
   -- Define a state for the state machine
   -- (from *FSM*)
  require
   state_supplied: *st* /= *Void* ;
   not_duplicate: **not** *has* (*st*)

 input (*in*: *PROTOCOL_IPC_EVENT*)
   -- Apply an input to the fsm.
   -- (from *FSM*)
  require
   input_exists: *in* /= *Void* ;
   machine_started: *current_state* /= *Void*

   -- (from *LEG_STATE_CONSTANTS*) :
Max_state_id: *INTEGER is 23*
Min_state_id: *INTEGER is 0*

 my_name: *STRING*
   -- The name of this BCSM for debugging

 new_state (*state*: *INTEGER*)
   -- Change the state of the machine (from *FSM*)
  require
   state_valid: *state* >= *Min_state_id* **and** *state* <= *Max_state_id*
  ensure
   new_state_defined: *current_state* /= *Void*

the_call: *CALL*
>   -- The call associated with this BCSM

the_connection: *CONNECTION*
>   -- The connection associated with this BCSM

the_leg: *LEG*
>   -- The leg that owns this BCSM

the_port: *PORT*
>   -- The port associated with this BCSM

the_routing_table: *ROUTING_TABLE*
>   -- The routing table associated with this BCSM

the_sig_chan: *SIG_CHANNEL*
>   -- The signalling channel associated with this BCSM

the_ssp: *SSP*
>   -- The ssp associated with this BCSM

invariant
>   *Min_max_ok*: *Min_state_id* >= 0 **and** *Max_state_id* >= 0 **and**
>   *Min_state_id* <= *Max_state_id*;
>   *state_defined*: *current_state* != *Void* **or** (*current_state.id* <=
>   *Max_state_id* **and** *current_state.id* >= *Min_state_id*
>   **and then** *has* (*current_state*));

current_state_defined:	*current_state* != *Void*;
the_leg_defined:	*the_leg* != *Void*;
the_sig_channel_defined:	*the_sig_chan* != *Void*;
the_port_defined:	*the_port* != *Void*;
the_connection_defined:	*the_connection* != *Void*;
the_call_defined:	*the_call* != *Void*;
the_ssp_defined:	*the_ssp* != *Void*;
the_routing_table_defined:	*the_routing_table* != *Void*;

end interface -- class *BCSM*

Figure 4.17: Class interface for *BCSM*

deferred class interface FSM [T –> ANY] *feature specification*

   current_state: FSM_STATE [T, *like* Current]
        -- The fsm's current state

   define_state (*st*: *like* current_state)
        -- Define a state for the state machine
     require
        state_supplied: st /= Void ;
        not_duplicate: **not** has (st)

   fsm_name: STRING
        -- Name of this fsm
     deferred

   has (*st*: *like* current_state): BOOLEAN
        -- Does this FSM have state st ?

   input (*in*: T)
        -- Apply an input to the fsm.
     require
        input_exists: in /= Void ;
        machine_started: current_state /= Void

   max_state_id: INTEGER
        -- Highest state id value for this fsm.
     deferred

   min_state_id: INTEGER
        -- Lowest state id value for this fsm.
     deferred

   new_state (*state*: INTEGER)
        -- Change the state of the machine
     require
        state_valid: state >= min_state_id **and** state <= max_state_id
     ensure
        new_state_defined: current_state /= Void

invariant
   named: fsm_name = Void;
   min_max_ok: min_state_id >= 0 **and** max_state_id >= 0 **and**
          min_state_id <= max_state_id;
   state_defined: current_state = Void **or else** (current_state.id <=
          max_state_id **and** current_state.id >= min_state_id
          and then has (current_state))

end interface -- class FSM

Figure 4.18: Class interface for FSM

deferred class interface LEG_STATE feature specification

   act_on (*in*: *PROTOCOL_IPC_EVENT*): *INTEGER*
        -- Act on the input specified and return the next state.
    require
       input_supplied: *in* /= *Void*

   id: *INTEGER*
        -- Unique identifier for this state (from *FSM_STATE*)
    deferred

   state_name: *STRING*
        -- Text description of state (from *FSM_STATE*)
    deferred

invariant

   d_ok: $id >= 0$;
   state_name_defined: *state_name* /= *Void*;

end interface -- class *LEG_STATE*

Figure 4.19: Class interface for *LEG_STATE*

5

Static network resource allocation by simulated annealing in Eiffel

Paul Johnson
GEC-Marconi
United Kingdom

5.1 INTRODUCTION

This chapter describes an application program which uses the technique of simulated annealing to solve the problem of optimising the allocation of processes to nodes in a heterogeneous wide area network.

The discussion covers three aspects:

1: The problem of optimising the network and why simulated annealing was used to solve it. The physical process of annealing metals is outlined and the operation of simulated annealing is demonstrated by drawing a detailed analogy between thermodynamics and the consumption of resources on a network.

2: The "Builder" — the application program which was implemented to solve this problem.

3: The implementation. This includes my personal account of the decisions made during the design process and the problems encountered during development. It also includes some conclusions about the suitability of simulated annealing and Eiffel for optimising wide area networks.

The problem

The problem is that of optimising the allocation of processes to nodes in a wide area network. In a wide area network such as a telephone system, numerous processes have to be run on a range of different machines (called nodes). Each node in the network provides a set of resources such as CPU power and data storage. The nodes are connected by links, each of which provides a bandwidth resource for communication. In parallel with this network is a "soft" network of processes connected by "channels". Each process must reside on a node, where it will consume some fixed amount of that node's resources. Similarly, each inter-process channel must be routed through the links between nodes and will consume a fixed amount of bandwidth on each one. A particular arrangement of processes on nodes and channels on links is known as a "network state" or "configuration". The number of possible states makes an exhaustive search for the best state impractical even for small networks.

5.2 SIMULATED ANNEALING

Simulated annealing is a technique for finding near-optimal solutions to large combinatorial problems such as the Travelling Salesman Problem. This problem and the basic technique simulated annealing are explained in [Press 1988], which also provides a program written in C for optimising the Travelling Salesman's route, both in the classical problem and with extra constraints such as minimising or maximising river crossings. [Johnson 1989] describes an empirical study of simulated annealing applied to the problem of partitioning a connected graph into two sets of nodes with a minimum number of edges going between the two sets.

The details of simulated annealing and how it was applied to the network allocation problem are described later in this chapter. In brief, it attempts to optimise the network by making changes to the configuration, applying a costing function to both the new and old configurations, and then using these two costs to generate a probability of adopting the new configuration in preference to the old one. This process is repeated many times and the system gradually evolves towards a low cost state. The algorithm generates a probability of moving to the new state rather than always choosing the cheaper of the two in order to avoid becoming trapped in a local minimum state. In such a state all single changes to the network would result in a higher cost but a sequence of changes might produce a cheaper state.

Simulated annealing does not require any deep understanding of the problem domain in order to provide solutions. This was important in the application under consideration because the nature of the problem was complex and subject to change during the project. It seemed unlikely that time spent on mathematical analysis would be productive. Any such analysis would depend on many aspects of the problem, any of which might change during or after the project. This could render the whole analysis invalid. Finally, a range of combinatorial optimisation problems have had simulated annealing applied to them, with generally good results [Genman 1984, Jepsen 1983, Johnson 1989, Press 1988, Laarhoven 1987]. Problems solved with simulated annealing include the placing of circuit blocks on integrated circuits, finding the structure of protiens and machine vision.

The amount of CPU time used by simulated annealing tends to be higher than for other methods, but there were no strong performance constraints on the solution to the problem. A program which took several hours to produce a good configuration would have been acceptable.

5.3 OPTIMISATION BY SIMULATED ANNEALING

Simulated annealing is based on the real-life process of annealing metals. If a molten metal is cooled slowly, the atoms line up into crystals which can extend for billions of atoms. This is remarkable because the only source for this order is the random movement of the atoms as they cool down (i.e. slow down: atomic velocity is equivalent to temperature).

5.3.1 Real annealing

When a metal is cooled slowly the atoms gradually settle into a low energy state. In this state all atoms are near to the optimum distance from their neighbours so that the energy in the solid as a whole is minimised. This produces a crystalline solid. On the other hand, if the metal is cooled quickly then the atoms become stuck in a random or *amorphous* structure where atoms are in general not at optimum distances from one another but the resultant force on each atom from all its neighbours is zero. In such a material there is energy stored in the tensions between the atoms and this energy can be used as a measure of how disordered the atoms are.

If an atom becomes part of the lattice, it is possible for it to escape again, thus temporarily raising the energy of the system. It is more likely to escape from a high energy position than from a low energy position. Since irregular arrangements of atoms have a higher energy than regular crystals, the irregular amorphous state is less stable and tends to disappear over time.

5.3.2 Simulated annealing

Optimisers using simulated annealing use an algorithm which is analogous to real annealing. The "energy" of the system is the cost or other quantity to be minimised, while the "temperature" of the system controls the amount of change between measurements of energy.

For those interested in the mathematics, the distribution of energy over the atoms in real matter is given by

$$p = e^{\frac{-E}{kT}}$$

where p is the probability of an atom having at least energy E at temperature T and

k is Boltzmann's constant. If an atom forming part of a solid needs an amount of energy E to escape from its position then this equation gives the probability that it will do so.

So in a simulated annealing system, if there is an existing configuration and the optimiser generates a variation on it with a higher energy, the probability that the new configuration will be adopted is

$$p = e^{\frac{(E_n - E_o)}{kT}}$$

where E_n is the energy of the new state, E_o is the energy of the old state, T is a measure of the amount of change between the old and new states, and k is set to the expected range of energy levels in the system divided by the range of temperatures. If $(E_n - E_o)$ is negative then p is arbitrarily n o set to 1. Hence the algorithm always adopts the new state if it has a lower energy and might adopt it if it has a higher energy. This is known as the Metropolis Algorithm after the first author of [Metropolis].

The way in which this algorithm minimises the energy is shown in figure 5.1. This shows the operation of simulated annealing for a problem with a continuous one dimensional state space. Real problems such as the Travelling Salesman or the network allocation problem do not have such simple state spaces, but the same principles apply. If the current state of the system is at A then a randomly chosen state which is "near" to A in some sense will have either a slightly higher or a slightly lower energy. The optimiser may sometimes move to a higher energy, but will always move to a lower energy. Hence over a large number of iterations it will slide down towards B. B is at a local minimum, so the optimiser cannot slide any lower and all the nearby states have higher energy levels. Sometimes one of these will be adopted by the optimiser, and so it will climb a little up one side or another. The average height of these excursions is controlled by the temperature. At high temperatures the optimiser will quickly jump out of a local

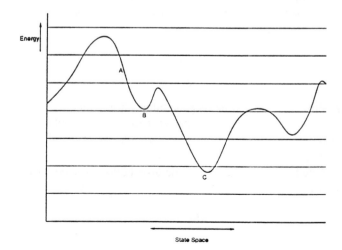

Figure 5.1: Hypothetical energy/state-space graph

minimum. At lower temperatures it will be stuck. In simulated annealing the movement across the state space at each iteration is also related to the temperature by the value of k. At high temperatures more distant states will be explored by the optimiser, and so it can escape from the local minimum in two ways. Either it can climb the hill by adopting a series of ever-higher energy configurations, or it can jump through the hill by adopting a more distant configuration on the other side. Either way, provided the temperature is high enough, the optimiser will eventually move to C. Since C is the global minimum the optimiser will tend to stay there, although it will make occasional excursions up the sides of the valley.

5.3.3 Temperature curves

The way in which temperature is decreased in a simulated annealer is an important trade-off. If the decrease is too fast then the system will "freeze" in an inefficient state. If the decrease is too slow then CPU time will be wasted.

[Johnson 1989] describes experiments in which the temperature was multiplied by a constant value slightly less than 1 at regular intervals, thus producing an exponential decay curve. These experiments suggested that at high temperatures very little optimisation occurs. The average energy level stays fairly constant, but with a large standard deviation. At low temperatures the system "freezes" and again the average energy level stays constant but the standard deviation is very small. In-between these two extremes was a band of temperatures where optimisation occurred.

The behaviour of the system tested in [Johnson 1989] was reminiscent of phase changes between liquid and solid in real materials, hence the use of the term "freezing" above (although the authors noted that the physical model may not be the best one to use). Some adaptive temperature schedules were tried by [Johnson 1989] to exploit this behaviour, but their performance was no better than for conventional cooling schedules.

5.3.4 Simulated annealing for resource allocation

In the resource allocation problem, the network state is analogous to the arrangement of atoms in a metal. The cost of a particular state is analogous to the energy of a particular configuration of atoms. Temperature is a number between 0 and 1, representing the probability that any single change to the state will occur. For instance, if $T = 0.2$ then when the new state is modified 1/5 of the processes will be moved onto new nodes and 1/5 of the channels will be rerouted. Hence k is a number approximately equal to the expected range of costs for a particular network.

The term "Boltzmann's constant" is kept for k, even though it is no longer very accurate. The value of k must be set for each network to be optimised. Similarly the value T is still referred to as "temperature", even though it is a probability value. Terms such as "cooling" and "freezing" which stress the analogy with real annealing are also used. T was measured in this way in an attempt to avoid making the cooling curve parameters dependent on the size of the network.

The cooling schedule is the same one used in [Johnson1989a]. Three values are required: the initial temperature, the rate of cooling and the temperature at which the process terminates.

Because simulated annealing is a stochastic process (another name for it is Monte Carlo annealing), it is not guaranteed to give the best configuration. Indeed, for a large problem it is very unlikely to find the absolute best configuration. All that can be said is that if the annealing is done slowly enough, the configuration is likely to be close to optimal, and that the more slowly the system is cooled, the closer it is likely to be to the optimal state.

There is a clash of terminology in this paper which reflects a similar problem in the application. Simulated annealing is based on an analogy with the annealing of metals. This leads to the use of the term "energy" to describe the cost of a particular network state and "temperature" to denote the severity of the change made to the network configuration for each iteration. On the other hand "energy" is not an intuitive term for the cost of a network configuration. Hence the terms "cost" and "energy" are used interchangeable in this paper. There is no application-specific term for the severity of the change at each iteration, so "temperature" is used throughout.

The builder and the network description file

The network to be optimised is specified to the Builder in a Network Description File (NDF). This lists the nodes, links, processes and channels that make up the network. Parameters to control the optimisation process are also included in this file for convenience, although they are not actually part of the network.

5.3.5 Nodes

Nodes provide the resources which are consumed by processes. A node has a name and a resource list. Each resource has a name and "cost curve". The cost curve is the function relating the total usage of a resource on a node to the cost of providing the resource.

At present two cost curve types have been implemented. They are named *LINEAR* and *EXPENSIVE*. Both take two parameters:

threshold
    Resource usage below this value is free (cost of zero).
rate Resource usage above *threshold* units is charged at *rate* per unit.

The program does not require any particular units for either *threshold* or *rate*. The only requirement is that the units employed be consistent. The meaning of "consistent" is explained below.

LINEAR and *EXPENSIVE* produce the same result, but *EXPENSIVE* has the side effect of printing a warning message on the final output if its threshold value is exceeded.

For example, the following is a valid node:

```
Blue{
     CPU: LINEAR (100, 2);
     Disk: LINEAR (20, 20);
     Core: LINEAR (1, 50)
     };
```

This describes a node called "Blue" with resources named "CPU", "Disk" and "Core". There are 100 units of CPU available, where a unit might be a million-instructions-per-second (MIPS), and additional CPU units cost 2 units each. Cost units are usually financial, such as pounds sterling, dollars or ECUs.

The cost function for the network sums the results from all the cost curves for the current configuration, so the units of cost in all cost curves must be the same. For instance, suppose that CPU is measured in MIPS while Disk and Core are measured in megabytes and the cost is measured in hundreds of dollars. The CPU threshold is 100 MIPS and the cost of extra CPU is 200 dollars per MIPS, while the Disk threshold is 20 megabytes and extra disk costs 2,000 dollars per megabyte. Processes can be placed on any node, so for each resource the units employed must be the same across the whole network.

Since simulated annealing places processes onto nodes at random, it is necessary that a cost can be calculated for any combination of process and node. This implies that every node must provide a cost curve for every resource. A special node called "DEFAULT" can be used to specify the cost curves for resources on all nodes. If a process requires a resource that is not supported by a node, the resource from the default node will be used instead. The default resources are usually *EXPENSIVE* with a small or zero threshold and a high rate to reflect the cost of installing new resources in nodes not intended to handle them. The program reports an error and halts if a process uses a resource which is not supported either by the default node or by every other node. For instance if the default node is specified as

```
DEFAULT{
     CPU: EXPENSIVE (50, 5);
     Disk: EXPENSIVE (2, 50);
     Core: EXPENSIVE (0.2, 200);
     FP: EXPENSIVE (0.1, 200)
     }
```

and a process requiring some of the "FP" (floating point) resource is placed on node "Blue", the cost curve used to calculate the cost of providing the floating point resources will be the one in the "DEFAULT" node. This facility avoids the need to specify every resource on every node.

5.3.6 Links

Links provide bandwidth between nodes on the network. A link has two end-points and a cost curve. For instance

> Blue-Green: EXPENSIVE(100, 1);

describes a link from the "Blue" node to the "Green" node with an expensive cost curve, a capacity of 100 units of bandwidth and a cost of 1 per extra unit of bandwidth. Although the cost curves for links do not have any names, they should be considered to be a separate resource for the purposes of the unit consistency rules given above.

5.3.7 Processes

Processes use the resources provided by nodes. In the simplest case a process consists of a name and a list of resource usages. A resource usage consists of a name and an amount. For instance

> Foo{
>   CPU: 30;
>   Core: 0.4;
>   FP: 0.1
>   };

specifies a process called "Foo" which uses 30 units of CPU, 0.4 units of Core and 0.1 units of FP. The units for each resource usage should be the same as those used to provide the resources in the node specifications.

Processes can be replicated. Each replica acts as a separate process and will be moved around the network by the optimiser. For instance

> 4: Bar{
>   CPU: 140;
>   Disk: 1.3333;
>   Core: 0.43
>   }

specifies that there will be four processes called "Bar", each of which consumes 140 units of CPU, 1.3333 units of Disk and 0.43 units of Core.

Processes can be pinned to individual nodes. A pinned process will stay on its node and not be moved around during optimisation. Pinnings can be combined with replication. For instance

> 5: Baz [Orange, Indigo, Silver] {
>   CPU: 40;
>   };

specifies five copies of a process called "Baz", three of which will be pinned to nodes "Orange", "Indigo" and "Silver". The optimiser is free to move the remaining two around the network.

More complex relationships between processes and nodes can be specified by creating dummy resources which make it very expensive to violate the desired relationships. For instance a process "Foo" might have a number of replicas of which not more than one may be on any single node. By specifying a default resource

Supports foo: EXPENSIVE (1, 1000);

and giving process "Foo" a resource usage such as

Supports foo: 1;

any attempt to place more than one "Foo" on any node will be made highly non-optimal.

5.3.8 Channels

Channels consume the bandwidth provided by links. Each channel connects two processes. For instance

Foo-Bar: 40;

specifies a channel between processes "Foo" and "Bar" that consumes 40 units of bandwidth on every link that it passes through. If the two processes are on the same node then no bandwidth will be consumed. If several links must be traversed then the channel will consume 40 units of bandwidth on each.

The routing of channels through links is the job of the optimiser. There is no requirement that the route taken by a channel be the one with the fewest "hops" through links. If the most direct route for a particular channel is already overloaded, the optimiser may send the channel by a more indirect route. The only rule is that a route may not visit the same node more than once.

If one or both of the processes are replicated then the channel is replicated as well. A replica of the channel is constructed for each pair of the two end-points. In the example channel above, if "Foo" has two replicas and "Bar" has three, then there will be six replicas of the channel between them. Each of these replicas will consume 40 units of bandwidth on each link through which it passes.

There is no facility for pinning channels to links or ensuring that replicated channels are not routed through the same link. There is also no way to specify limits or costs associated with the latency of channels. Latency calculations could be added to the Builder if necessary by specifying a latency for each link and charging these to the channels that are routed across them. Each channel would have a latency cost-curve which would describe the urgency of the data it carried.

5.3.9 Parameters

The following parameters must be specified in the network description file. They control the behaviour of the simulated annealing.

temperature
>   The state change probability at which the cooling process starts. A typical value is 0.25.

rate The rate at which the temperature is reduced. Every 50 iterations the temperature is multiplied by this value. It must be a number between 0 and 1, with 0.99 being a typical value.

terminate
>   The temperature at which the annealing stops. This must be a number between 0 and the temperature. The best value is the reciprocal of the total number of process and channel replicas. This total is the number of possible changes which the optimiser can make in one iteration. Since the "temperature" is the approximate proportion of possible changes which will be made, at temperatures less than this the network modification code is unlikely to make any changes.

boltzmann
>   "Boltzmann's Constant" for this network. It should be set to the expected range of costs for this network.

The number of iterations for each level of temperature is set at 50. This provides a large enough number of iterations for a mean and standard deviation to be computed. Apart from the accuracy of these statistics, altering this number would only affect the rate at which the temperature is reduced. Hence it was felt that making this a parameter in the network description file was not necessary.

5.4 PROCESSING THE NETWORK

After the NDF has been parsed, an initial network configuration is generated at random. Each process is assigned to a random node and each channel is given a random route between the nodes where the processes it connects have been placed. No attempt is made to create a better-than-random initial configuration.

At each iteration of the optimiser, the network state is copied and the copy randomly modified to generate a new state. The following modifications can be performed by the optimiser.

- Any process replica which is not pinned to its node can be moved to an adjacent node. An adjacent node is one connected to the current node by a link. This link is added to the route of all the channels connected to the process and the channels are then checked to ensure that this has not introduced any loops in the route of the channel. A loop occurs if a node appears more than once in the route list. When this happens the loop is eliminated by removing the nodes between the two references. In order to check for such loops in linear time, a "visited" flag is tested and then set in each node on the route.

- Any channel may be rerouted. When a channel is rerouted the old route is destroyed and a new route generated at random. The only restrictions on the new route are that it may not contain loops and must have the same end-points as the old route.

- It is possible that large networks will need a less drastic way of modifying routes in order to be optimised efficiently. When a route is close to being optimal, it is very unlikely that a new route will be an improvement on the existing one. An algorithm that replaced small sections of a route with new sections of a similar length would probably be better.

There is nothing fundamental about these operations. They were chosen because they constitute a spanning set of operations on the network through which any network configuration can be transformed to any other, and because they could be implemented efficiently and easily.

5.5 PROGRAM OUTPUT

The Builder sends output to two files, and also prints progress reports to the standard output.

The final network configuration is printed in an output file. It contains a report on the network state which lists the same information as the Network Description File and also adds information about the allocation of nodes and links, and the resource usages and costs. Some excerpts from an output file are shown below.

Node Blue costs 230 and has the following resources:
Core: LINEAR (Thres = 1, Rate = 50). Usage = 0.93, Cost = 0.
Disk: LINEAR (Thres = 20, Rate = 20). Usage = 4.3333, Cost = 0.
CPU: LINEAR (Thres = 100, Rate = 2). Usage = 215, Cost = 230.
FP: EXPENSIVE (Thres = 0.1, Rate = 200). Usage = 0, Cost = 0.

This describes the node "Blue" and shows that more "CPU" capacity is needed.

The description combines the static information from the original Network Description File and the dynamic informa- tion generated by the optimisation process. The name of the node, the resource names and their cost curves are static information. The usages and the resulting costs are the dynamic information.

The usage figures are the total resource usages from all processes located on this node. The cost figures are the result of passing these usages through the cost curves.

Process Bar (x5) pinned to Silver, Indigo and Orange uses:
FP: 0.3
Core: 1.342
Disk: 2
CPU: 40
Located on: Silver, Indigo, Orange, Yellow, Violet.

This describes a process "Bar" with 5 replicas, three of which are pinned to nodes and the remaining two of which have been allocated to nodes "Yellow" and "Violet".

> Orange-Gold: Cost curve: EXPENSIVE (Thres = 100, Rate = 4.4).
> Usage = 142, Cost = 184.8. Warning: resource limit exceeded.

This describes the link from node "Orange" to node "Gold" and gives its cost curve and usage levels. Because this is an *EXPENSIVE* cost curve where the usage threshold has been exceeded, a warning message is also printed.

> Foo-Bar: 73
> 1, 1: Route Gold-Silver.
> Via Gold-Silver.
> 1, 2: Route Gold-Indigo.
> Via Gold-Magenta-White-Silver-Indigo.
> // Other routes omitted.

This gives the routing for two replicas of the channel between processes "Foo" and "Bar". Each replica consumes 73 units of bandwidth. The first is between the adjacent nodes "Gold" and "Silver", while the second is from "Gold" to "Indigo" and is routed through four links. The numbers before the word "Route" are the process replica indices. Replica 1 of process "Foo" is located on "Gold". Hence both routes start there. Replica 1 of process "Bar" is located on "Silver" and replica 2 is located on "Indigo". Hence these are the destinations of the two routes.

The Builder also produces a log file containing four columns of real numbers. Every 50 iterations the current temperature, the average energy, the standard deviation of the energy and the minimum energy so far are recorded in this file for later analysis.

5.6 POSSIBLE EXTENSIONS TO THE BUILDER

5.6.1 More kinds of cost curve

New kinds of cost curve can be added by minor modifications to the program source code. The Builder contains a class *COST CURVE* with the deferred function *cost*. A new class can be derived from *COST CURVE* which defines the cost function, and a new clause added to the parser to create the instances of the new cost curve. These cost curves can be arbitrarily complicated functions with variable numbers of parameters. The only requirement is that they map resource usage onto cost. Possible new cost curves include step functions and multi-point linear interpolation. For instance, disk space is usually purchased in units of about 100 megabytes, and larger disks usually cost less per megabyte than smaller ones. These things cannot described by the existing linear model.

It has been suggested that node-level cost function customisation might be needed. For instance if the CPU requirement passes a certain threshold then a new physical CPU would be required. This would come with more core storage, and so the core threshold would be increased. The current system of cost-curves which are local to resources could not handle such a situation. The largest problem here would be the addition of new syntax to the network description language. The definition of a new derivative of the *NODE* class which could handle such cost functions would be a simple modification.

5.6.2 Non-random modification strategies

One way to improve performance of the Metropolis algorithm might be to modify the network in an intelligent way, rather than simply making random changes. It is true that in the final stages of annealing almost all the changes made to the network result in higher costs, but intelligent modifications bring a serious danger.

Such a modification strategy would have a set of rules which are expected to lower the cost of the configuration. These rules would be applied at every iteration. If a rule was wrongly applied, the new configuration would have a higher cost and would probably be rejected. Hence on the next iteration the network configuration would be the same, and the same rule would be applied. Thus the optimiser would become trapped in an endless loop.

Two possible approaches to solving this problem are given below.

- Rules might be constructed with a random element, so that the behaviour of the rule varied with each application. This would reduce the probability of becoming stuck in such a loop, but would not eliminate it. It also moves away from the concept of intelligent modification back towards the stochastic technique of simulated annealing.

- The rule base could have a scoring system implemented so that a rule which failed to work well would not be applied again for some number of iterations.

- These solutions might be made to work, but they introduce new variables into the problem. In the first solution, a balance between stochastic processes and hard rules must be found. This is made difficult by the lack of any way to quantify the balance. In the second approach, the way in which the scoring system operates would have a considerable affect on the behaviour of the optimiser. In both cases the choice of rules would also have a significant effect.

Evaluating such a system would be difficult. Given two slightly different optimisers, the only way to decide which is the best overall would be to test both on a large enough number of networks to provide a statistical universe while also varying the cooling parameters in order to find the best combinations for each optimiser. This would be a very slow and expensive process.

5.6.3 Better-than-random starting configurations

[Johnson 1989] applied simulated annealing to the graph partitioning problem. They compared the results from using a purely random initial configuration with a configuration generated by other algorithms, and found that the source of the starting configuration was crucially important to the efficiency of the annealing. There are two possible sources of such a starting configuration for the network builder.

- An expert system could be used. Testing would be much easier than for the iterated rules considered in the previous section, but would still require a statistical universe of networks.

- Human experts could provide hints about where various processes would be best located. It seems likely that human system designers would have access to information about the network being optimised which is not explicitly described in the NDF, and so would be able to generate a much better initial configuration than a random allocation procedure or expert system. A GUI tool which shows a map of the network and indicates which nodes and links are being overloaded would be useful for this, and it seems likely that the existing Eiffel classes for representing the network state and calculating the cost could be reused in such a tool.

5.6.4 Different termination conditions

It has been suggested [Waddington1991a] that the annealing process should include a more intelligent termination decision. For example the annealing could be stopped if no improvement has been made for a certain number of iterations. This may be added to the Browser in the future.

5.7 IMPLEMENTATION: WHY EIFFEL

I chose to implement the Builder in Eiffel [Meyer 1988, 1992] for the following reasons:

- The problem contains some immediately recognisable objects (nodes, links, processes and channels). Hence it seemed likely that an object-oriented language would be suitable. The only two such languages available to me were Eiffel and C++ [Ellis 1990].

- The objects in the problem would be described using complicated data structures which would need to be manipulated in a variety of ways. It seemed likely that the assertion mechanism and code reuse facilities of Eiffel would help to keep the data structures consistent.

- The copying and modification of the network state at every iteration seemed likely to be a complicated operation. Eiffel provides the functions deep clone and deep copy which can duplicate arbitrarily complex data structures, and also includes a garbage collector which can reclaim old objects. A C++ implementation would have required these functions to be written by me.

- The project sponsor wanted to find out about the suitability of Eiffel for use on medium and large scale projects. Implementing this application in Eiffel was to provide useful information about the language.

The major concerns about Eiffel were the reliability of the compiler and libraries, and the efficiency of the generated code.

At the start of the project I was using ISE Eiffel 2.2 on a Sun 3/260 running Sun-OS 4.0.3. By the end of the project I had migrated to ISE Eiffel 2.3 on a Sun 4/260 running Sun-OS 4.1.1.

5.8 DESIGN

The first step was to agree with the client exactly what problem would be solved. I produced a brief report which outlined the problem, explained the simulated annealing technique, and listed the input and output requirements for the program [Johnson 1991].

The design process was very basic. I identified the major object classes by intuition and described their interfaces in a file of design notes. The major responsibilities of each class and the relationships between the classes were listed at this stage.

Many authors [Booch 1991, Meyer 1988, Ellis 1990] have emphasised that object-oriented programs are best developed incrementally or in a bottom-up manner. The lack of detailed design at the beginning of the project followed this philosophy. My aim was to develop a flexible framework into which later, more detailed design decisions could be fitted.

An extract from the design file, along with the flat version of the final class, is included in the appendix at the end of this chapter.

The main problem was divided into three major sub-problems.

- A language for the network description was needed, and a parser for this language would have to be written.
- The network would need to be represented using Eiffel data structures.
- The network state would need to be manipulated by the optimiser.

At this time I decided that the static data about the network (such as the links between nodes and the channels between processes) would be held in one structure and the dynamic data (such as the current mapping from processes to nodes) would be held in a parallel structure. This decision was to cause problems later on, but at the time it seemed likely that the most expensive part of the optimisation process would be the copying of the network state every iteration. It therefore made sense to keep the dynamic network state structure as small as possible. Accordingly I designed pairs of classes such as "Node" and "Node_state". "Node" held a printable name, a list of resources and a list of links. "Node_state" held a reference to its "owner" node, a list of resource states (giving total usage for each resource), and a list of process states. Processes, links, channels and networks were also divided in this way.

Object-oriented design and modular design both bring code and data structures together. Where a particular piece of functionality is associated with a number of data structures object-oriented design also splits up the code between the data structures, using dynamic binding to organise the navigation between different parts. To see how this works in the Builder, consider the *PRINTABLE* class and its descendants.

PRINTABLE contains two deferred procedures, *print_short* and *print_long*. Every class which contributed to the final output file inherits from *PRINTABLE* and effects these two procedures. The only restrictions are that *print_short* should not output a new line, and that *print_long* should always end with a new line. In the case of simple classes such as *USABLE*, which stores resource usage information, the two print procedures both produce the same information. In the case of the *NODE* class *print_short* produces a one-line summary of the name, total cost and list of resource names, while *print_long* prints the name and total cost and then calls *print_long* for each resource. Hence every object in the network can print a description of itself, possibly in terms of lower level objects. An example of the output from the *NODE* version of *print_long* is:

> Node Blue costs 230 and has the following resources:
>   Core: LINEAR(Thres = 1, Rate = 50). Usage = 0.93, Cost = 0.
>   Disk: LINEAR(Thres = 20, Rate = 20). Usage = 4.3333, Cost = 0.
>   CPU: LINEAR(Thres = 100, Rate = 2). Usage = 215, Cost = 230.
>   FP: EXPENSIVE(Thres = 0.1, Rate = 200). Usage = 0, Cost = 0.

The *NETWORK* class *print_long* procedure calls the *print_long* procedure for each node, link, process and channel in the network and so produces the final output file.

This approach of distributing functionality through the classes contrasts with the common approach in a modular language such as Modula-2 [Wirth 1985a]. Under this system, a *print_configuration* procedure would have been written which navigated a data structure defined elsewhere. Any change to the data structure would have required a change to this procedure, along with any other procedures which also navigated the structure.

5.9 THE NETWORK DESCRIPTION LANGUAGE

The language grammar was designed by checking the contents of each static data class and reflecting this in the syntax of each grammatical construct. The ISE Parsing and Lexical Analysis libraries [Meyer 1990] were used to implement the parser.

The ISE Parsing library requires the programmer to define a new class for each syntactic construct. A once function is defined which returns the construct as a list of sub-constructs, and other procedures are defined to handle the semantic actions.

I found this mechanism rather clumsy. Each class needed a large amount of "boilerplate" code to specify ancestors and redefined functions. Even the syntax definition code itself was verbose: each sub-construct had to be created and then explicitly appended to a list. During the definition of the language syntax I spent most of my time typing rather than thinking. A tool which could take some kind of BNF syntax description and generate the classes automatically would have saved time.

I found the documentation for the parsing libraries to be very poor. The manual [Meyer 1990] dealt with the definition of syntax, but described the "commit" mechanism purely in terms of optimisation. In fact this mechanism is used for syntax error detection and reporting. The manual also left the relationship between the parser and the lexical analyser rather vague, as was the relationship between the parsing operation and the semantic actions. I eventually discovered how to arrange these by reading the library source code and studying the example program.

The four semantic action routines in each construct class are called

semantics, pre_action, in_action and *post_action.*

Routines *semantics* and *in_action* are normally not redefined. *semantics* calls *pre_action, in_action* and *post_action. in_action* calls *semantics* on each sub-construct. This is documented in the manual, but not very clearly.

There was no advice on how best to arrange for the semantic actions in the parser to produce the data structures and symbol tables from the parse tree. I eventually decided to use a global stack for each construct in the language. The *pre_action* routine for each construct notes the stack count for each type of sub-construct. After the *pre_action* procedure is called, the sub-constructs are automatically constructed and pushed onto their stacks. The *post_action* routine then pops off enough instances of each sub-construct to restore the stack counts to their previous states. These sub-constructs are used to create the new construct which is then pushed onto its own stack.

The libraries handle syntax error detection and reporting fairly well. When an error is detected, a message is printed on the standard error stream giving the line number where the error was detected, the lexical token that was found and the token or construct name that was expected. No attempt at syntax error recovery is made. Instead the parser aborts and clears a flag to signal an error to the application.

There was no support provided for semantic error messages. For these I defined a class *PARSABLE* which is inherited by all data structures created by the parser. This provides source file, line number and column number information. Tokens such as identifiers and numbers take this data from the lexical analyser. Higher level constructs copy the data from one of their lower level constructs, usually the first. *PARSABLE* also defines a procedure *report_error*. This takes a string argument and prints it out as an error message with the location data.

I found some bugs in the version 2.2 Parsing libraries available at the start of the project. These were fixed in the version 2.3 libraries. I have not found any more bugs in the Parsing or Lexical Analysis libraries.

5.10 REPRESENTING THE NETWORK

Representing the static information about the network was not difficult. The design notes were translated into Eiffel, expanding the English language descriptions both into assertions and procedural code. Each grammatical construct in the Network Description

Language was mapped to a class in the network data structure, and a construction routine for each class was called from the parser. This construction routine was not just the class *Create* feature, since the creation of *LINK* and *CHANNEL* objects required references to their end points to be looked up in a hash table. These end-points were passed to the *Create* features for the new objects but the end-points were not informed by the *Create* features that they had new connections, so the parser's semantic routines also had to connect the nodes to the links and the processes to the channels.

It became apparent that I had not thought hard enough about how objects were to be created and modified. The philosophy of "software contracting" behind Eiffel [Meyer 1988] emphasises the specification of invariants which hold true at all times. Many of the invariants and postconditions I had written into my design were to ensure mutual consistency. For instance if a *NODE* had a *LINK* attached then one of the end-points of that link should be equal to the node, and similarly the node at the end of a link should have the link connected to it. Unfortunately such an assertion pair is violated when one side of the structure is modified before the other. Hence it was impossible to construct or modify the network as it was originally designed, since any attempt had to involve an inconsistent intermediate state. The solution was to keep one side of the consistency constraint, relax the other half, and not write other code which assumed that the relationship between a node and a link was mutual.

Another potential solution was to have constructors which updated other objects to reflect the new object's existence. Under this scheme the *LINK* constructor would call the *add_link* operation on each of it's end points. This was rejected because it would make it very difficult to create temporary objects. Any link would automatically have the same visibility and lifetime as its end-points. Hence modular software using the *LINK* class would be very difficult to build.

In the final design when a node is connected to a link it ensures that the link has an end-point at that node (this is awkward to specify in invariants, so other checks are used). No corresponding guarantee is made for a link with nodes at its end points. Any valid link must have nodes at its end-points but those nodes do not necessarily know about the link. This functionality was implemented by a generic class *END_POINTS[T]* which managed connections to end-points of any type.

The relationship between nodes, links, processes and channels is shown in figure 5.2. The horizontal arrows denote static information and the vertical arrows show dynamic information. Each node has a list of links, and each link has two nodes. Similarly each process has a list of channels and each channel has two processes. Each node also has a list of resources and each process has a list of usages. Each process is allocated to one node and each channel to a number of links.

Once these classes had been written the Builder could be compiled and executed. It could read a network description, generate a data structure containing the static network information and print the structure out. Debugging this took about a week, and is described in the section on debugging in Eiffel.

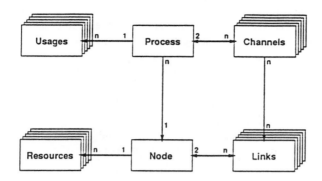

Figure 5.2: Architecture of the builder

5.11 THE NETWORK STATE

Before starting to write the code to manage the dynamic state of the network, I spent two months exploring the possibility of a library of classes which could maintain consistent relationships between objects in such a way that the consistency constraints could not be violated. I expected that since modifying the dynamic state of the network would involve manipulating many relationships in a consistent way, such a class library would be useful. The resulting library is described in [Johnson 1991].

When I came to use this library in the Builder I discovered that it made modular software construction very difficult, since any temporary objects would automatically make bidirectional links to other permanent objects. The library was therefore not used.

The network state needed to support three operations.

1. It had to be copied.
2. It had to be changed randomly, with the severity of the change depending on the progress of the optimisation (temperature).
3. The cost (energy) of the current configuration had to be measured.

The most obvious and efficient way to copy the state was by the built-in Eiffel function *deep_clone*[1]. However this function copies all the objects which can be reached directly or indirectly via references in the structure being copied. This implied that there could be no references from the network state to the static information about the network. The only alternative was to write a specialised copy function which would work through the network state selectively copying objects. This would mean having a description of the network data structures held in two different formats. One would be a set of type declarations and the other would be the instructions for copying it. This would make the process of modifying the data structures difficult and error-prone.

---

[1] Technically the *deep_clone* function is not built into the language. It is inherited from the universal ancestor class *ANY*

The state modification code needed access to the static and dynamic data about each object. Since references from the dynamic to the static data were not feasible, I considered references from the static to the dynamic. The problem here was that there might be several dynamic states under consideration at any one time. The only solution to this problem involved each static object having a list of references to the various dynamic states. This would be complex and inefficient, so I rejected the idea.

In the end I merged the static and dynamic classes. This meant that the copies of the network state contained redundant information, but it made everything else very simple. New states could be generated by the *deep_clone* function, and all the information needed by the state modification code was kept in one set of classes rather than two.

The measurement of cost was fairly easy. The *NODE* and *LINK* classes had cost functions, and the *energy* function of the *NETWORK* class totalled up the results from these functions. They in turn operated by passing the current usage levels for each resource object to its cost curve object.

The change of name from "cost" to "energy" at the network level is due to the way in which the Metropolis Algorithm was implemented. The class *ANNEALER* takes a generic parameter constrained to inherit from *ANNEAL_STATE*. *ANNEALER* contains the main loop of the Metropolis algorithm, and its creation procedure takes as arguments the parameters which control the annealing and an object of type *ANNEAL_STATE* to anneal. *ANNEAL_STATE* contains deferred functions required by *ANNEALER* and is an ancestor class for any system which is to be optimised by simulated annealing. Hence *NETWORK* defines *energy* rather than *cost* because it conforms to the terminology of simulated annealing rather than network resources.

5.12 FINE GRAIN INHERITANCE

In a previous paper [Johnson 1991] Dr. Ceri Rees and I have proposed the concept of Fine Grain Inheritance (FGI). This suggests that classes written in languages which support multiple inheritance should inherit their interfaces from a large number of very small base classes. The Builder was the first non-trivial program where this idea was applied.

All classes were divided into read-only and write-only superclasses, except where one of these superclasses would have been empty. Whenever concepts in a class could be separated they were described in superclasses, even if the class contained only one or two features.

In most cases this did not contribute to the reuse of existing sections of code, partly because the only libraries available were ISE classes that come bundled with their compiler [Meyer 1990], and partly because the general design of the Builder was foreseen from the outset. FGI is intended to help during later modifications which were not foreseen. I would expect the use of FGI to start paying off if the Builder ever needs alteration or enhancement. Despite this two observations are worth making.

A number of people have predicted that programs built using FGI would become overly complex and that mundane problems like the need for complicated name-schemes for classes would make it awkward to use. I did not find this to be a problem. For instance, the ancestor tree for class *NODE* is:

```
HAS_LINKS
  HAS_LINKS_READ
HAS_RESOURCES
  HAS_RES_READ
  COST_CENTRE
  HAS_RES_WRITE
NODE_READ
  HAS_RES_READ
  HAS_LINKS_READ
  COST_CENTRE
  NAMED
  PRINTABLE
  PARSABLE
  VISITABLE
    VISITABLE READ
    VISITABLE WRITE
NODE_WRITE
  HAS_RES_WRITE
  HAS_LINKS_WRITE
  VISITABLE_WRITE
```

This tree was generated by the Eiffel *ancestors* command. Despite the number of ancestor classes, naming has not been a problem and locating the definitions of particular features was not particularly difficult. The *short* and *flat* commands in the Eiffel environment [Meyer 1990a] were very useful for this. However the tree contains a few irregularities which need explanation.

- *HAS LINKS* fails to inherit from *HAS_LINKS_WRITE*. This was due to a problem with the Eiffel type checker, which rejected an attribute links with a type of *HAS_READ* in one ancestor, *HAS_WRITE* in another, and *HAS* in the *HAS_LINKS* class.

- *COST_CENTRE* (which contains the single deferred attribute *cost*) is directly inherited by *HAS_RESOURCES*. Since *COST_CENTRE* only has a readable attribute, it should be inherited via *HAS_RES_READ*. Strict following of FGI would have required another base class for the other attributes of *HAS_RES_READ*. The arrangement above was adopted out of laziness.

- *NODE_READ* inherits from *VISITABLE* rather than *VISITABLE_READ*. The *VISITABLE* classes defined a boolean flag with two operations *set_visited* and *clear_visited* for use by the channel routing algorithm. Since the routing function did not change the network, it took an argument of type *NETWORK_READ* , and hence could only access the features of *NODE_READ*. I decided that it made more sense for the visit flag to be be writable in *NODE_READ* than it did for the routing algorithm to take a generally writable network.

The finished Builder contains 10,100 lines of Eiffel in 123 classes. The line count includes comments, blank lines and a standard header comment of 25 lines per class.

When compiled in unoptimised form with all assertions and debugging instructions enabled, the executable Builder was about 2.5 Mbytes long. When compiled via a C package with no assertions or debugging instructions, the executable was 600 Kbytes long. Both these figures are for a Sun 4.

5.13 DEBUGGING UNDER EIFFEL

The system was compiled and debugged under ISE Eiffel version 2.3.

The biggest problem when debugging was the lack of a proper source-level debugger. The Eiffel environment includes a *VIEWABLE* class which can display classes and follow references, but this cannot access local variables in routines that fail and does not support breakpoints or other execution control. Tracing is available and could be turned on or off at the class level, but it often produced either too much information or too little. I kept having to resort to inserting print statements or extra assertions in the code when the ability to examine a few local objects would have answered my questions.

The ISE Eiffel 2.3 compiler is not completely type-safe. In particular Eiffel allows the programmer to redefine a feature argument as a descendant of its original type. This facility can result in an entity with one type refering to an object with the type of an ancestor. When a feature of this object is called, the run-time system fails with a segmentation violation.

The Builder failed in this manner twice during development. When this occurred it was necessary to use the Unix "dbx" utility to find out what had gone wrong. The location of the bad feature call provided a clue to the nature of the type violation. Hence the application had to be recompiled with the C compiler "-g" debug flag on. The type violations were not difficult to find once the problem was understood and a stack trace had been obtained, but a novice Eiffel programmer would find this difficult and confusing.

Recompilation during development was slow. The most time-consuming part was the linking of the final executable, which was taking several minutes towards the end of the project. A full compilation of all the Builder classes but excluding the libraries took 19 minutes on a Sun 4/330 with all files held on a local disk.

Despite these problems the Builder was still easy to debug. Because of the emphasis placed by Meyer on software contracting and the corresponding assertions in the program, many bugs were found by examining the exception trace. This was printed automatically when an assertion was violated. Often these were bugs which would have resulted in inconsistency in the network data structures. If the program had been written in languages such as C [Kernighan 1978] or C++ [Ellis 1990], which lack the Eiffel assertion mechanism, these bugs would have silently left the data structures inconsistent, causing strange behaviour minutes or hours later. Tracking such bugs using dbx would have been very difficult. This showed up most dramatically after the Builder had first run through 50 iterations of the Metropolis Algorithm and had produced its first set of statistics. Only three bugs were found after this. One was due to a problem with the garbage collector failing to run often enough, so that the program ran out of memory. The other two were rounding errors which resulted in slightly negative values violating assertions that required values greater than or equal to 0. The Builder has now been run for many hours and has behaved perfectly.

Many bugs were caught by the Eiffel type checker which would have been missed by the C or C++ type systems. In both languages the programmer must override (coerce) the type of pointers extracted from container objects such as hash tables or lists. Eiffel does not require this, and so programs can be constructed in a type-safe manner. I found it useful to put a partly modified version through the compiler in order to locate code segments which still needed changing, especially argument lists. If the modification involved a change to the interface of a class, the compiler could be relied upon to locate all the out of date uses.

C++ now includes a facility for generic types (templates) described in [Ellis 1990]. This would have solved the problem with the C++ type system described above, but it is still experimental and was not available for this project.

5.14 OTHER TOOLS

The Builder source code was written using the GNU Emacs [Stallman 1988] editor in Eiffel mode [Omohundro]. Use was also made of an Eiffel Browser [Johnson 1990] running under Emacs and complementing the Eiffel mode functions. This system had the following advantages.

- The Browser made it very easy to move from one class to another while editing under Emacs. When editing a group of classes, I did not need to remember which directory the classes were stored in.

- The *short* and *flat* versions of the classes [Meyer 1990] could be loaded into Emacs buffers by the Browser. This gave more flexibility than the ISE Browser, which merely allows the user to page through the class text.

- The Eiffel mode includes commands which insert templates for Eiffel structures such as classes, functions, procedures and loops.

- The editor provides automatic line indenting. This saved time and was also useful for checking the proper nesting of control structures without having to compile the program.

- The multiple window feature of Emacs helped when writing code which referred to other classes. The short-flat form of the server class was kept in one window for reference while the code being edited was displayed in another.

The Unix SCCS system was used to maintain an audit trail of modifications to the software. It would have been useful had the Eiffel compiler been able to access code stored using SCCS. This would have avoided the need to extract files manually before compiling, and would also have avoided unnecessary recompilations after edited files were checked in.

5.15 PERFORMANCE MEASUREMENTS

The test file used for the measurements contained 16 nodes, 15 processes, 21 links and 56 channels. These figures include replicated process and channels. A map of the nodes and links is shown in figure 5.3. The resources supported by each node are not shown, but the figures attached to the links are the thresholds and rates for the bandwidth cost curves.

Name	Value
temperature	0.25
rate	0.95
terminate	0.025
boltzmann	3000

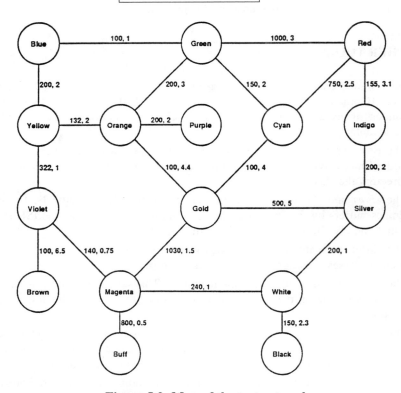

Figure 5.3: Map of the test network

During performance testing, the Builder was run for 2250 iterations. At the start the average cost of the network was 20331.8 units and the minimum cost found during the first 50 iterations was 16026.5. At the end of the optimisation, the average cost was 6895.75 and the minimum cost was 6052.25. The optimised network configuration was inspected by hand. Some non-optimal routes were found. The annealing parameters for this test are shown in the above table.

The problem with simulated annealing is that when the network has reached a state which is close to being optimal, almost all the random changes made by the algorithm result in a higher cost. At present the route modification algorithm reroutes a channel at random, ignoring the existing route. It seems likely that a smaller modification which replaces part of the existing route with a similar number of "hops" might be a good idea.

The following measurements were taken on a Sun 4/330 running Sun-OS 4.1.1. They were obtained by use of the Unix "gprof" command.

In another test, the Builder was run for 3150 iterations. This took 5035.44 CPU seconds, including initialisation, reading the input file and formatting the output file. The actual optimisation consumed 4864.77 seconds and this is used as the base for the following percentages. Of the optimisation time, 2265.17 seconds (47%) were taken by the garbage collector and 1990.68 seconds (40%) were taken by the *deep_clone* function. The network mutation procedure took 541.51 seconds (11%). Hence these three operations accounted for 98% of the computation time, and the two system operations accounted for 87% of the time.

These measurements were made with the "C-package" option of the Eiffel compiler, all assertions switched off, and optimisation switched on. The incremental garbage collector was turned off, and a full collection made once every fifty iterations.

These measurements are limited by having been made on a single network which was constructed for test purposes rather than from real-life data. Little seems to be known about how the time required for simulated annealing varies with the size of the problem, although [Press 1988] notes that simulated annealing scales "as a small power of [the size of the problem]". More extensive testing with real-world data is planned.

5.16 REUSABILITY

None of the classes from the Builder have been reused so far. However there are two clusters of classes which might be reused in the future.

The *ANNNEALER* and *ANNEAL_STATE* classes were designed to describe the concept of a simulated annealer. *ANNEAL-STATE* can act as an ancestor class for simulated annealing algorithms in other applications.

Other approaches to network optimisation can be explored using the network description classes. For instance a tool which allows manual optimisation to be performed on a graphical representation of the network could be based on the existing classes. The basic operations of moving processes, rerouting channels and finding the cost of a configuration are already supported.

5.17 CONCLUSIONS

Simulated annealing is an effective technique for dealing with the problem of allocating resources on a wide area network. Further work is needed to explore the way in which optimisation time varies with the network size.

The fact that simulated annealing works well on a problem with such a complicated cost function suggests that it can be applied to other complicated problems. Previously the technique was open to the accusation that it might only work on problems with simple cost functions.

Eiffel was a good choice of language for this application. The concept of software contracting [Meyer 1988] is a powerful tool for organising functionality in large programs, and Eiffel was designed to support this concept with its assertion mechanism and the short and flat tools. I would recommend Eiffel as a language for medium and large scale software development.

The current implementation of Eiffel (version 2.3) suffers badly from a slow garbage collector and a lack of debugging facilities. These should improve in the next version. If the garbage collector does improve then the performance of the Builder should improve by a corresponding amount, and it will be worth while spending time optimising the network modification code. The lack of debugging facilities has to be set against the excellence of the Eiffel language itself.

Eiffel may lack a proper environment at present, but this will improve. Its main rival, C++, has better programming environments available but is a much weaker language for software engineering. While Eiffel vendors can easily produce better tools, C++ can only be improved by changing the language. As Eiffel matures it will become increasingly superior to C++.

5.18 ACKNOWLEDGMENTS

This report forms part of the FOOD (Framework for Object-Oriented Design) project. The work was commissioned by GPT.

APPENDIX: FROM DESIGN TO EIFFEL

The following is an extract from the original design notes produced at the start of the project, followed by the class as it was finally implemented. The two classes in the notes became a single class in the final implementation so that *deep_clone* could be used to copy the network state. The *state_copy* , and *state_copy_done* features were originally intended to support this copying, and so were never implemented.

Node: *Named_object, Printable, Has_resources, Has links*
   Name: *String*
   Resources: *Array_read* [*Resource*]
   Links: *List_read* [*Link*]

   Add_resource
   Add_link
   Print_short
   Print_long

Node_state: *Problem_state, Printable, Owned, Has_resource_states,*
Has_process_states
   Owner: *Node*
   Resource_states: *Array_read* [*Resource_state*]
   Process_states: *List_read* [*Process_state*]
   Fixed: *List_read* [*Process_state*]
   Unfixed: *List_read* [*Process_state*]
     Processes = *union* (*Fixed, Unfixed*)
     union (*Fixed, Unfixed*) = {}

   Add_fixed_process
   Add_process
   Remove_process
   State_copy
   State_copy_done
   Print_short
   Print_long

These two class outlines were eventually unified into the *NODE* class. The following class text was produced by the Eiffel "flat" filter. A number of features such as:

   Visitable_sccs_id: *STRING* **is** "%W%" ;

have been removed. These were part of the version control and have no other function.

The occasional notes placed in the code below always describe the feature immediately above.

class *NODE* **feature**

```
        -- Feature from HAS_RESOURCES
add_usages (proc: USES_RES_READ) is
        -- Add this consumer to the set being supported on this object
    require
        valid_consumer: proc /= Void;

    local
        this_usage: USAGE;
```

```
    do
      from
        proc.usages.list.start
      until
        proc.usages.list.offright
      loop
        this_usage := proc.usages.list.item;
        resources.item (this_usage.obj_name).add_usage (this_usage.amount);
        proc.usages.list.forth;

    end;
```

This started out as the *add_process* feature in the design document. The *USES_RES_READ* class is an ancestor of *PROCESS* which encapsulates read-only data on the use of resources. This is the only aspect of *PROCESS* which this procedure needs to know about.

The procedure examines each resource usage in the process, and looks up its name in the hash table of resources maintained on this node. It then adds the amount used onto the resource with the same name. The feature *remove_process* performs the opposite operation.

```
          -- Feature from VISITABLE
    clear visited is
          -- Clear the visited flag.
      require
        visited_count > 0;

      do
        if visited then
          count_imp.put (count_imp.item–1);
        end;

        visited := false

    ensure
      not visited
    end;
```

Nodes can be "visited" by the routing algorithms. This routine clears the visited flag on this node and decrements the count of visited nodes. This counter is used to check that the router clears all the visited flags after it finishes.

```
          -- Feature from PARSABLE
    column number: INTEGER;
          -- Column in which this object was found.
```

```
        -- Feature from NODE_READ
construct name: STRING is
        --Node name
    local
        tname: STRING;

    do
        tname := obj_name;
        Result.Create (tname.count + 6);
        Result.append ("node " );
        Result.append (tname);

    end;


        -- Feature from PARSABLE
copy_location (other: PARSABLE) is
        -- Copy the source location from other to this construct.
        -- Used for example to locate a procedure construct at the
        -- first line of its declaration: just copy the location from
        -- the name of the procedure.

    require
        other exists: other /= Void;

    do
        line_number := other.line_number;
        column_number := other.column_number;
        file_name := other.file_name

    end;
```

The *construct_name* feature originally comes from the *PARSABLE* class as well, but in *NODE_READ* there is enough information to give it a full definition. These features are used by the *raise_error* procedure to print out meaningful error messages.

```
        -- Feature from HAS_RESOURCES
cost: REAL is
        -- Cost of keeping all these processes on this node.
    do
      from
        resources.list.start
      until
        resources.list.offright
      loop
        Result := Result + resources.list.item.cost;
        resources.list.forth;
```

end;

ensure
  Result >= 0.0;

end;

This function returns the cost of keeping all the processes currently on this node. It iterates over the list of resources, adding the cost for each resource onto the total.

The **ensure** clause for this feature is one of those that had to be disabled as a workaround for rounding errors.

    -- Feature from *VISITABLE*
count_imp: *CELL [INTEGER]* **is**
    -- Storage for the visited count.
  once
    !! Result;
  end;

make (*n: STRING*; *where: PARSABLE*) **is**
    -- Create a node named *n* in network *net*.
  require
    name_exists: *n* /= *Void*

  do
    obj_name := n;
    line_number := where.line_number;
    column_number := where.column_number;
    file_name := where.file_name;
    !! resources;
    !! links;
    debug
      io.error.putstring ("Creating node");
      io.error.putstring (n);
      io.error.putstring (".0 ");

    end;

  ensure
    obj_name = n;

  end;

    -- Feature from *PARSABLE*
file_name: *STRING*;
    -- Source file in which this object was found.

```
        -- Feature from PARSABLE
line_number: INTEGER;
        -- Line on which this object was found.


        -- Feature from HAS_LINKS
links: HAS [LINK];
```

The ISE hash table class lacks a facility for iterating over the contents of the table. The *HAS* class was created as a workaround. It simply contains a hash table and linked list which contain the same data. Since this is only needed for static data, the problem of deleting items in such a container does not arise.

```
obj_name: STRING;
        -- Name of this node.


        -- Feature from NODE_READ
print_long (f: FILE) is
        -- Prints out the long form of this node.
    require
        valid_file: f /= Void

    do
        f.putstring ("Node ");
        f.putstring (obj_name);
        f.putstring ("has the following resources:");
        from
            resources.list.start
        until
            resources.list.offright
        loop
            f.putstring (" ");
            resources.list.item.print_long (f);
            resources.list.forth;

        end;
        f.new_line;

    ensure
        resources.list.offright
        -- Last character to f was new line.
    end;


        -- Feature from NODE_READ
print_short (f: FILE) is
        -- Print short form of this node.
    require
        valid_file: f /= Void
```

```
do
    f.putstring ("Node");
    f.putstring (obj_name);
    f.putstring ("supports");
    from
        resources.list.start
    until
        resources.list.offright
    loop
        f.putstring (resources.list.item.obj_name);
        if not resources.list.islast then
            f.putstring (", ")
        else
            f.putstring (" ");

        end;
        resources.list.forth;

    end;

ensure
    resources.list.offright
    -- No new_line issued to f.
end;
```

See the text for an explanation of the print procedures.

```
    -- Feature from PARSABLE
raise_error (mess: STRING) is
    -- Print message to standard error with line number information.
    require
    valid_message: mess /= Void

do
    io.error.putstring (file_name);
    io.error.putstring (" (line " );
    io.error.putint (line_number);
    io.error.putstring ("): " );
    io.error.putstring (construct_name);
    io.error.putstring (": " );
    io.error.putstring (mess);
    io.error.new_line

end;
    -- Feature from HAS_RESOURCES
```

remove usages (proc: USES_RES_READ) is
    -- Remove this consumer from the set being supported on this object.

require
    valid_process: *proc /= Void*

local
    this_usage: *USAGE*

do
    from
        proc.usages.list.start
    until
        proc.usages.list.offright
    loop
        this_usage := *proc.usages.list.item*;
        resources.item (*this_usage.obj_name*).*add_usage* (*this_usage.amount*);
        proc.usages.list.forth

    end

    end;
See the *add_usages* procedure for details about this.

        -- Feature from *HAS_RESOURCES*
resources: *HAS* [*RESOURCE*];
    -- Resources for this object.

Like links, *resources* needs to support both sequential and keyed access. The *remove_usages* routine above shows an example of keyed access, and the print routines show sequential access.

        -- Feature from *VISITABLE*
set_visited **is**
        -- Set the *visited* flag.
    do
        if not *visited* **then**
            count_imp.put (*count_imp.item+1*);

        end;
        visited := **true**

    ensure
        visited

    end;
        -- Feature from *VISITABLE*

visited: *BOOLEAN*;
    -- Flag to indicate whether this object has been visited by
    -- a router yet. It is important that routers clear this
    -- flag when leaving a node, otherwise subsequent routing
    -- operations will fail in funny ways.

    -- Feature from *VISITABLE*
visited_count: *INTEGER* **is**
    -- Number of nodes with *visited* set true. Used to check
    -- that the routing algorithms leave them all clear.
do
    Result := *count_imp.item*
end;

invariant

    --| Invariant from *PARSABLE*
file_name_exists: *file name* /= *Void*;

    --| Invariant from *NAMED*
valid name: *obj_name* /= *Void*;

    --| Invariant from *VISITABLE_READ*
visited count >= *0*
end -- class *NODE*

6

A layered-modelling tool for the integration of computer applications

Bart Luijten and Bart Luiten
TNO/Delft University of Technology/Ballast Nedam
Delft (The Netherlands)

To support the design and manufacturing process of industrial and architectural products, many computer applications are available. One of the main problems industrial automation is faced with is the communication between those applications. Integration of computer applications can be achieved by integrating the data transferred between the applications. Data integration can be realised through conceptual information models, like product models. For reasons of maintenance, reuse and model integration, these models generally have a layered structure, in which functionality is split into more generalised and more specialised layers.

This chapter describes the development and implementation of a tool to support the implementation of these layered conceptual models in an object-oriented system. The modelling tool provides an easy to use graphical user interface for the specification and implementation of layered conceptual models. To facilitate the integration of applications international accepted standards for the exchange of data are supported. The tool has already proven to bridge the gap between specification and implementation by using rapid prototyping. The possibilities for the integration of applications are promising.

6.1 INTRODUCTION

For the 1990s one of the main research issues in computer science is the integration of the islands of automation that emerged from the 1980s. Since 1985 the Dutch research institute TNO Building and Construction Research is working on this issue for the

Building and Construction Industry. Islands of automation, like Computer Aided Design and Computer Aided Manufacturing, are integrated by integrating the computer applications of these islands. Computer applications are integrated by integrating the data that is transferred between these applications. To realise data integration the product modelling approach of ISO/STEP developed by ISO TC184 SC4 is followed. ISO is the International Organisation for Standardisation and STEP is the STandard for the Exchange of Product model data.

6.1.1 A brief history of product modelling

During design and manufacturing of industrial and architectural products many computer applications are used. Communication between these applications forms a substantial problem. This problem generally leads to ad hoc solutions, where two translators are made for every pair of applications. This results in a large number of translators (in the worst case $(n-1)*n$ translators for n applications), which are hard to maintain. Systems of integrated applications also tend to be very inflexible with regard to extensions; for the integration of a new application with n other applications $2*n$ translators have to be developed (in the worst case). To overcome these problems the STEP Framework approach [Kirkley 1991] suggests a neutral database containing all data of the product, a so-called product model. Every application will have only two translators with this product model, one to and one from the product model. Information can be extracted from it and new information can be stored into it. When the number of applications is larger than three, which is normally the case, this approach requires less translators than the ad hoc solutions. This product modelling approach is also more flexible because every new application requires only two new translators.

The problem of integration of applications is now 'reduced' to the problem of implementing the theory on product modelling. According to the STEP Framework approach product models are developed in a layered structure. Every layer contains functionality on a certain level of abstraction. Functionality on a higher layer is more general while functionality on a lower layer is more specific. An example of this layered structure is shown in figure 6.1.

The first layer, the object layer, is the most general layer and is generally applicable. It contains for example functionality with regard to database management and user interface control. The second layer contains functionality as standardised in the STEP resource models, like topology and geometry models. This layer also contains the graph model for modelling networks and deriving subsystems and aspect systems. The models of the second layer are applicable to all products. The second layer is used in the third layer, which contains reference models for the different branches of industry, in our case the Architecture, Engineering and Construction (AEC) industry. For this layer, TNO developed GARM (General AEC Reference Model) [Gielingh 1988] which is part of a draft proposal for the STEP standard. Such a reference model can be used in the next layer to model a family of products in a product type model, e.g. the Road Model Kernel [Williams 1990] for a family of highways. An instance of a product type model is a

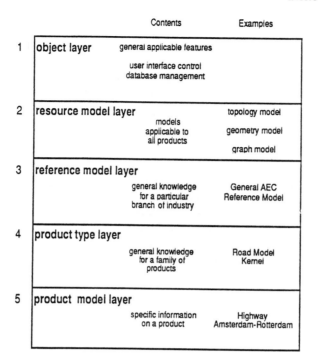

Figure 6.1: Example of the layered structure of the STEPFramework approach

product model, which is the last layer. For instance, the model of the Amsterdam–Rotterdam highway is an instance of the Road Model Kernel.

Most tools used in the 1980s do not support the implementation of the layered structure of the STEP Framework approach very well. They separate data and functionality too much and they lack an inheritance mechanism. Because tools cannot implement the layered approach in a satisfactory way, a significant problem appears: for every product type model the programmer has to start from scratch. This makes it nearly impossible to reuse previously implemented functionality, which means that for every product type model the functionality of the (STEP) resource model layer and of the (AEC) reference model layer has to be implemented again. This leads to complex models, extra work and problems with maintenance of the systems. It is also very difficult to keep the product type models consistent with each other, so integration between models of different product types becomes hard to realise. This integration between product type models is useful when one product type model incorporates another, e.g. a model for high rise office buildings incorporates a model for concrete structures and a model for heating installations.

Fusion of functionality of different abstraction levels in one product type model not only leads to programming problems, like extra work and maintenance and consistency problems, but also to organisational problems. Because every product type model requires a new implementation from scratch, a large gap between specification and implementation arises. The new models are so complex that only specialists can implement them, and they take a long time to realise. Therefore, specification and implementation are done by different people and with a large time gap in-between. In this way there is no direct feedback and no rapid prototyping.

6.1.2 An object-oriented modelling tool

Experience has shown that the above mentioned problems can best be solved by using an object-oriented environment. But using an object-oriented language alone is not enough: it is still possible to make inflexible, inconsistent, hard to maintain systems that are only usable for experts. That is why we chose to develop a layered-modelling tool. This tool should support the layered modelling principles of the STEP Framework approach. The tool is developed for product modelling, but most of the principles are applicable to any tool for the support of the implementation of layered conceptual models. The ideas behind this modelling tool were introduced previously in [Luiten 1991] and [Willems 1991].

6.1.3 A road map for this chapter

In section 6.2 requirements for a layered-modelling tool are given. The alternative approaches to implement the layering mechanism are discussed and compared with each other in section 6.3. The main characteristics of the chosen mechanism, 'specialisation by instantiation', are worked out here. Section 6.4 discusses some implementation considerations for the prototype implementation of a layered-modelling tool, PMshell. Some implementation details are given in section 6.5. Section 6.6 deals with the system architecture of PMshell. The last section of this chapter contains an example of the use of PMshell as a tool for implementing geometric models and the integration of a 2D graphical query tool. The chapter ends with conclusions.

6.2 REQUIREMENTS

The implementation of the STEP product modelling approach not only requires an object-oriented environment, but also a tool to support and guide the modelling process. This modelling tool should fulfil requirements dealing with the following topics: (1) layered modelling, (2) integration of applications, (3) exchange of data, (4) independence of the object-oriented environment, (5) graphical user interface and (6) programming and modelling. The six topics are described below.

6.2.1   Layered modelling

The main principle of object-oriented system development is the ability to design new structures based on existing structures. In this way the complexity of a system can be reduced by generalising common parts of the system and specialising other parts. This principle is used for layered modelling. The idea behind layered modelling is that the functionality of a model can be divided into different aspects. Every aspect of that functionality is implemented as a group of classes. Such a group of classes is called a domain. The classes of a domain can inherit features from other classes, thereby forming a class inheritance hierarchy. Domains can be based on more abstract domains, thereby forming a domain hierarchy. When domains are designed to have well defined interfaces (as suggested by the STEP Framework committee in [Kirkley 1991]), the development and maintenance of software can be managed more easily. In this way the concept of a class with an inheritance hierarchy and exported and hidden features is extended to the level of a domain with a domain hierarchy and exported or hidden classes. A layer consists of a set of domains with functionality on the same abstraction level. Different models can be based on the same (domains of a) layer, thereby having a common structure, which makes the exchange of information more easy. The tool must support this layered modelling approach.

6.2.2   Integration of applications

Users of computer applications, such as a geometric modeller or a Finite Element Method application, want to use information stored in a model and to store new information in that model. To make this possible mechanisms must be defined to integrate an application in the layer the model on which is based. The successful integration of an application into a layer depends on the availability of a clear interface between the application and the outside world. Another option is to enable the application to exchange data through one of the standards described in the next paragraph. The mechanisms for an easy integration of computer applications must be available in the modelling tool.

6.2.3   Data exchange standards

One of the important aspects of the integration of applications is the ability to exchange data. In the ISO/STEP community several standards have been developed to facilitate the exchange of data between applications. One of these standards is the EXPRESS [ISO 1990] information modelling language, which is used for describing data structures and functionality. EXPRESS can be used to describe a layer in a standardised way. The modelling tool must therefore be able to generate a EXPRESS schema of a layer and to generate a layer from an EXPRESS schema. In this way an existing EXPRESS schema can be used to generate a corresponding layer with the modelling tool. Another standard is the STEP physical file format [ISO 1991], which defines the syntax for a ASCII file used for the exchange of data between databases and applications. Several applications in the field of CAD/CAM already use this standard to exchange data. Reading and writing the STEP physical file format is an essential requirement of the modelling tool.

6.2.4   Independence of the object-oriented environment

The implementation of the modelling tool should not depend too much on the specific possibilities of the chosen object-oriented language and computer platform. In this way porting the modelling tool to another environment, e.g. for reasons of efficiency, is possible. This requirement results in the implementation of a lot of specific mechanisms of the chosen object-oriented language in a more general way in the modelling tool itself.

6.2.5   Graphical user interface

Because a model can become very complex, a graphical presentation is needed. The user interface must provide an interactive use of this graphical presentation. Because each layer represents a different level of abstraction of a model, a different diagram technique can be helpful. Each layer in the modelling tool must have the possibility to define a diagram technique, corresponding to its specific functionality.

6.2.6   Programming and modelling

Two kinds of users of the modelling tool can be distinguished. The programming user specifies a new domain (as part of a layer), by defining a set of new classes, all related to the same field of interest. This domain is based on already existing domains. He specifies a new class by defining a set of new features. The modelling user constructs a new model by creating objects out of the classes of the domains. Therefore, the general functionality of the modelling tool must contain mechanisms to cover programming as well as modelling demands.

6.3 LAYERING MECHANISM

The most important characteristic of the modelling tool is the possibility to implement layered models. The way such a layered model is implemented is critical for the modelling tool. Therefore, a choice has to be made between alternative approaches towards the implementation of the layering mechanism.

6.3.1 Source code versus data items

The implementation of a mechanism to specify and implement the layers of a model is not trivial. At least four alternative approaches can be distinguished. A choice has to be made between (1) specifying and implementing the layers as source code, i.e. as groups of classes, (2) specifying and implementing the layers as data items, i.e. as groups of objects, (3) specifying all layers as data items and generating the source code for all the layers together or (4) specifying each layer as data items and generating the source code per layer. The four approaches and their advantages and disadvantages are described below.

(1) Specifying and implementing the layers as groups of classes

This is the way most programmers implement an object-oriented model. The model is stored directly as program code in files. The advantage of this solution is that the object-oriented mechanisms of the environment can be used and that the classes can be compiled directly. Tools such as a browser or a repository can be used to help the programming user. However, this approach has several disadvantages too. Detailed knowledge of the syntax and semantics of the implementation language is required for the programming user. Grouping the classes of a domain in one directory, which helps to keep the structure clear, is a matter of discipline of the programming user. Furthermore the modelling tool becomes very inflexible. Every change in the model results in editing a number of classes. Another disadvantage is that for every model a suitable tool (or user interface) has to be developed for the modelling user.

(2) Specifying and implementing the layers as groups of objects

The specification of the system under construction, with data structure and functionality, is stored as data items in groups of objects. This specification is interpreted when a modelling user uses the system to create and handle a model. It is a very flexible solution, because the specifications of the object types, stored as data items, can be changed easily. Furthermore, no generation and compilation of program code is needed. The disadvantage of this approach is that all object-oriented mechanisms have to be implemented, with features for the storage of the specification as well as features for the interpretation of this specification. Also performance problems can be foreseen, because during execution of the system every action must be interpreted first.

(3) Specifying the layers as groups of objects and generating source code for the complete model

This is the way a conventional CASE tool is designed. The specification of the complete system under construction is stored as data items in groups of objects. From these data items the source code for all classes is generated and compiled into a system, which can be used to create models. This solution is very flexible, because the specification of classes, stored as data items, can be changed easily. A disadvantage of this approach is that the object-oriented mechanisms have to be implemented in the modelling tool, to make sure that the specification of the system and thereby the generated code are correct. Another disadvantage is that functionality specified in a layer cannot be used to support the design of other layers. For the programming and the modelling user two completely different tools have to be developed.

(4)   Specifying each layer as a group of objects and generating the source code for each layer

The idea is that each layer has the ability to store the specification of a new layer. The specification of the classes of a layer is stored as data items. From this data the source code of the classes can be generated and compiled and the layer can be added to the system. Implementing the layer under construction as a group of objects (created from the classes of the parent layer), and the other layers as groups of classes, combines the advantages of the other solutions. The specification of the classes can be changed easily. The compiled system can be used by the programming user to base new layers on it, or by the modelling user to create and handle models. The object-oriented mechanisms of the object-oriented environment can be used, because every layer is compiled separately.

The fourth layering mechanism has a sort of evolutionary approach. Specification of a system, using all kinds of data modelling techniques, implementation of a system in an object-oriented environment and using a system to create models is supported with one tool. This approach is the most promising, and is worked out in the next section.

6.3.2 Specialisation by instantiation

As mentioned above the main principle behind the selected layering mechanism is that every layer has the ability to store the specification of a new layer. This new layer is automatically based on the layers where the specification is stored. This principle is also true for the classes of a layer, i.e. every instance of a class has the ability to store the specification of a new class. This new class automatically inherits from the class where the specification is stored. This means that an instance of a class not only can be interpreted as an object in a model for the modelling user, but also as a specification of a new class in a new layer for a programming user. This is not so strange, since an object in a model can be seen as the last step in a specialisation course. Take for example a class *BUILDING* with an attribute *id* of type *STRING*. This class can be instantiated while setting the value of *id* to "house", which can be denoted as *BUILDING* ("house"). Other instances could be *BUILDING* ("church"), *BUILDING* ("office") or building ("hospital"). Each instance can be considered as a specilisation of a building.

To realise this principle of 'specialisation by instantiation', two transformations must be implemented:

- A transformation from class to object.
- A transformation from object to class.

The first transformation is easy to realise, because it corresponds with the procedure to create instances of a class. To instantiate a class into an object can be interpreted as the first step in the specialisation course. The second step in the specialisation course is to generate program code for the new class. When both steps are executed, the new class can be compiled so it can be specialised again. In this way a new generation of classes in the inheritance hierarchy is implemented. Now the decomposition of a system is complete: a system consists of layers for each abstraction level, each layer consists of domains for each aspect of functionality and each domain consists of one or more generations of classes.

Each class must have a feature to generate the program code from the state of an instance of that class. It is only a matter of efficiency to define this *generate* feature in a common root class in the modelling tool. Suppose this root class is called *OBJECT*. The generation of the first layer in a system can be specified by instantiating *OBJECT*.

A simple and realistic example for the first layer is an implementation of a model for graphs. In this simple system we will only distinguish nodes and links. A link connects two nodes, a source node and a target node. *OBJECT* has an attribute field called *id* to identify the objects (and it references three lists for (1) attribute definitions, (2) function definitions and (3) procedure definitions respectively). For the first step in the specialisation course the creation procedure of *OBJECT* is executed twice and the *id* fields are set. This results in the objects *OBJECT* ("link") and *OBJECT* ("node"). Furthermore, two attributes of type "node" are defined, which represent the source node and target node of a link. This step is shown in the upper part of figure 6.2. The square symbol with a circle inside represents a class. A circle represents an object.

For the second step a transformation procedure is needed to generate the program code for classes *NODE* and *LINK* from the states of *OBJECT* ("node") and *OBJECT*

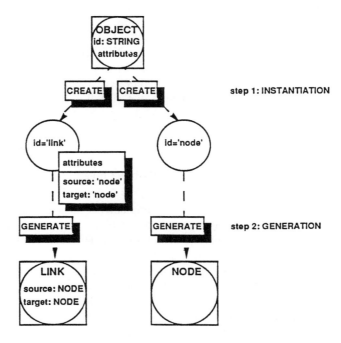

Figure 6.2: Specialisation: instantiation and generation

("link"), as can be seen in the second part of figure 6.2. This *generate* feature has several components:

- The *id*-field becomes the name of the new class.
- The class of the object becomes the parent of the new class.
- The three lists of feature definitions result in the declaration of new features.
- An attribute value is interpreted as a redefinition of the attribute type.

This last component of the *generate* feature needs some clarification. Suppose this graph model is specialised, in another layer, into *NODE* ("station"), *NODE* ("airport"), *LINK* ("railway") and *LINK* ("airline"). In that case an airline may not be connected with a railway station. This can be achieved by setting the attribute value of *source* (and *target*) of *LINK* ("airline") to *NODE*("airport"). The *generate* feature uses this information to redefine the attribute type of source (and target) of *AIRLINE* to *AIRPORT*.

Of course, there is a lot more to say about the *generate* feature. This example however has been restricted to demonstrate the main principles. Details are worked out in the next sections, where a prototype version of a layered-modelling tool is reviewed.

6.4 IMPLEMENTATION CONSIDERATIONS

The principles introduced in the sections 6.2 and 6.3 are implemented in a prototype version in a system called PMshell (from 'P' Modelling shell, where 'P' stands for Product, Process, Project or Production). PMshell is implemented with Eiffel version 2.3.4 on a SUN Sparc station 1 and a SUN Sparc station 2. The reason why Eiffel was chosen for an object-oriented language was the paradigm of programming by contract and the possibility of multiple and repeated inheritance. Throughout the rest of this chapter the object-oriented paradigm of PMshell is considered to be equivalent with the object-oriented paradigm of Eiffel and the notion of a domain in PMshell is equivalent to the notion of a cluster in Eiffel.

6.4.1 Data structure of the PMshell object layer

The most general layer of PMshell, implements most of the requirements stated in the previous section. This layer is called the object layer in figure 6.1. The object layer contains one domain, called the kernel domain. The data structure of the kernel domain is shown in figures 6.3 and 6.4. The diagram technique is a variation on NIAM (Nijssen's Information Analysis Method [Nijssen 1989]). In NIAM entities are represented by circles and facts (or relations between entities) by lines with boxes. In this variation dashed circles represent basic types. A subset relation is represented by an arrow from the subset entity to the superset entity. A subset entity inherits the characteristics of its superset entity or entities. Entities, facts and subset relations in a NIAM schema can be regarded as classes, properties and inheritance relations in an object-oriented system. Constraints with regard to client relations can be defined. Multiplicity constraints are represented by two numbers: the lower bound and the upper bound. A zero as second number indicates an unspecified upper bound. The type of a property is indicated by the direction of the arrow in the relation box. The kind of property (Attribute, Function, Redefined Attribute or Redefined Function) is denoted by the capitals (A, F, RA or RF) in the relation box.

In figure 6.3 the inheritance relations of the classes of the object layer are shown. *DOMAIN_INTERFACE*, *DOMAIN*, *OBJECT*, and *FEATURE* all inherit from *TOP*, which is a deferred class. By introducing *TOP*, general mechanisms for the generation of program code, the exchange of data, database management and user interface control can be introduced in one superclass and implemented in a number of subclasses. *FUNCTION* inherits from both *PROPERTY* and *ROUTINE* and *ASSERTION* inherits from *FUNCTION*, because it is a special function with a *BOOLEAN* result type. *ARGUMENT* inherits from *PROPERTY* because of practical reasons (an argument is similar to a property). *FEATURE*, *PROPERTY* and *ROUTINE* are deferred classes and therefore will never be instantiated.

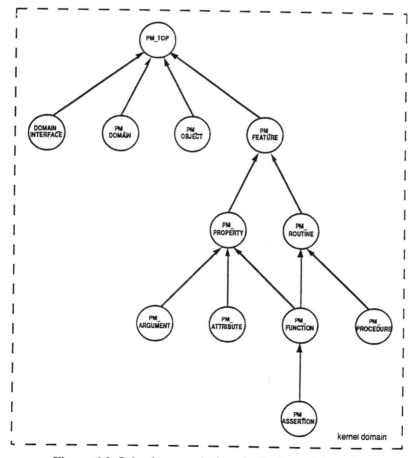

Figure 6.3: Inheritance relations in the kernel domain

In figure 6.4 the client relations are shown. Every *TOP* has an *implementor*. A *DOMAIN* can be based on other *DOMAINS* via a *DOMAIN_INTERFACE*. This mechanism implements the layered architecture of PMshell. A *DOMAIN* contains zero or more *OBJECTS*. An *OBJECT* with zero *partners* defines a single inheritance relation and an *OBJECT* with one or more *partners* defines a multiple inheritance relation. An *OBJECT* contains zero or more *ATTRIBUTES*, *FUNCTIONS*, *PROCEDURES* and *ASSERTIONS*. These *ASSERTIONS* are the *invariants*. The *type* of a *PROPERTY* is defined by an object conforming to *TOP* . Invariants of *PROPERTY* restrict this *type* to a basic type, a property type, or an object type. A basic type is one of the types *BOOLEAN, INTEGER, REAL, DOUBLE, CHARACTER* or *STRING*. A property type corresponds with the association type of the Eiffel language and an object type corresponds with the complex type of the Eiffel language. Furthermore, a *PROPERTY* has a *lower bound* and an *upper bound*, which are the minimum and maximum number of values of a property (also called the multiplicity of a property). A *ROUTINE* has a *body*, zero or more *ARGUMENTS* and lists of *ASSERTIONS*, which are the *pre-* and *postconditions*.

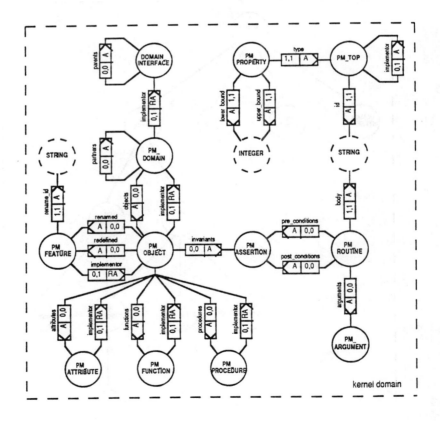

Figure 6.4: Client relations in the kernel domain

6.4.2 General functionality of the PMshell kernel domain

The general functionality of PMshell is located in the kernel domain. There are four groups of features in this domain: (1) features for the administration of the specification of a new class, (2) features for the description of the interface of a class, (3) features for the generation of program code and documentation for new classes, and (4) features for the management of databases. The four groups of features are worked out in this subsection.

(1) Features for the administration of the specification of a new class

The specification of a new class requires an administration of the identifier, the partners, the features, the invariants and the renamed and redefined inherited features. Part of the administration concerns the definition of features, the selection of parents and the renaming of features of a new class. This part is realised with the data structure of *OBJECT* (described in the previous subsection) which is inherited by every object. Another part of the administration concerns the redefinition of property types. This part is realised via the fields in an object. Every property has a corresponding field in an object. A redefined type of an inherited property is stored as a value in that field. Because only objects conforming to the type of a field can be stored in a field, a redefinition of a property type always makes sense. The types of arguments and functions can also be redefined in this way, because arguments and functions are also properties and also have a field in an object. The final part of the administration concerns the definition and redefinition of the body of routines. The body of a routine is stored in a file with the name of the routine and placed in a directory with the name of the class. If such a file exists for an inherited routine, this is interpreted as a redefinition of the body of the routine. To handle the three parts of the administration routines are implemented.

(2) Features for the description of the interface of a class

To enable the user to handle objects of different classes in a uniform way, a description of the interface of a class is required. Therefore, *OBJECT* contains extra lists of *ATTRIBUTES*, *FUNCTIONS* and *PROCEDURES* as well as a list of *ASSERTIONS*. These lists contain inherited features and invariants that are implemented as once functions, because they are the same for every object of the same class. With this description the features of every object are known and the user interface can handle every object in the same way. A distinction must be made between the administration of the specification of a new class and the description of the interface of objects of a class. The first is based on the data structure of the object layer and is different for every object of a class, because every object contains the specification of a new class. The second is the same for all instances of a class, therefore implemented as a set of once functions, and is generated as part of the program code for a new class.

(3)   Features for the generation of program code and documentation for new classes

To add a generation of new classes to the system, the program code for the classes must be generated and compiled. The administration is used for the generation of the Eiffel code. Features for the generation of program code are located within the classes *DOMAIN*, *OBJECT*, *ATTRIBUTE*, *FUNCTION*, *PROCEDURE* and *ARGUMENT*.

Apart from the generation of Eiffel code, it is also useful to be able to generate a neutral specification of the newly defined domain and its classes. For this the information modelling language EXPRESS [ISO 1990] is used. An EXPRESS schema is generated using information from the administration of the definitions. The reverse generation is also possible, i.e. a domain can be generated from an existing EXPRESS schema. So, an EXPRESS schema forms the neutral specification of a domain.

(4)   Features for the management of databases

To enable a user to store instances of a class in a database, an entity corresponding to the class is defined in the database. Hence every class is stored in the database in two different ways: firstly as an instance of its parent class for its specification and secondly as a corresponding entity for the storage of its instances. In this way the modelling user can use the same database structure as the programming user, because entities corresponding to every class are available in the database. To define an entity corresponding to a class in the database the administration is used.

An important purpose of PMshell is the ability to integrate different applications, through the exchange of data. The exchange of data can be realised with databases as well as with ASCII files in a more environment independent way. The format of ASCII files is described in the STEP physical file format [ISO 1991], which is used by many applications in the field of CAD/CAM. Therefore, a model in PMshell can be stored in and retrieved from a STEP physical file.

6.4.3   Graphical presentation of the user interface

Because conceptual models can get very complex, a graphical presentation is needed. Therefore, the PMshell User Interface is based on the CGE (Configurable Graphical Editor [Vogel 1991]). The CGE is an advanced diagram editor, which can be tailored to many different diagram techniques. One of the diagram techniques is a NIAM-like diagram technique used in PMshell for the specification of data structures of domains. PMshell has layers on different levels of abstraction. In PMshell a diagram technique can be defined for every abstraction level. As an example, the layers of figure 6.1 and their graphical presentations are shown in figure 6.5.

For the graphical presentation of a conceptual model the programming user has the ability to choose one of the diagram techniques defined in the layers the conceptual model is based on. For example, for the Reference Model layer one can use the NIAM-

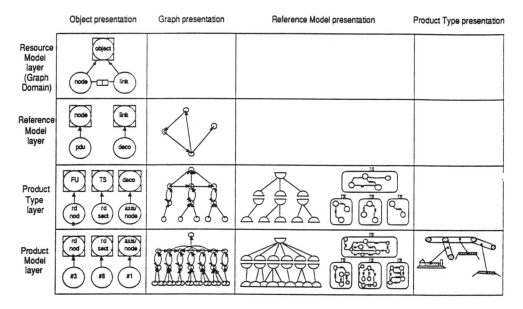

Figure 6.5: An example of PMshell layers with their graphical presentations

like diagram technique, inherited from the Object layer, or the diagram technique defined in the Graph domain of the Resource Model layer. For the Product Model layer the modelling user can use a variety of different graphical presentations, including the one defined in the Product Type layer, which looks much like the actual geometry of his model. In the example of figure 6.5 the Product Model of a highway is presented in the diagram technique defined in the domain for the Road Model Kernel [Willems 1990]. In this way, the different graphical presentations bridge the gap between abstract symbols and actual geometry.

6.5 IMPLEMENTATION DETAILS

The implementation of PMshell in Eiffel contains some details which can be interesting for other programmers of modelling tools. The main issue are the generated Eiffel code, the extensions to the Eiffel library classes and the methodology for interfacing with a database manager.

6.5.1 Generation of Eiffel code: basic class definition

The generation of Eiffel code for a new class is best explained with an example. The domain for geometrical models (see section 6.7 for more information) is taken as an example in the next subsections. The main classes are *GEO_OBJECT* and its subtypes *GEO_VERTEX*, *GEO_EDGE* and *GEO_FACE*. In this section we will have a closer look at the generated Eiffel code of *GEO_EDGE*. *GEO_EDGE* inherits the attributes *presentation* and *boundary* from *GEO_OBJECT* and defines a new attribute *orientation*, a new function *length* and a new procedure *SET_VERTICES*. The attribute *presentation* references the presentation of the edge in a graphical query tool and the attribute *boundary* defines the two end vertices of the edge. The attribute *orientation* determines whether the edge goes from the first to the second vertex or vice versa. The function *length* determines the distance between the two vertices. The procedure *set_vertices* is defined to set the two end vertices. To define this new class the programming user creates an object of type *GEO_OBJECT* with the name "geo_edge". He also adds information about new features and redefinitions of inherited features. From this definitions Eiffel code is generated for the new class.

First of all the skeleton of the new class *GEO_EDGE* is generated which consists of the export clause, the inheritance clause and the feature definition clause, as can be seen in figure 6.6. These clauses are filled, partly with user added information, partly with automatically generated code. In the export clause the exported features of *GEO_OBJECT* and the new features are exported. In the inheritance clause

```
class GEO_EDGE creation
      make
inherit

   GEO_OBJECT
      rename
         make as geo_object_make
      redefine
         boundary, class_parents, local_class_features, local_class_fields,
         local_class_attributes, local_class_functions, local_class_procedures
      end
feature {NONE}

   make (act_id: STRING) is
      do
         geo_object_make (act_id)
      end;
feature

   ... See below ...

end -- class GEO_EDGE
```

Figure 6.6: Generated skeleton of *GEO_EDGE*

GEO_OBJECT is made parent, and redefined and renamed features are declared. The renaming of the creation procedure *make* and the redefinition of the so-called class features are generated automatically. The first feature defined in the feature clause is the *make* procedure. This procedure is always generated and its execution consists of the creation procedures of the parent classes, followed by the initialisation of fields with a multiple value (these fields are implemented as *LINKED_LIST*, which must be initialised before usage). The creation procedures of the parent classes are automatically renamed, so they can be used in the new *make* creation procedure. Furthermore, a *make* creation procedure always has one argument, the *id* of an object. The other features are discussed in the rest of this section: new features in section 6.5.2, redefined and renamed features in section 6.5.3 and class features in section 6.5.4.

6.5.2. Generation of Eiffel code: definition of new features

The next step is to generate the definitions of the new features. For *geo_edge* this results in the definition of the attribute orientation, the function length and the procedure *set_vertices* (see figure 6.7). For every attribute a field is generated of the right type. This type can be a basic type, a property type, or an object type. In this case a boolean field for orientation is defined. For the newly defined routines the standard definitions are generated with arguments, a comment line, preconditions, an optional external clause, a local entities clause, the body and postconditions. Pre- and postconditions are generated automatically to ensure the right multiplicity for the arguments and the function result. The user writes the code after the generated preconditions and before the postconditions in a separate file, so he or she can give extra pre- and postconditions, declare external defined routines, declare local entities and the body. This body-file is read during the generation of code. The generated features can be referenced to in the normal Eiffel way in the body of other routines.

As shown in figure 6.8, not only code for the routines but also code for some extra fields and procedures are generated. These extra features are defined to enable the user to set arguments, execute routines and inspect function results at run-time. For every argument of a routine a field is generated. The name of the field, the *field_id*, is a concatenation of *routine.id* and *argument.id*. In this example the fields *set_vertices_start_vertex* and *set_vertices_stop_vertex* are generated automatically. For every function another extra field is generated for the result value, in this case the field *length_result*. The *field_id* of this result field is a concatenation of *routine.id* and "*_result*". The types of the arguments and results of the normal routines refer to the types of the generated fields by association. When the fields are redefined, the type of the arguments and the results are also redefined.

Furthermore, for every routine an extra procedure is generated, which is used for executing the routine at run-time in a uniform way, regardless of the arguments and the result type, in this case the procedures *pm_length* and *pm_set_vertices*. When for example a user wants to execute *set_vertices* he or she first sets the argument fields *set_vertices_start_vertex* and *set_vertices_stop_vertex* and then calls the procedure *pm_set_vertices* with features provided by *X_INTERNAL* (see subsection 6.5.7). Another

```
orientation: BOOLEAN
      -- True: from first GEO_VERTEX in boundary to second

length: like length_result is
      -- The length of the edge
   require
      -- user-defined preconditions
   local
      -- local entities
   do
      -- routine body
   ensure
      -- user-defined postconditions
   end; -- length

set_vertices (start_vertex: like set_vertices_start_vertex;
              stop_vertex: like set_vertices_stop_vertex) is
      -- Set boundary to start_vertex and stop_vertex.
   require
      min_card_start_vertex: start_vertex /= Void;
      min_card_stop_vertex: stop_vertex /= Void;
      -- user-defined preconditions
   local
      -- local entities
   do
      -- routine body
   ensure
      -- user-defined postconditions
   end
```

Figure 6.7: New features of *GEO_EDGE*

example is the execution of the function *length* by a user at run-time. No arguments have to be specified. The procedure *pm_length* is called and the result of *length* is put in *length_result*. This field can be inspected with features provided by *X_INTERNAL*. As will be shown in the next subsection the extra defined fields are also used for the redefinition of types of arguments of a routine and the type of the result of a function.

6.5.3 Generation of Eiffel code: redefinition and renaming

Part of the strength of the object-oriented paradigm of Eiffel is the ability to rename and redefine inherited features, e.g. redefinition of the type of an inherited attribute, to restrict

```
length_result: REAL;

pm_length is
  do
    length_result := length;
  end;


set_vertices_start_vertex: GEO_VERTEX;

set_vertices_stop_vertex: GEO_VERTEX;

pm_set_vertices is
  do
    set_vertices (set_vertices_start_vertex, set_vertices_stop_vertex);
  end
```

Figure 6.8: Extra fields and procedures for new features of GEO_EDGE

the possible values of the attribute in a new class. In this example the type of *boundary* is redefined to the class *GEO_VERTEX*. In the object "geo_node" the programming user sets the field *boundary* to the object "geo_vertex". This is interpreted as a redefinition of this field. The redefinition of an attribute is declared in the inheritance clause (see figure 6.6) and is defined in the feature clause of the new class (see figure 6.7).

Arguments and result types of inherited routines are redefined in the same way: the

```
boundary: LINKED_LIST [GEO_VERTEX];
  -- Bounding objects
```

Figure 6.9: Redefinition of inherited feature in GEO_EDGE

programming user sets the fields to a certain value which is interpreted as redefinition. The implementation of a routine is redefined by editing a new body file. The generator inspects for every inherited feature·whether there is a new body file. If so, the routine is redefined in the normal way. Of course, also a combination of redefinition of types and implementation is possible.

For renaming inherited features *OBJECT* has the attribute *renamed_features*. *FEATURE* has an attribute *rename_id* to store the new name. For all features in the list *rename_id* must be specified. Renaming is not used in this example[1].

---

[1] In Eiffel version 2.3.4 renaming and redefinition of one feature results in a duplication of this feature. This is conceptually questionable, and in Eiffel version 3.0 this possibility has been eliminated.

6.5.4 Generation of Eiffel code: description of the class interface

To be able to handle objects of different classes in a uniform way, a description of the interface of the classes has to be available. This description is implemented by a set hash tables containing the parents, inherited *ATTRIBUTE*s, *FUNCTION*s and *PROCEDURE*s of an object. The features referring to these tables are called class features and are generated automatically. The items in the tables can be retrieved through their *id*.

Let's have a closer look at the class features generated for the description of attributes of *GEO_EDGE* in figure 6.10. In *geo_edge_attributes* first the attributes of the parent are merged. The routine *merge* is a new procedure of *X_HASH_TABLE* (an extension of *HASH_TABLE*) to merge two tables of the same type. Then the inherited attributes are redefined in the table; in this case the type of *boundary* is redefined. Finally the newly defined attributes are added to the table; in this case *orientation*. For the type definition, an object with *id* "BOOLEAN" is created. Also the multiplicity (i.e. the lower and upper bound) is set. The table is implemented as a once function, so only one table of attributes is created for all objects of this class. *OBJECT* has a function

```
    geo_edge_attributes: X_HASH_TABLE [PM_ATTRIBUTE, STRING] is
      local
        attribute: PM_ATTRIBUTE;
        object: PM_OBJECT;
        parent_features: X_HASH_TABLE [PM_ATTRIBUTE, STRING];
      once
        !! Result.make (100);
        parent_features := deep_clone (geo_object_attributes);
        Result.merge (parent_features);
        Result.item ("boundary").set_type (templates.object_with_class_name
            ("GEO_VERTEX"));
        object.Create ("BOOLEAN");
        attribute.Create ("orientation", object);
        attribute.set_min_card (1);
        attribute.set_max_card (1);
        Result.put (attribute, attribute.id);
        Result.item ("presentation").set_type (templates.object_with_class_name
            ("GQT_EDGE"));
      end;
    local_class_attributes: X_HASH_TABLE [PM_ATTRIBUTE, STRING] is
      do
        Result := geo_edge_attributes
      end
```

Figure 6.10: Description of interface for attributes in *GEO_EDGE*

local_class_attributes to reference the inherited attributes in a uniform way. This function is redefined and addresses *geo_edge_attributes* now. It is not possible to make *local_class_attributes* a once function, because once functions cannot be redefined. Similar class features are generated for the functions and the procedures of this class.

For the parents a class features are defined too (see figure 6.11). In this way a list of parents is always available without using Eiffel-dependent classes such as *E_CLASS*. This table is used among others for the definition of entities in a database (see section 6.5.8).

```
geo_edge_parents: X_HASH_TABLE [PM_OBJECT, STRING] is
    once
        !! Result.make (10);
        Result.put (templates.object_with_class_name ("GEO_OBJECT"),
            "GEO_OBJECT");
    end;

class_parents: X_HASH_TABLE [PM_OBJECT, STRING] is
    do
        Result := geo_edge_parents
    end
```

Figure 6.11: Description of interface for parents in *GEO_EDGE*

It has proven to be convenient to have two extra once functions, one for all features of a class (i.e. all attributes, functions and procedures) and one for all fields of a class (i.e. all attributes, arguments and result fields). Code for the definition of the once functions *geo_edge_features* and *geo_edge_fields* and code for the redefinition of *local_class_features* and *local_class_fields* is generated, as shown in figure 6.12. In this way the time-consuming concatenation functions *give_local_class_features* and *give_local_class_fields* are executed only once for every class.

6.5.5 Generation of Eiffel code: multiple inheritance

An important characteristic of the object-oriented paradigm of Eiffel is multiple inheritance. This is also supported in PMshell. The first parent of a new class is the class of which the object with the class definition is an instance. Instances of the other parents are stored in the attribute *partners* defined in *OBJECT*. All partners together form the parents of the new class. New features of the new class are stored in the first partner, a redefinition of a feature is stored in the instance of the first class with that feature. Multiple inheritance has influence on the generated code in the export clause, the inheritance clause, the creation procedure and the description of the class interface.

```
geo_edge_features: X_HASH_TABLE [PM_FEATURE, STRING] is
  once
     Result := give_local_class_features
  end;
geo_edge_fields: X_HASH_TABLE [PM_PROPERTY, STRING] is
  once
     Result := give_local_class_fields
  end;

local_class_features: X_HASH_TABLE [PM_FEATURE, STRING] is
  do
     Result := geo_edge_features
  end;

local_class_fields: X_HASH_TABLE [PM_PROPERTY, STRING] is
  do
     Result := geo_edge_fields
  end
```

Figure 6.12: Extra functions for description of interface in *GEO_EDGE*

Section 6.5.3 discusses class features such as *local_class_attributes* that give information about features inherited from an object with one parent. The function *class_attributes*, defined in *OBJECT*, merges the *local_class_attributes* of all partners into one table with all inherited attributes. This table is used in the user interface controller, among others.

The multiple inheritance mechanism can also be used by the modelling user to model an object that inherits features from two or more classes. In this way it is not necessary to make a new class for every specialisation. Consider for example the class *HUMAN_BEING* and its subtypes *MALE*, *FEMALE* and *MINOR*, *ADULT*, each with their own features. If, for the object of a boy, only properties from *MALE* and *MINOR* are inherited and no new properties are added, it is not necessary to make a new class. In that case a so-called compound object can be instantiated with two parents. This subject has not been worked out and tested yet in all details, but we think it is a promising feature of PMshell.

6.5.5 Generation of Eiffel code: domain interface

Not only code for the new classes has to be generated: code for the interface of the domain under construction must also be generated. This interface class, named *DOMAIN_INTERFACE*, contains information about the parent domains on which the working domain is based. This information is stored in *parent_interfaces*. *DOMAIN_INTERFACE* also contains information about the classes of this domain which are available to other domains. This information is stored in *classes*. The geometry domain in the example of section 6.7 is based on the object layer and the Graphical Query Tool domain, as can be seen in figure 6.13. In the *Create* procedure of *DOMAIN_INTERFACE parent_interfaces* and *classes* are filled.

When a new domain is started, only *parent_interfaces* is filled. During the specification of the domain the newly defined classes are inserted in *classes*. When a domain is closed the code for a new class is generated, in this example *GEOMETRY_INTERFACE*. This class has the same contents as *DOMAIN_INTERFACE*, only another class name. Other domain_interfaces can refer to this class so that the corresponding domains are based on this geometry domain. In the same way the Graphical Query Tool domain is used in the geometry domain by a reference to *GQT_INTERFACE*.

6.5.6 The class *TEMPLATES*

While developing and working with PMshell it became evident that quite a lot of procedures are executed with information that is only available at run-time. For instance, it is only known what class the user wants to instantiate when the user has chosen the name of a class from a list of names of available classes. At run-time the user chooses a class name and wants that class to be instantiated during the same run (i.e. without compilation). Creation of a class with the name of that class only available at run-time also happens when a database or a STEP physical file is read.

In Eiffel it is not possible to create an object from a class with the classname only available at run-time[2]. That is why the class *TEMPLATES* is introduced. *TEMPLATES* is a subtype of the class *HASH_TABLE* and contains instances of all classes of PMshell that conform to *TOP* and are all retrievable by a key of type *STRING*. The value of the key is the name of the class. *TOP* has a once function *templates* of type *TEMPLATES*, so all classes in the system have this function. *Templates* is filled once at the beginning of a PMshell session. For this filling information from the *DOMAIN_INTERFACE*s is used.

6.5.7 The class *X_INTERNAL*

The Eiffel library contains the class *INTERNAL* which has features that give information about the internal structure of a class. They give information about such things as the

---

[2] As stated before the current version of PMshell is implemented in Eiffel version 2.3.4. In this Eiffel version only one creation procedure can be defined. Creation procedures of the used classes have different numbers and types of arguments, so a C-call to the C-routine *eif_create* ("*classname*", arg_1, ..., arg_n) can not be used in a flexible manner. In Eiffel version 3.0 it is possible to define more creation procedures per class [Meyer 1992]. In that case a simple creation procedure without arguments can be defined for runtime use and a more complex one for normal use. In that way *TEMPLATES* will not be necessary any more.

```
class DOMAIN_INTERFACE creation
 make
inherit
 PM_INTERFACE
   rename
    make as pm_interface_make
   end
feature
 make is
   local
     object_interface: OBJECT_INTERFACE;
     gqt_interface: GQT_INTERFACE;
     geo_object: GEO_OBJECT;
     geo_vertex: GEO_VERTEX;
     geo_edge: GEO_EDGE;
     geo_face: GEO_FACE;
   do
    pm_interface_make;
    set_id ("geometry");

    !! object_interface.make;
    parent_interfaces.append (object_interface);

    !! gqt_interface.make;
    parent_interfaces.append (gqt_interface);

    !! geo_object.make ("GEO_OBJECT");
    current_classes.put (geo_object, "GEO_OBJECT");

    !! geo_vertex.make ("GEO_VERTEX");
    current_classes.put (geo_vertex, "GEO_VERTEX");

    !! geo_edge.make ("GEO_EDGE");
    current_classes.put (geo_edge, "GEO_EDGE");

    !! geo_face.make ("GEO_FACE");
    current_classes.put (geo_face, "GEO_FACE");
   end
 end -- class DOMAIN_INTERFACE
```

Figure 6.13: *DOMAIN_INTERFACE* **of geometry domain**

available features, the field type of a property and the dynamic type of the value of an attribute. For the implementation of PMshell only information about the internal structure of a class is not enough: also procedures on the internal structure of a class are necessary. These are procedures for setting the value of a field or executing a routine. These features are implemented in the class *X_INTERNAL*, which inherits from *INTERNAL*. The procedures *from_structure* and *to_structure* of *INTERNAL* on the physical object structure are not used because they are too primitive. See the appendix of this chapter for a short version of *X_INTERNAL* without assertions.

The features in *INTERNAL* that give information about logical fields and routines in an object generally work with field or routine numbers for identification. This proves to be rather inconvenient, so functions are defined for the conversion from feature names to field or routine numbers. These functions are *which_field*, to determine the field number of a field name in an object, *which_bool*, to determine the position of a field name in a list of packed-booleans of a field in an object, and *which_routine*, to determine the routine number of a routine name in an object. *X_INTERNAL* has two versions of every feature: one using the field or routine numbers for identification, the other using feature names. In the former the connection with C is established, the latter only uses the former with the conversion functions. The name of the latter is always the name of the former preceded by "*n_*".

6.5.8 Interface with database manager

Programming users of PMshell want to be able to interface with a database to save and retrieve specifications of domains. Also modelling users want to save their work in a database to back-up their work and to realise data communication with applications. For these reasons PMshell provides an interface with Exis [de Bruijn 1991]. Exis stands for EXPRESS Instancing System, a product of TNO. Exis is meant to close the gap between conceptual information modelling in EXPRESS and implementation of such models in databases. Exis is a database manager interface to a variety of back-ends for storing data. For the moment only a FILOS back-end is supported, but in the future other database systems, like Oracle, will be supported. FILOS (FILe Organisation System) is also a product of TNO. Exis supports some object-oriented mechanisms, like multiple inheritance. Alas, type redefinition and attribute renaming is not supported.

For the modelling user his or her working domain, the objects of this domain and the attribute values are saved. For the programming user not only the domain (for the specification of a new layer), the objects (for the specification of new classes) and the attribute values (for the redefinition of attribute types) are saved, but also the administration (for the definition of new features), the renamed features, the argument field values (for the redefinition of argument types) and the result field values (for the redefinition of result types of functions) are saved. A programming user defines a new class by instantiating an existing class and adding new features and renaming and redefining inherited features. When he or she generates Eiffel code from this instance for the new class, the instance is saved in the database and a new entity, corresponding to the new class, is defined in the database. This database entity can be used to save instances with definitions of subtypes of the new class. In this way a domain is not only defined generation by generation in the Eiffel system, but also in the database. For every class, Eiffel has an object and a class, and the database an instance and an entity. The modelling user can use the final database of the programming user, with database entities for all the classes, to store his model in it.

The interface between PMshell and Exis is concentrated in the object layer. As all layers generated with PMshell inherit from the object layer, they inherit the database features too. For the interface with Exis two extra classes are defined: *EXIS_C_CALLS* which contains low-level C-calls to Exis routines and *EXIS_FUNCTIONS* which contains more complex features. All classes in the object layer have some Exis features.

EXIS_C_CALLS has an Eiffel feature for every (exported) routine of Exis. It does not add any functionality to Exis but it takes care of the type conversion between Eiffel, C and Exis. There are features for opening and closing a database, for defining the data structure with entities and attributes, for inspecting the data structure, for adding, removing and changing instances and for inspecting instances.

Initialisation of new entities in an Exis database requires two actions: declaration and definition. First a new entity must be declared. As a result of the declaration an entity is given an *exis_entity_id*. This id is used for referencing the entity definition in the database. Every subtype of *TOP* has an attribute *exis_entity_id* for this id. For the definition of an entity the supertypes and the attributes must be given. For the definition of attributes the kind (single or LIST) the upper- and lower bound and the type must be given. There is no renaming or redefinition of inherited attributes possible in Exis. This causes no problems when an extra attribute is defined for a renamed attribute. Redefinition is not strictly necessary, because type checking is already done in Eiffel.

For saving and loading instances *EXIS_FUNCTIONS* has a field *exis_administration* to store references to saved and loaded objects. This is a *HASH_TABLE* with *TOP* instances, retrievable by an *INTEGER*. The key is the instance number in the Exis database. This administration is necessary to enable a recursive saving and loading of instances. For example, when an attribute value is loaded from the database, the system first checks whether the attribute value is already loaded by checking whether *exis_administration* has the Exis instance number. If so, the value of the attribute is set to the instance in *exis_administration* retrievable by the Exis instance number. If not, the instance is loaded from the database, added to *exis_administration* and the value of the attribute is set to the loaded instance. When a new instance is loaded, first the classname of the instance is retrieved from the database. This classname is used for getting an empty Eiffel instance from *TEMPLATES* (see subsection 6.5.6). Then the attribute values for this new instance are loaded. *EXIS_FUNCTIONS* has features for loading and saving all kinds of attribute fields, single, *LINKED_LIST* and *HASH_TABLE* fields, and for these kinds seven different types, *TOP* and the six basic types. These features use features from *EXIS_C_CALLS*, for the connection with Exis, and *X_INTERNAL*, to inspect and set Eiffel fields. Therefore, *EXIS_FUNCTIONS* inherits from these two classes.

All classes in the object layer have the routines *exis_save_declaration* (to declare a new entity in the database), *exis_save_definition* (to define a new entity), *exis_save* (to save an instance) and *exis_load* (to load an instance). These features are redefined for every class in this layer. In *OBJECT* these features are redefined in such a way that instances of subtypes of *OBJECT* interface with Exis, using the administration of new features and the description of a class interface for the inherited features. This mechanism is general enough to make sure that in all subtypes of *OBJECT* no redefinition of the Exis features is required.

6.6 SYSTEM ARCHITECTURE

The system architecture of PMshell can be divided into several parts. These parts are shown in figure 6.14. First of all there is the object layer, which forms the kernel of the system. The object layer provides all the functionality that is needed to design new layers based on the object layer. The object layer has been discussed in detail in the previous sections. Another part of the system architecture is called the system interface. This part controls the interaction of a user with PMshell through a user interface. The communication between the system interface and a user interface is described in a protocol.

6.6.1 The protocol between PMshell and user interface

One of the main problems with the design of a user interface is the mixture of user interface functionality with the functionality of a system. This problem has been solved

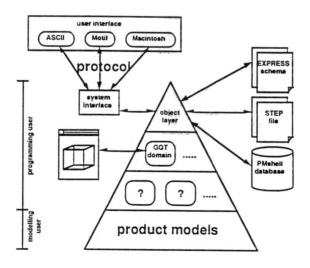

Figure 6.14: The PMshell system architecture

satisfactorily in PMshell by the use of a protocol between the user interface and the system interface.

The user interface and the system interface are separate processes. These processes communicate with the UNIX pipe mechanism. This communication consists of sending and receiving commands and is formalised by the description of a protocol. The protocol is defined in such a way that the commands can be parsed, to ensure easy interpretation by both sides. There are several advantages to this approach. Once the protocol is agreed upon, the system interface and a number of user interfaces can be developed independently of each other. Also, the mixture of user interface functionality and system functionality is avoided.

At the moment three user interfaces are developed for PMshell. The ASCII user interface is developed as a prototype to be used in different locations. This interface uses only ASCII characters and can be used on nearly all terminals. The Macintosh user interface is developed to be able to use a graphical interface without depending on an X-window. This user interface is connected with PMshell through a modem connection. The Macintosh user interface transfers only protocol commands through the modem connection while the ASCII user interface transfers the complete stream of characters used for printing the menus. The OSF/Motif user interface is considered to be the ultimate user interface. It can only be used on an X-window terminal. This interface has been developed with the help of the TeleUSE user interface builder [Telesoft 1990]. The Motif user interface can be used in combination with the CGE (Configurable Graphical Editor) [Vogel 1991] for the graphical presentation of a model.

The protocol is divided into a set of commands. As an example, the format of two commands is described below. The syntax of the protocol is defined in Wirth's Syntax Notation [Wirth 1977]. The 'send' part is the command from 'system interface' to 'user interface' and the 'receive' part is the answer from the 'user interface'. The words in upper case are keywords of the protocol, while the words in lower case refer to other constructs of the protocol. For example the word "feature" is a definition of an attribute, function or procedure, including the name of the feature, the kind of feature, the property type and routine arguments.

In the first protocol example the user is asked to give the definition of a feature. The name of the command DEFINE_FEATURE is sent together with an existing definition and lists of object types and property identifiers, as shown in figure 6.15. These lists can be used to define the type of a property or argument by referring to an object or to another property. The user is presented a form (see for example the session with PMshell, shown in figure 6.17) in which the kind of feature can be selected (attribute, function or procedure). If the feature is a property, the type and multiplicity can be selected and if the feature is a routine, a set of arguments can be defined. This interaction is controlled by the user interface. When the definition is complete, the user can choose to select the CANCEL, OK or BODY button. In case the feature is a routine and the BODY button is pressed, the system interface will continue the definition of the feature with an edit session. In this edit session the body of the routine can be defined and the definition of the feature is complete.

```
send:          DEFINE_FEATURE
               feature
               '(' { object_type } ')'
               '(' { property_id } ')' ';'

receive  1:    CANCEL ';'
         2:    OK feature ';'
         3:    BODY feature ';'
```

Figure 6.15: Protocol for *DEFINE_FEATURE*

In the second protocol example the INSPECT_OBJECT command gives the user the opportunity to examine the state of an object. The object identifier is sent together with the feature identifiers and the attribute values, as shown in figure 6.16. The user is presented a form, containing all the features of the object. With this form, properties can be inspected and routines can be executed. The execution of a routine requires the system interface to take over the control from the user interface. Therefore, the system interface receives an EXECUTE command together with the routine identifier. The routine will be executed and the system interface will send the INSPECT_OBJECT command again. If the value of a property is another object, this object can be inspected and the system interface receives an INSPECT command together with the property identifier and the object identifier. The object identifier is used for giving the INSPECT_OBJECT command again for the corresponding object. In this way a user can browse through the objects of a model. The path through the objects is stored (because of the recursive nature of the INSPECT_OBJECT command) and can be traversed backwards.

```
send:          INSPECT_OBJECT
               object_id
               '(' { attribute_id type upper_bound value } ')'
               '(' { function_id } ')'
               '(' { procedure_id } ')' ';'

receive  1:    CANCEL ';'
         2:    INSPECT property_id object_id ';'
         3:    EXECUTE routine_id ';'
```

Figure 6.16: Protocol for *INSPECT_OBJECT*

Functions are treated in a special way in the INSPECT_OBJECT command. Because the value of a function is derived from the state of an object, a function value may not be valid after this state has been changed. However, directly after a function has been executed, the value is valid and the function can be treated in the same way as an attribute. This function is called the active function and is sent together with the attributes of an object. Once a procedure has been executed the active function loses its special status and is treated as a normal function again, because the state of the object might have changed.

6.6.2 The system interface

The system interface is a program, which uses the functionality of the object layer. The different commands of the protocol are translated into corresponding routines in the object layer. The system interface controls the dialogue between user and system. The protocol between the system interface and user interface is defined in such a way that no knowledge about the sequence of actions is implemented in the user interface. After answering a command the user interface is always in the same idle state. From the last answer the system interface determines which command has to be answered next. This has the advantage that a change in the sequence only has to be implemented in the system interface. The different user interfaces will all follow this change.

6.6.3 The user interface

The user interface can be considered as a set of functions, which are used by the system interface to communicate with a user. These functions range from displaying a simple warning message to displaying a model in a number of different diagram techniques. Because no knowledge of the sequence of actions is expected in the user interface, different interfaces for different users can be maintained easily. Every user interface has to be able to interpret the commands of the protocol and nothing more. In addition to the standard set of functions, the user interface has a special function for displaying so called generic forms. These generic forms can be used by the programming user to construct forms for presenting or questioning information.

6.7 A DOMAIN FOR GEOMETRIC MODELS

As an example of the use of PMshell, a simple domain for geometric models is implemented. This domain is based on a domain called *GQT,* which encapsulates a Graphical Query Tool in PMshell. The Graphical Query Tool [Balkenende 1990] is a simple interactive 2D drawing application, which can visualise geometric models in three side views and one perspective view. With the Graphical Query Tool the user can set eye and view point, zoom in and out of the model and select geometric objects like vertices, edges and faces for inspection.

In a session with PMshell, shown in figure 6.17, the domain for geometric models is constructed. The domain consists of the classes *GEO_OBJECT*, *GEO_VERTEX*, *GEO_EDGE* and *GEO_FACE*. The root class of this domain is *GEO_OBJECT*. This class defines two attributes. The first attribute is *presentation*, which is a reference to a geometric model *GQT_MODEL* in the Graphical Query Tool. In *GQT_MODEL* a number of routines are defined for opening a window, defining the views and drawing the model. The second attribute is *boundary*, which forms the relation between an object and a number of bounding objects. The attribute *boundary* is redefined in the classes *GEO_EDGE* and *GEO_FACE*, because an edge is bounded by exactly two vertices and a face is bounded by three or more edges. Furthermore, *GEO_VERTEX* defines an attribute coordinates and *GEO_EDGE* defines an attribute *orientation* and a function *length*. The function *length* is being defined in the session with PMshell, shown in figure 6.17.

Other domains can be based on the geometry domain. These domains can form a Product Type layer, which inherits the functionality of the geometry domain. In this way the Graphical Query Tool is integrated in the Product Type layer and can be used for visualisation of a Product Model.

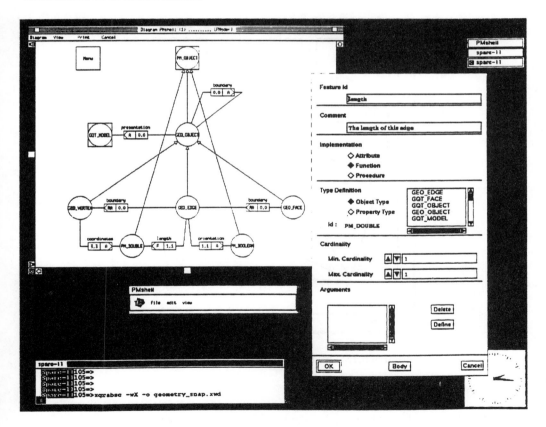

Figure 6.17: A session with PMshell

With the geometry domain a simple model of a box can be made. First the eight vertices of the corners of the box are created. These vertices are used as the bounding objects of twelve edges, which represent the edges of the box. With two extra edges a face can be defined diagonal in the box.

Because every object has a reference to *GQT_MODEL*, the model of a box can be visualised by the Graphical Query Tool. This visualisation is shown in the snapshot of figure 6.18. The capital letters 'A' through 'H' at the corners of the box correspond with the identifiers of the instances in the STEP physical file, e.g. 'VERTEX_A', 'EDGE_AB' or 'FACE_AFGD'. As mentioned before, the Graphical Query Tool is an interactive application, which enables the modelling user to select geometric objects and return the selection to PMshell. This selection can be used in PMshell to present information about the selected geometric objects to the modelling user for inspection. In this way the modelling user can retrieve more than just geometric information from a product model.

The model of the box can be saved in a STEP physical file. This file contains the

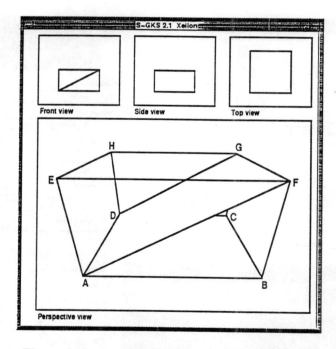

Figure 6.18: A snapshot of the graphical query tool

data of the model and can be used as an alternative for the database. An example of the STEP physical file for the model of the box is shown in figure 6.19.

The syntax is straightforward. First a header is given with an identification of the

```
STEP;
HEADER;
FILE_IDENTIFICATION('CUBE.STEP','19920121.103635',(),
('TNO Building and Construction Research','Department of Computer Integrated
Construction'),
'STEP VERSION 1.0','','PMshell v0.9');
FILE_DESCRIPTION('');
IMP_LEVEL('');
ENDSEC;
/*
GEO_OBJECT(id,presentation,boundary);
GEO_VERTEX(id,presentation,boundary,x_coordinate,y_coordinate,z_coordinate);
GEO_EDGE(id,presentation,boundary,orientation);
GEO_FACE(id,presentation,boundary);
GQT_MODEL(id);
PM_OBJECT(id);
PM_DOMAIN(id);
*/
DATA;
@1=PM_DOMAIN('BOX',(#2,#3,#4,#5,#6,#7,#8,#9,#10,#11,#12,#13,#14,#15,#16,
#17,#18, #19,#20,#21,#22,#23,#24,#25));
@2=GEO_VERTEX('VERTEX_A',#25,(),1,1,1);
@3=GEO_VERTEX('VERTEX_B',#25,(),1,2,1);
@4=GEO_VERTEX('VERTEX_C',#25,(),2,2,1);
@5=GEO_VERTEX('VERTEX_D',#25,(),2,1,1);
@6=GEO_VERTEX('VERTEX_E',#25,(),1,1,1.5);
@7=GEO_VERTEX('VERTEX_F',#25,(),1,2,1.5);
@8=GEO_VERTEX('VERTEX_G',#25,(),2,2,1.5);
@9=GEO_VERTEX('VERTEX_H',#25,(),2,1,1.5);
@10=GEO_EDGE('EDGE_AB',#25,(#2,#3),.F.);
@11=GEO_EDGE('EDGE_BC',#25,(#3,#4),.F.);
@12=GEO_EDGE('EDGE_CD',#25,(#4,#5),.F.);
@13=GEO_EDGE('EDGE_DA',#25,(#5,#2),.F.);
@14=GEO_EDGE('EDGE_EF',#25,(#6,#7),.F.);
@15=GEO_EDGE('EDGE_FG',#25,(#7,#8),.F.);
@16=GEO_EDGE('EDGE_GH',#25,(#8,#9),.F.);
@17=GEO_EDGE('EDGE_HE',#25,(#9,#6),.F.);
@18=GEO_EDGE('EDGE_AE',#25,(#2,#6),.F.);
@19=GEO_EDGE('EDGE_BF',#25,(#3,#7),.F.);
@20=GEO_EDGE('EDGE_CG',#25,(#4,#8),.F.);
@21=GEO_EDGE('EDGE_DH',#25,(#5,#9),.F.);
@22=GEO_EDGE('EDGE_AF',#25,(#2,#7),.F.);
@23=GEO_EDGE('EDGE_DG',#25,(#5,#8),.F.);
@24=GEO_FACE('FACE_AFGD',#25,(#22,#15,#23,#13));
@25=GQT_MODEL('MODEL_BOX'); ENDSEC; ENDSTEP;
```

Figure 6.19: The STEP physical file for the geometric model of a box

file, the time and date of creation and the creator. Following the header, a description of the entities of the model is given in comment (this is necessary for PMshell to be able to read the sequence in which attributes are stored in an instance). Finally the instances of the model are listed. Every instance begins with '@' and an instance number, followed by the entity type of the instance and a list of attribute values. For a boolean value the notations '.F.' and '.T.' are used. Character values and string values are denoted by single quotes. The elements of a list are placed between brackets and separated by a comma. The notation for a reference is '#', followed by an instance number.

6.8 CONCLUSIONS

Experience with the implementation of layered models, like the STEP product model, proved the necessity of a supporting tool to develop and use these models. In a layered model general features have to be implemented only once in a general layer, so all other layers can inherit these features. Important general features are the generation of data in a standardised format to communicate with other systems and the extraction of information from standardised formatted data generated by other systems. One can think of the communication via a database manager, via a data modelling language like EXPRESS or via a data exchange format like the STEP physical file format. If layered modelling is supported with a tool the gap between specification and implementation can be bridged.

PMshell is a prototype implementation of a layered-modelling tool. PMshell proved that it is possible to implement such a tool. In PMshell the programming user and the modelling user are supported in one system. The programming user uses features that are normally used by modelling users. These features are interpreted as actions that define new classes or redefine inherited features. While developing and using PMshell it was shown that modelling users can use programming features as well. Another interesting choice made for the implementation of PMshell is the separation of the system itself and its user interfaces into different processes. The processes communicate via a protocol. In this way a number of user interfaces for different users can be developed parallel, independently from the system. The protocol can also be used for more sophisticated interfaces, e.g. for an application that controls processes on product models.

The first implementation of a layered-modelling tool is promising but a lot of work still has to be done. The tool should be used at a larger scale to have a better view on its potentials and limitations. The interactive integration of larger applications realised via PMshell should be implemented and tested. Problems can be foreseen with the performance of the system and with data handling. At this moment complete models are kept in core during execution but when models grow bigger parts of models must be stored in a database. How to work with data partly stored in a database and partly in core is not clear yet.

The graphical user interface of the current version only supports one modelling technique, a NIAM-like diagram technique. It is the intention to make the user interface configurable to any graphical modelling language. Another issue for the future is that

Eiffel version 2.3 has some problems with repeated inheritance that also influence the current version of PMshell. Hopefully with Eiffel 3 [Meyer 1992] these problems are solved. A third issue is the theoretical and practical elaboration of the possibilities of compound objects. The last interesting point for theoretical and practical research is a general mechanism for data inheritance. This type of inheritance can be used for objects which inherit attribute values from other objects.

APPENDIX: Class *X_INTERNAL*

Note: Assertions have been omitted.

Ancestors of class *X_INTERNAL*:

    INTERNAL

class interface X_INTERNAL ***feature specification***

which_field (*obj*: *ANY*; *field_id*: *STRING*): *INTEGER*
  -- Position of *field_id* in list of logical fields in *obj*.

which_bool (*obj*: *ANY*; *field_id*: *STRING*): *INTEGER*
  -- Position of *field_id* in list of a packed_booleans field in *obj*.

which_routine (*obj*: *ANY*; *routine_id*: *STRING*): *INTEGER*
  -- Position of *routine_id* in list of routines in *obj*.

stringfield (*i*: *INTEGER*; *obj*: *ANY*): *STRING*
  -- String referenced by the *i*-th field of obj.

n_field (*obj*: *ANY*; *attr_id*: *STRING*): *ANY*

n_stringfield (*obj*: *ANY*; *attr_id*: *STRING*): *STRING*

n_intfield (*obj*: *ANY*; *attr_id*: *STRING*): *INTEGER*

n_realfield (*obj*: *ANY*; *attr_id*: *STRING*): *REAL*

n_doublefield (*obj*: *ANY*; *attr_id*: *STRING*): *DOUBLE*

n_boolfield (*obj*: *ANY*; *attr_id*: *STRING*): *BOOLEAN*

n_charfield (*obj*: *ANY*; *attr_id*: *STRING*): *CHARACTER*

set_field (*i*: *INTEGER*; *obj*: *ANY*; *val*: *ANY*)
  -- Set *i*-th field of *obj* to reference to *val*.

set_stringfield (*i*: *INTEGER*; *obj*: *ANY*; *val*: *STRING*)
  -- Set *i*-th field of *obj* to reference to string *val*.

set_intfield (*i*: *INTEGER*; *obj*: *ANY*; *val*: *INTEGER*)
  -- Set *i*-th field of *obj* to integer *val*.

set_realfield (*i*: *INTEGER*; *obj*: *ANY*; *val*: *REAL*)
  -- Set *i*-th field of *obj* to real *val*.

set_doublefield (*i*: *INTEGER*; *obj*: *ANY*; *val*: *DOUBLE*)
  -- Set *i*-th field of *obj* to double *val*.

set_boolfield (*i*: *INTEGER*; *obj*: *ANY*; *which*: *INTEGER*; *val*: *BOOLEAN*)
  -- Set *which*-th boolean of *i*-th field of obj to boolean *val*.

set_charfield (*i*: *INTEGER*; *obj*: *ANY*; *val*: *CHARACTER*)
  -- Set *i*-th field of obj to char *val*.

n_set_field (*obj*: *ANY*; *attr_id*: *STRING*; *val*: *ANY*)

n_set_stringfield (*obj*: *ANY*; *attr_id*: *STRING*; *val*: *STRING*)

n_set_intfield (*obj*: *ANY*; *attr_id*: *STRING*; *val*: *INTEGER*)

n_set_realfield (*obj*: *ANY*; *attr_id*: *STRING*; *val*: *REAL*)

n_set_doublefield (*obj*: *ANY*; *attr_id*: *STRING*; *val*: *DOUBLE*)

n_set_boolfield (*obj*: *ANY*; *attr_id*: *STRING*; *val*: *BOOLEAN*)

n_set_charfield (*obj*: *ANY*; *attr_id*: *STRING*; *val*: *CHARACTER*)

n_procedure_exec (*obj*: *ANY*; *procedure_id*: *STRING*)
  -- Execute procedure with name *procedure_id* of object *obj*.
  -- The procedure does not have arguments.

end interface -- class *X_INTERNAL*

7

Building an interactive 3D animation system

**Enrico Gobbetti, Jean-Francis Balaguer,
Angelo Mangili and Russell Turner
Swiss Federal Institute of Technology
Lausanne (Switzerland)**

7.1 INTRODUCTION

The continued improvement and proliferation of graphics hardware for workstations and personal computers has brought increasing prominence to a newer style of software application program. This style relies on fast, high quality graphics displays coupled with expressive input devices to achieve real-time animation and direct-manipulation interaction metaphors. Such applications impose a rather different conceptual approach, on both the user and the programmer, than more traditional software. The application program can be thought of increasingly as a virtual machine, with a tangible two- or three-dimensional appearance, behavior and tactile response.

Dynamic graphics techniques are now considered essential for making computers easier to use, and interactive and graphical interfaces that allow the presentation and the direct manipulation of information in a pictorial form are now an important part of most of modern graphics software tools. The range of applications that benefit from this techniques is wide: from two-dimensional user interfaces popularized by desktop computers like Apple's Macintosh or the NeXT machine, to CAD and animation systems that allow the creation, manipulation and animation of complex three-dimensional models for purposes of scientific visualization or commercial animation. Future possibilities include the latest virtual environment research that permits an even more intuitive way of working with computers by including the user in a synthetic environment and letting him interact with autonomous entities, thanks to the use of the latest high-speed workstations and devices.

In this chapter we will present the design and implementation of an interactive key-frame animation system based on these dynamic graphics techniques. Key-frame animation is the standard technique used to generate most current commercial computer animation. In its simplest form, key-framing consists of placing the 3D objects to be animated in successive *key* positions and then interpolating some form of spline to generate a smooth motion. One major problem with building key-frame animation systems is that it is difficult to make them easy to interact with and control. We therefore set as a primary goal of this project the achievement of a direct manipulation system in which the user would at all times be able to see, move around within and interact with the animation environment in real time.

7.2 KEY-FRAME ANIMATION

Computer animation is closely related to movie making. A scenario describes the story, defines the actors, how they interact, and what emotions the film has to convey. The scenario is subdivided into a succession of scenes and a story board is realized giving the first general impression of the visual appearance of the film. Once these steps are accomplished, the animator can define the animation for each of the scenes of the movie. Then the animation is rendered and recorded frame by frame to video tape or film.

One way to define an animation is to use some kind of key-framing system, where the animator defines the animation of each actor independently by specifying key values over time of the parameters to animate, and the system interpolates those keys to generate the in-between values of the parameters. This technique is inspired from the way traditional commercial animations are done and is therefore fairly close to the way animators are used to working. A large spectrum of other techniques for creating computer-animated movies exists: from scripting, where the animation is defined by a program in a specialized high-level language, to simulation, where animation results from the evolution of a world's model according to some predetermined laws. However, all these other techniques can be in some way be considered as different front-ends to a key framing system.

The production of good quality animation by direct use of a key framing system requires that the animator be able to control all the finer details of the scene and the motion in a very interactive way, so that it is possible for him to refine his work as many times as needed. The first step of the animator's work is the scene composition. Components of a scene are the animation camera, a set of lights of various types, and a set of geometric shapes. The animator must be able to specify the position, orientation and scaling of each component of the scene, to specify any other parameter of any type of object (such as the angle of view of the camera and the color of the lights) and to organize these components into a hierarchy.

Once a scene is assembled, the animator can start to work on the definition of the motion. The animator describes the animation on an object by object basis. For each object, a sequence of key values of its parameters is specified and the system generates the in-between values using some interpolation technique. Each animation parameter must be stored in a separate track to perform various kinds of interpolation. The animator must be able to choose the kind of interpolation he desires depending on whether he wants continuity of speed and acceleration or not. The interpolation of key values over time is, however, a rather ill-defined problem. The animator has to choose one type of curve among many, and the first choice is not generally the right one to generate the kinds of paths or timing desired by the animator.

Therefore an interactive key-frame animations system must provide real-time playback for the animator to be able to evaluate the animation from various points of view. The first animation is generally a first draft and the animator must be given very interactive tools to edit and refine through many iterations the curves which define the animation and the timing.

7.3. DESIGN APPROACH

The design and implementation of dynamic graphics applications such as the interactive key-frame system described here are complex tasks: these systems have to manage an operational model of the virtual world, and simulate its evolution in response to events that can occur in an order which is determined only at run time. In particular, this kind of application must be able to handle the multi-threaded style of man-machine dialogue that is essential for direct manipulation interfaces, and makes extensive use of many asynchronous input devices (from the ubiquitous keyboard and mouse to more sophisticated devices such as the SpaceBall or DataGlove).

The relevance of object-oriented concepts for solving this kind of problems has already been noted by several authors (see [Gobbetti 1991] and [DeMay 1991] for a discussion of this). From a software-engineering point of view, dynamic graphics applications have many aspects that can benefit from object-oriented techniques: for example, data abstraction can be used to support different internal data representations, several graphics drivers can be encapsulated in specific objects, different subclasses can offer the same interface for the manipulation of graphical objects, and information distribution can help to manage the inherent parallelism of dynamic graphics programs. From the point of view of a user, the direct manipulation metaphor of modern dynamic graphics programs is consistent with the fact that object-oriented applications are designed so as to manipulate objects related in type hierarchies. All these considerations led us to the choice of an object-oriented technology for the design and implementation of our key-frame animation system.

Prior to this project, we already had another experience building object-oriented software. This was a user interface toolkit developed on Silicon Graphics workstations using a custom-made object-oriented extension to C based on the concepts of Objective C [Cox 1986]. This experience was successful but also showed us the limitations of using a hybrid language for the implementation of an object-oriented design. Because the language was hybrid, it was difficult to enforce the object-oriented paradigm completely, and programmers sometimes mixed procedural and object-oriented styles, obtaining in this way components that were hard to reuse. Furthermore, the language provided no multiple inheritance, no static typing and no genericity, limiting in this way its expressiveness and sometimes influencing our design decisions. For example, code duplication was necessary in cases where multiple inheritance should have been used and many errors showed up only at run-time in the form of features being applied to objects that were not supposed to implement them. Another big problem with this system was its lack of garbage collection, which required us to spend inordinate amounts of time chasing memory bugs (dangling pointers, memory never being deallocated, etc.) and devising complex algorithms to destroy object structures.

All of this convinced us of the importance of using a pure object-oriented language for our work, and Eiffel [Meyer 1988] was chosen for this new project because of its characteristics (multiple inheritance, static typing, dynamic binding, and garbage collection) that corresponded to our needs. Our previous experiences convinced us of the appropriateness of object-oriented technology for building libraries of reusable components. What was interesting for us when starting to work on the project of building the animation system was to know if it is possible to use this approach for creating applications and if reusable components can be created as a side-effect of using object-oriented techniques during the development of a program. Furthermore, we wanted to test if it was possible to use a pure object-oriented language such as Eiffel for the creation of an application with such large constraints on performance as an interactive animation system.

7.4 SYSTEM DESIGN

7.4.1 Identification of principal class clusters

To promote code-reuse and to allow several people to work on the project simultaneously, class libraries had to be designed so to provide efficient, reusable and extensible components for composing applications. At the beginning of the design process, a large amount of time was spent up front in group discussions about the design of the system. The problem was split into several principal clusters to be developed in parallel by different people, with each cluster carried through the design process to implementation.

The identification of these clusters was based on an analysis of the problem statement and on our previous experience designing other graphical systems. The practice of starting with the creation of the basic libraries instead of directly starting to analyze the functionalities required is typical of the bottom-up approach that object-oriented design favors [Meyer 1987]. The clusters we selected for further design by this preliminary analysis were:

- A **mathematical cluster**, to contain useful basic mathematical abstract data types.
- A **spline cluster**, to provide means to animate these basic data types.
- A **modeling cluster**, to represent the various components of graphical scenes.
- A **rendering cluster**, to provide several rendering facilities.

- A **dynamic cluster**, to provide ways to encode interactive and animated behavior.
- A **user-interface cluster**, to provide standard interaction widgets and devices.

We find it very useful to describe the structure of our class clusters in term of object- relation diagrams, as in [Rumbaugh 1991]. The definition of the static structure of our software is always the first step of our design process, and these diagrams allow us to give a schematic presentation of this structure that combines within the same diagram instance relations and inheritance relations. These diagrams have thus become for us a standard way for exchanging our ideas during the design meetings about the creation of our class clusters.

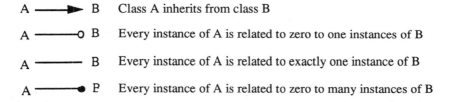

Figure 7.1: Object-relation diagrams

Object-relation diagrams are the only formal technique we use for describing our design process: no other types of diagrams or special notations were used during the design of the key-frame animation system. We find these diagrams useful but we do not insist too much on using other formalized schemes (data flow diagrams, for example) for representing other important aspects of our software. These other techniques could be of some use (especially if used in conjunction with some tool for keeping all these other representations up-to-date with respect to the code), and we will perhaps consider them in the future. Eiffel, with assertions and invariants, offers a way to represent the programming contracts between the different components of the system and their required behavior. Fragments of Eiffel code are therefore sometimes used by us quite early in the design in place of pseudo-codes or data-flow diagrams to define the functional model of some components.

In the next section we will, for each of the clusters composing the animation system, give an overview of the reasoning that guided its design, analyze its structure, and discuss the results obtained in terms of performance and reusability. The class libraries as presented here are the result of multiple iterations of our design process.

7.5 OVERVIEW OF THE PRINCIPAL CLUSTERS

7.5.1 Mathematical cluster

Analysis

The mathematical foundation of the animation system, as for most non-trivial graphics applications, comes from linear algebra. The first step in the design was to provide an encapsulation of the basic concepts of this branch of mathematics.

Matrices and vectors are two of the most important abstractions found in graphics programming. Three-dimensional vectors, are needed to store and manipulate information such as the vertices of a faceted object or its normals, and four-dimensional matrices are the most common technique for representing the projective transformation defined by a virtual camera and the linear transformations used for positioning, orienting and scaling graphical objects. So, a *MATRIX* and a *VECTOR* are usually standard classes in any object-oriented graphics system, but most graphical libraries do not offer more than these two algebraic data types.

Four-dimensional matrices can be used to represent affine transformations (linear combinations of scaling, translation and rotation operations). However, not all instances of a four-dimensional matrix are affine transformations. Furthermore, this representation is not the only possible one and its exclusive use can make it difficult to perform some important operations like interpolating between transformations, a feature that is definitely needed for an animation system! What an animator usually wants to do when interpolating between two affine transformations is to separately interpolate their components (the rigid body transformations, translation and rotation, and the scale factors of the three axes). It is therefore important to be able, at any moment, to extract these parameters from a transformation.

For these reasons, we decided to include in our system a class of transformation objects able to consistently maintain and manipulate their four-dimensional matrix representation and their translation, orientation, and scale components through a well defined interface, thus ensuring, through a proper set of assertions, the affine nature of the transformation. Two of the transformation's components, translation and scaling, can be easily represented as three-dimensional vectors, and no new class needs to be added to the system. There are, however, several different possible solutions for representing rotations, the more frequently used being quaternions and Euler angles. Quaternions are, in fact, four-component homogeneous coordinates for orientation, and they are now becoming increasingly prevalent in animation systems because of their well-behaved mathematical properties ([Shoemake 1985] discusses several issues related to this topic). A class for representing quaternions was therefore included in our design for a mathematical cluster.

The other type of basic mathematical entity that is usually found in graphical software is color, and a *COLOR* class is included in our system. Although colors are often represented as Red-Green-Blue triplets, there exist other representations and the color class has the ability to convert between these.

By making all these types of mathematical objects available to the designers and implementors of the key frame animation system, we aimed at providing a solid set of abstractions to be used together with the other basic Eiffel classes [ISE 1989] in order to simplify the task of writing large dynamic graphics applications.

Object model

The following diagram shows the most important classes of our mathematical cluster and their relations (classes in parentheses are deferred):

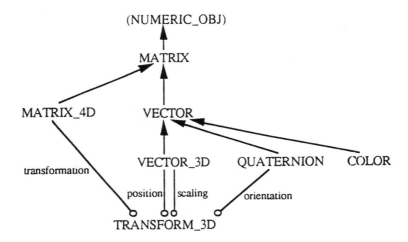

Figure 7.2: Mathematical cluster

The *NUMERIC_OBJ* deferred class defines objects on which the usual arithmetic operations such as "+", "-", "*", "/" are defined and provides a common interface for all these features. Most other classes of this cluster inherit from it, covariantly redefining features to ensure correct typing. A finer distinction between different types of numerical objects with respect to the behavior of the operations applied to them could be made, and *NUMERIC_OBJ* should perhaps be separated into different inheritance levels to represent fundamental mathematical types. However, we felt that the effort for designing this kind of more formal set of abstract classes was too great.

Instances of the *MATRIX* class can represent arbitrary rectangular matrices, and vectors of arbitrary dimension can be represented by instances of *MATRIX*'s heir *VECTOR*. Features for performing all sorts of computations, from basic arithmetic operations to solutions of arbitrary linear systems, are exported from these classes. In this design vectors are rectangular matrices with one of the two dimensions equal to one, consistently with the mathematical definition of the concepts they represent, and a proper class invariant of *VECTOR* ensures that this basic property is always verified. In this way, most of the operations on vectors are just inherited from matrices, and the system is able to distinguish between row vectors and column vectors.

Since four-dimensional matrices and three-dimensional vectors are widely used in graphical programming, the two classes *MATRIX_4D* and *VECTOR_3D* are provided with additional operations and more specific and faster implementations of ancestor's features. The concept of color, linear transformation, and quaternion, mentioned in the analysis, are represented by the *COLOR*, *TRANSFORM_3D*, and *QUATERNION* classes respectively.

Object design

The object design of such basic classes as the ones present in this cluster is very important. These kinds of object have to be used as basic building blocks for the rest of the system and it is therefore very important to have them both simple to use and highly efficient to improve the performance of the applications.

In order to provide regular interfaces, and therefore improve the usability of our classes, we follow some conventions for naming features. Some of these conventions are:

- Features that return an alternate representation of an object always begin with *as*, as for *as_quaternion*: *QUATERNION* which can be applied to instances of *MATRIX_4D*.

- Features that modify the value of *Current* as a result of some computations based on the parameters always begin with *to*, as in *to_sub* (*left*, *right*: **like** *Current*), which can be applied to instances of *NUMERIC_OBJ*.

- Features that store the results of their computations in one of their parameters always contain the indication _*in*, for example *row_in* (*i*: *INTEGER*; *v*: *VECTOR*) which can be applied to instances of *MATRIX*.

As a result of these conventions, the class features use as often as possible the style of modifying *Current* or one of the parameters instead of returning a new object as a result. In this way, it is the client's responsibility to allocate all the objects needed, therefore reducing the overhead due to allocation and collection of unnecessary temporary objects.

All the routines and the classes of our libraries are enriched with a set of preconditions, postconditions and invariants that specify their programming interface contract. We put some effort into defining these assertions, because we believe that they are a key element for promoting reusability. Assertions formally define the behavior of our components (and therefore we use them during the design phase), provide a certain form of documentation and help during debugging. Another interesting fact we noted about assertions is that their use helps to produce efficient software: by clearly defining the responsibilities of each component, we can avoid using defensive programming techniques, and therefore obtain more readable and at the same time more efficient code.

In order to implement the mathematical operations defined in the various classes of this cluster, and especially the *MATRIX* and *VECTOR* classes, we decided to use two standard Fortran libraries that are well known in the scientific programming community: BLAS [Lawson 1979] and LAPACK [Anderson 1990].

BLAS, or Basic Linear Algebra Subprograms, is a set of public domain routines able to perform basic numerical computations on one and two-dimensional arrays interpreted as vectors and matrices. This set of routines operates at a very low level and represents a general purpose kernel library. Highly optimized versions exists on specific machines (for example, they're now included in the Cray SCILIB).

LAPACK, or Linear Algebra Package, is designed as a portable and efficient linear algebra package implemented on top of BLAS. It provides routines for solving systems of simultaneous linear equations, finding least-squares solutions of overdetermined systems of equations, and solving various eigenvalue problems.

These two libraries offer high-quality implementations of numerical algorithms but are rather difficult to use in application programs because of the flat structure of these packages and the fact that the client of these routines has to take care of maintaining all the state information in auxiliary data structures between different calls (for this reason, some of the routines have tens of parameters!). These drawbacks are typical of libraries developed using standard procedural languages.

These two libraries are encapsulated as Eiffel classes whose routines are simple interfaces to the Fortran ones. All these routines have preconditions and postconditions that define their contract, ensuring that these external operations are properly used. For example, the Eiffel interface to the BLAS routine *samax* is

```
samax (n: INTEGER; sx: ARRAY[REAL]; lowx: INTEGER; incx: INTEGER): REAL is
        -- REAL FUNCTION SAMAX (N,SX,INCX)
        -- Returns the maximum absolute value of all entries in SX.
        -- N       Input, INTEGER N, number of elements in SX.
        -- SX      Input, REAL SX (N), vector to be searched.
        -- INCX        Input, INTEGER INCX, increment between elements of SX.
        --              For contiguous elements, INCX = 1.
        -- SAMAX Output, REAL SAMAX, the maximum abs. value of all
        --              entries in SX.
    require
            n_non_negative: n>=0;
            sx_exists : sx = Void;
            sx_low_valid : in_int_range(sx.lower+lowx, sx.lower, sx.upper);
            sx_high_valid : in_int_range(sx.lower+lowx+incx*(n–1),
                                        sx.lower, sx.upper);
    do
            Result:= C_samax(@n, sx.to_c+Word_size*lowx, @incx);
    ensure
            -- Result is the maximum absolute value in the specified range of ofsx
    end;


C_samax(n: INTEGER; sx: POINTER; incx: POINTER) is
    external
            language "c" alias "samax"
    end
```

These encapsulated routines are then used in the various classes of the mathematical cluster as internal implementations of various higher-level operations, Eiffel being used as a packaging tool that offers all the benefits of a pure object-oriented language. State information required by these routines is handled inside mathematical classes and these details are hidden to the client of the mathematical cluster.

We believe that this ability to reuse components written in other languages is a key feature of Eiffel. After all, isn't one of our main goals reusability? Many years of programming efforts have been spent in developing and testing large software libraries in various languages, and some of these libraries, like BLAS and LAPACK, provide a set of functionalities that is really worth reusing. Languages such as C++ and Objective-C try to encourage this reuse by allowing the programmer to continue developing their software in hybrid languages. However, we feel that this approach does not enforce a clean separation between the object-oriented and non-object-oriented portions of the software and therefore perpetuates the software engineering problems of the traditional languages.

The Eiffel approach, on the other hand, is to define clean and localized interfaces with external components, without making any compromise with the object-oriented paradigm the language is based on, obtaining in this way the best of these different worlds. In our case, the ability to reuse LAPACK and BLAS was an important aspect in our development. A lot of functionality was added in a relatively small amount of time and high performance was immediately obtained thanks to the use of these routines, without being forced to change the object-oriented nature of our mathematical components. Our mathematical library is just a starting point, and we hope that in the future, more work will be done for providing these kinds of tools to Eiffel developers.

7.5.2 Representing animation

Analysis

Animation can be defined as the description of the evolution of some parameters over time. We decided to build an interactive key framing system where this evolution is described by specifying key points at certain times, and an interpolator computes the values in-between. Having described how to represent the basic mathematical entities needed by the system using our mathematical cluster of classes, the next problem that we need to attack is the definition of their variation over time using interpolation techniques.

The simplest interpolation technique is linear interpolation. However, this presents the major disadvantage of discontinuities of speed and acceleration at the key points. Another technique is spline interpolation. Splines are curves described as a succession of polynomial segments defined over some parameter. These polynomials can be of any degree, but generally in animation, polynomials of degree three are used. We speak in that case of cubic splines.

Various families of spline curves exist. The most commonly used in the field of computer animation are Cardinal Splines and the Kochanek-Bartels superset. They both interpolate through the control points defining the segments. The major interest of the Kochanek-Bartels splines is that segments are defined by starting and ending points and starting and ending tangents. This allows easy definition of the curve, and permits the creation of local discontinuities by specifying different ending and starting tangents. Kochanek-Bartels and Cardinal splines are only C1 continuous, meaning they don't offer continuity of acceleration, which limits the control you have on the timing.

Another important family of splines are Basis splines, commonly called B-splines. B- splines offer global parameterization on the whole curve and their cubic form offers C2 continuity, i.e. continuity of speed and acceleration (more generally a B-spline of order k is a curve defined by polynomial segments of degree (k-1) and that presents C(k-2) continuity). Hence we can define very smooth paths but also create discontinuities at a point. Their major drawback is that B-splines do not interpolate through the control points and therefore an interpolation layer has to be built on top of them.

A B-spline combined with an interpolation layer is a very versatile tool. Its mathematical formulation is very general, allowing us to use genericity to build parametric curves of anything as a function of time or of any other parameter. These curves can be of any degree offering from linear interpolation to high continuity interpolation. The interpolation layer and the capability to go back and forth between the approximation and interpolation representation provide a very flexible tool for the programmer and designer.

In the case of computer animation, the spline curve represents the history of one parameter. As the timing is generally different for each parameter (translational parameters of a camera won't generally evolve over time in the same way as the field of view, for example) it is necessary to provide history for each parameter independently. We use in this case the term *track*.

For these reasons, we decided to create the *B_SPLINE* class and a subclass which offers the interpolation interface to the curve for the programmer. As pointed out earlier, the animation system has to deal with the evolution over time of several types of objects (affine transformations, colors, etc.) In order to be able to represent this fact, we decided to design subclasses of our mathematical objects which are able to store a history of their value. We call these objects animated variables. An animated variable is defined as being a variable of some type having some history information storage mechanism, which we decided to build on top of B-splines curves. Animated variables can be of any type as long as interpolation has some meaning on this type.

Object model

The animation cluster is composed of a set of classes that are used to represent the animated variables and the history storage information.

Three basic sorts of class can be identified:

- **B-splines** (subclasses of *B_SPLINE*) represent parametric B-splines of any dimension and any order defined over a knot vector giving the distribution of the parameter along the curve and a control polygon. This is an approximation curve. An important subclass is the *INTERPOL_B_SPLINE* class which offers the

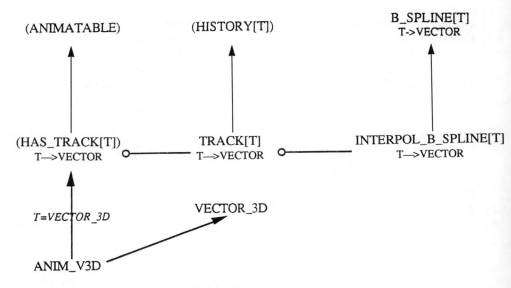

Figure 7.3: Basic animation classes

interpolation interface to the approximation curve. The basic mechanisms to go back and forth from approximation and interpolation representations are implemented here.

- **Histories** (subclasses of *HISTORY*) represent the history storage mechanism. A history is defined as a time ordered list of key values which is traversable over time. An important subclass is the *TRACK* class where B-spline curves are used to interpolate between the key values.

- **Animatable variables** (subclasses of *ANIMATABLE*) are variables having a time dependent value. They have a current value and a current time and mechanisms to update and retrieve information from their history. An important subclass is *HAS_TRACK* which implements the history using a *TRACK*.

In this architecture, history mechanisms and history storage are decoupled. A B-spline curve should not make any assumptions that the parameter used is time. On the other hand, a history should not make assumptions about how the history is stored. Intermediary classes such as *TRACK* make the link between history mechanisms and information storage. On the other hand, for animated variables, the type of the variable and the type of history storage used are also decoupled. This allows us to define, for example, an animated quaternion whose history is defined over a track of three dimensional vectors or an animated transformation defined as an aggregate of other animated variables.

Object design

The use of interpolation to compute the in-between values imposes two constraints on us. The first is that any animated variable should be interpolable. The second constraint is that, as we use parametric B-spline interpolation, a multi-dimensional variable should be interpolable on each dimension independently.

Object-oriented languages such as Eiffel offer a way to express these constraints in the classes by constraining the generic parameter. In order to perform animation, we must record a history and then play it back. History is recorded by specifying a list of key values which are interpolated for playback. However, some manipulation may be necessary before yielding the desired value at a given time. Hence, animated variables behave as windows on their history: setting the current time moves the window and changing the value of the variable changes the content of the window.

These general mechanisms are implemented in the deferred class *ANIMATABLE*. A *store* feature transmits the value of the window to the history, while an *update* feature sets the value of the window to the value of the history at the current time. A *set_time* feature makes the window move along the history.

When an *update* feature is applied to an animated variable, it applies the feature *value_in* to its history. In the case where the history is an instance of the *TRACK* class, the *value_in* feature is applied to instances of the *B_SPLINE* class, causing the evaluation of the polynomial function defining the segment for the current time. This choice of implementation led to the introduction of a *POLYNOM* class (a subclass of *NUMERIC_OBJ*) which implements symbolic polynomial calculus and evaluation. The problem of evaluating the history at a given time is then reduced to the search for the proper segment of the curve and the evaluation of the polynomial defining the segment.

7.5.3 The graphical model

Analysis

Since dynamic graphics applications must be able to respond to asynchronous input events as they happen, designers have to build their programs with little knowledge about when and in what order the events will occur. Therefore, at any moment during the execution of a dynamic application the entire state has to be explicitly maintained in a global data structure.

So, one of the first steps in building a graphics system is to design this data structure which is called the graphical model. This model consists of the set of classes used to represent the virtual objects to be manipulated. It is worth noting that rendering is not the only operation that needs to be done on these objects. In an interactive key-frame animation system, for example, graphical objects need to be animated and dynamically controlled in their shape and appearance. Thus, many different aspects have to be considered when designing the graphics model, which is implemented in the graphical cluster.

Several class structures have been proposed in the literature for representing three-dimensional hierarchical scenes. These designs strive to provide good encapsulations of the concepts useful for modeling, rendering and animating the types of complex objects that are necessary for dynamic graphics applications. Examples are proposed in [Fleischer 1988], which describes an object-oriented modeling testbed, [Grant 1986], which presents a hierarchy of classes for rendering three-dimensional scenes, and [Hedelman 1984] which proposes an object-oriented design for procedural modeling.

Key-frame animation systems are typically concerned with the animation of models arranged in a hierarchical fashion: a transformation tree defines the position, orientation, and scaling of a set of reference frames that transform the space in which graphical primitives are defined. This kind of hierarchical structure is very handy for many of the operations that are needed for modeling and animating a graphical tree (see [Boulic 1991]): objects can be easily placed one relative to another and the simulation of articulated figures, which is essential for any type of animation work, can be done in a natural way. Figure 7.4 shows an example of hierarchical scene representation.

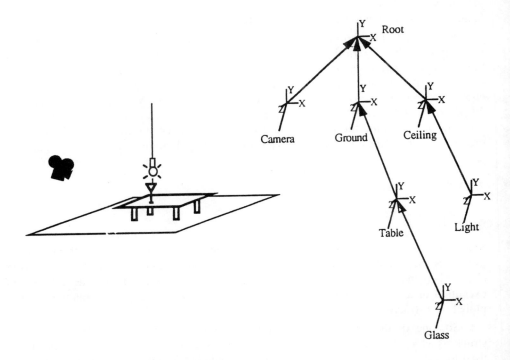

Figure 7.4: A hierarchical scene

Object model of the hierarchical world

The basic modeling classes of our system are modeled as an object-oriented representation of classical animation hierarchies. Its structure is presented in the following diagram:

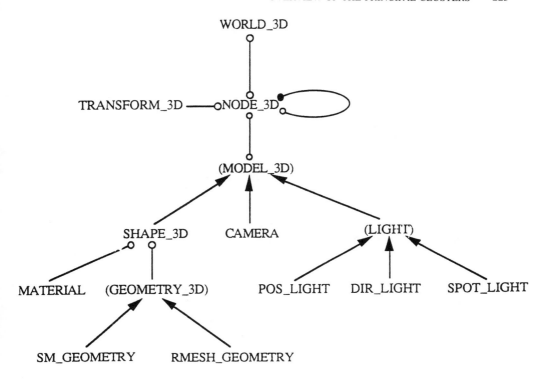

Figure 7.5: Basic modeling classes

The *WORLD_3D* class represents the three-dimensional scene that the animation system manipulates and contains all the global information: the environmental illumination parameters (packaged in instances of *AMBIENT*), and the geometric hierarchy being manipulated.

The transformation hierarchy is represented by instances of *NODE_3D* related in a hierarchical fashion, and is used to specify the position, orientation, and scaling of the reference frames to which the models are attached. This geometric information is packaged in *TRANSFORM_3D* objects, and animation paths are stored by replacing plain *TRANSFORM_3D* instances with instances of the subclass *ANIM_TRANSFORM_3D*, which are able to store a transformation history and to play it back.

To *NODE_3D* instances it is possible to attach instances of *MODEL_3D*, which defines the concept of three-dimensional models in the reference frame of their node. A scene can be composed of three basic types of *MODEL_3D*: lights, cameras, and shapes. It is worth noting that this design clearly separates the hierarchical structure of the scene from the models attached to them, and that models themselves are not hierarchical. This comes from the fact that it is common practice during the creation of an animation sequence to start by designing the hierarchical structure of the scene, and to attach to this structure some simple models to test the animation. These simple models can easily be replaced by more elaborate ones as work progresses. In this way, complex hierarchical structures like skeletons can be designed and reused several times with different shapes attached to them to change their look. The clear division in our design between nodes and models makes this work easier.

An instance of *LIGHT* represents a source of light, and maintains information about the color and intensity of the emitted rays. Subclasses of *LIGHT*, such as *DIR_LIGHT*, *POS_LIGHT* and *SPOT_LIGHT*, define various types of sources and maintain more specific information.

An instance of *CAMERA* represents a camera positioned in the scene, and maintains information about its viewing frustrum and its perspective projection.

An instance of *SHAPE_3D* is an encapsulation of the concept of a physical object having a shape and a material in the Cartesian space. Geometries and materials are defined in completely separate classes, to make them more reusable and to be able, for example, to manipulate a purely geometric object in a program that does not have to know about its possible material properties.

Subclasses of *GEOMETRY_3D* are provided to offer various ways to define the geometric properties of a physical object. Examples are: *SM_GEOMETRY*, which defines a geometric object by specifying a surface model as a set of triangular facets, and *RMESH_GEOMETRY*, which represents objects as rectangular grids of three-dimensional points.

Instances of *MATERIAL* are used to define the behavior of physical objects with respect to light. They contain information such as the color and intensity of emission, diffuse, and specular components as well as the shininess and transparency factors.

All the state information about the model being manipulated can be maintained within this graphical hierarchy. Inheritance and polymorphism are used to handle in a simple and efficient way the different types of graphical shapes. The addition of new types of geometries, for example, is done by defining new subclasses of *GEOMETRY_3D*, and specifying the relevant operations.

The Icon world

In a three dimensional scene, some models are not directly visible. A light, for example just emits some light into the scene, and a camera simply defines a viewpoint and a perspective projection. However, in a three-dimensional application based on direct manipulation, models such as cameras and lights, and purely user-interface constructs such as control points, may have to be made visible for the user to select and manipulate them.

These models exist only for means of user interface, hence they should not be part of the scene hierarchy. Therefore we decided to introduce the concept of three-dimensional icons, which is used to make visible, by some recognizable representation, models which are usually invisible when making the final rendering of the scene.

The introduction of the *ICON_3D* class led to the creation of *VIEWABLE_3D*,

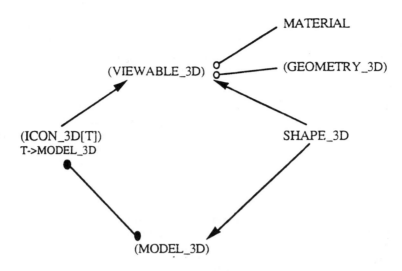

Figure 7.6: The icon world

which represents the capability of maintaining a geometric representation and a material. This abstract class defines characteristics that are common to its descendants *SHAPE_3D* and *ICON_3D*.

Object design

The implementation of the different classes composing the modeling cluster did not pose particular problems. Most of the responsibilities of these classes consist of handling some kind of data structure (like an n-ary tree of transformations for *NODE_3D* and a bi-dimensional array of points and normals for *RMESH_GEOMETRY*). Since we were able to directly use the basic data structures classes provided by Eiffel's library, this allowed us to concentrate most of our time on the purely mathematical side of geometric objects.

7.5.4 Rendering

Analysis

The modeling hierarchy presented in the previous section defines the way we organize and maintain the data structures representing a graphical scene for our dynamic applications. The next step in the object-oriented design process is to organize the types of operations defining how the data structures should be manipulated.

For an application such as key-frame animation, two of the most important types of operations are implementing the visual appearance and dynamic behavior of the different graphical objects. An important design question that arises is: where should the graphical appearance and dynamic behavior be encoded? Two possible solutions are: to encode these features directly in the model (for example by adding a specific *render* feature to the various graphical objects), or to design other sets of classes that are able to perform these operations.

In simple two-dimensional architectures, such as user-interface toolkits, these kinds of operations are usually encoded directly in the model. For more sophisticated applications, this kind of approach is not feasible because there is no simple and unique way for a graphical object to perform complex operations like drawing itself, or responding to events.

If we analyze the problem of rendering a three-dimensional scene, several reasons suggest the creation of auxiliary classes:

- Many different algorithms for drawing graphical scenes may coexist in the same system. Examples are: ray-tracing, radiosity, or z-buffering techniques. The details about these techniques should not be known by every graphical object.

- Rendering may be done using several different types of output units, such as a portion of the frame buffer or a file, and it is not necessary for all this knowledge to be spread out among all the graphical objects.

- Several rendering representations, such as wire-frame or solid, may be selectable on a per graphical object basis. The same object may be viewed by several different windows at the same time, each view using a different representation.

We can see that the rendering feature needs much more information than the type of the object to be rendered, and that the same graphical instance can be rendered in several different ways depending on the type of renderer and the type of representation. Therefore, we decided to design and implement new types of objects to maintain this additional information and to implement the various rendering algorithms.

Object model

The rendering cluster is composed of a set of classes that are used to display a scene. The following diagram shows the basic design of this cluster:

Five basic sorts of classes can be identified:

- **Renderers** (subclasses of the *RENDERER* abstract class), which represent a way to render entire scenes. The code for actually rendering three-dimensional scenes is implemented here. An important subclass of *RENDERER* is *LIGHTED_RENDERER*, which describes renderers that can take into account illumination parameters when computing a visual representation of the scene.

- **Cameras** (subclasses of *CAMERA*), which are objects able to return geometric viewing information such as perspective and viewpoint.

- **Worlds** (subclasses of *WORLD)*, which are objects able to return global illumination information.

- **Viewable models** (subclasses of *VIEWABLE_3D,* such as *MODEL_3D* and

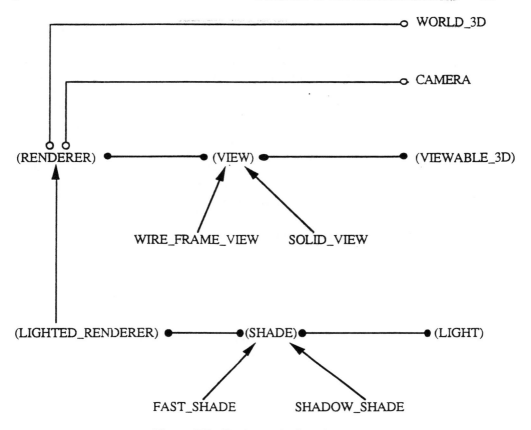

Figure 7.7: Basic rendering classes

ICON_3D in the modeling cluster) that are visible objects having position, orientation and scale in the Cartesian space, a geometry, and a material.

- **Views** (subclasses of *VIEW*), which define how a viewable object should be represented.

In this architecture, view objects act as intermediaries between the viewable models and the renderer, telling the renderer what technique (e.g. wireframe, solid) should be used to display each graphical object.

Object design

In order for a renderer object to be able to display a single graphical object, it must consult its views and the attached viewable object to determine the necessary drawing algorithm. This shows that the rendering feature is polymorphic on more than one type.

Object oriented languages like Eiffel, by means of its dispatching which is done on the basis of the target type at the moment of feature application, offer a way to select between different implementations of the same operation without using complicated conditional instructions which are difficult to maintain and extend. This is one of the major advantages of object-oriented programming and can be used even when the dispatching has to be done on more than one type. This is true for the rendering operation, which is implemented by applying a feature to each polymorphic variable we want to discriminate and let the dynamic binding make all the choices [Ingalls 1986].

To show how this method works, let's look at the various classes that form the rendering cluster. In order to render a scene, a render feature has to be applied to a renderer, which has the task of displaying all the objects that are attached to its views. To do this the renderer, after some initializations, has to set up the camera and apply a *render* feature to all its views with itself as a parameter. This algorithm is completely general and can be written in the abstract *RENDERER* class:

```
render is
        -- Render the current scene
    require
            not is_rendering
    do
            if camera = Void then
                    begin_rendering;
                    define_camera (camera);
                    from views.start until views.offright loop
                            views.item.render (Current);
                            views.forth;
                    end;
                    end_rendering
            end
    ensure
            not is_rendering
    end
```

When a *render* feature is applied to a view, its task is to know what kind of geometries are attached to it through its viewable objects, and to communicate back to the renderer all this specific information. This is done by storing the current renderer and applying a *view* feature to all the viewable objects known by the view. The viewable objects will do the same kind of operation to know about their geometry and respond to the view feature call from the view with a more specific feature call indicating all the type information needed: a *view_rmesh* feature will be applied by objects conformant to *RMESH*, a *view_sm* feature by objects conformant to *SM_GEOMETRY*, and so on. So, every subclass of *VIEW* will have to implement a new *view_...* feature for each of the types of geometries that need to be distinguished. The Eiffel code of the abstract *VIEW* class is as follows:

deferred class *VIEW* **inherit**
  GAP_LIST [*VIEWABLE_3D*]
       rename
           make **as** *gap_make*
       end

feature
  current_renderer: *RENDERER*;
       -- The renderer that is currently asking information to the view
  render (*r*: **like** *current_renderer*) **is**
       -- Apply back to *r* a more specific *render_*... feature with all
       -- the information needed for rendering each item of the list.
       require
           R_exists: *r* /= *Void*;
           Not_rendering: *current_renderer* = *Void*;
       do
           current_renderer := *r*;
           from *start* **until** *offright* **loop**
               item.view (*Current*);
               forth;
           end;
           current_renderer := *Void*
       ensure
           Not_rendering: *current_renderer* = *Void*
       end
  view_sm (*m*: *MATERIAL*; *t*: *TRANSFORM_3D*; **o**: *SM_GEOMETRY*) **is**
       -- Send back a *render_.._sm*(*Current, m, t, o*) to *current_renderer*
       require
           Rendering : *current_renderer* /= *Void*;
           Material_exists: *m.* /= *Void*;
           Transf_exists : *t* /= *Void*;
           Item_exists : *o* /= *Void*;
       deferred
       end; -- *render_sm*
  view_rmesh (*m*: *MATERIAL*; *t*: *TRANSFORM_3D*; *o*: *RMESH_GEOMETRY*) **is**
       -- Send back a *render_.._rmesh*(*Current, m, t, o*) to *current_renderer*
       require
           Rendering : *current_renderer* /= *Void*;
           Material_exists: *m* /= *Void*;
           Transf_exists : *t* /= *Void*;
           Item_exists : *o* /= *Void*;
       deferred
       end; -- *render_rmesh*
end -- *class VIEW*

Each of the specific view features is implemented in *VIEW* subclasses by applying back to the current renderer a specific *render* feature with all the information needed to display the object using the right representation, thus telling the renderer to actually display the object. So, for example, the *WIRE_FRAME_VIEW* class defines the *view_sm* feature as follows:

> *view_sm* (*m*: *MATERIAL*; *t*: *TRANSFORM_3D*; *o*: *SM_GEOMETRY*) **is**
>
> > **require**
> >
> > > *Rendering* : *current_renderer* /= *Void*;
> > > *Material_exists*: *m* /= *Void*;
> > > *Transf_exists* : *t* /= *Void*;
> > > *Item_exists* : *o* /= *Void*;
> >
> > **do**
> >
> > > *current_renderer.render_wf_sm* (*Current, m, t, o*);
> >
> > **end**; -- *render_sm*

Figure 7.8 shows a typical example of feature invocation when the render feature is applied to a renderer.

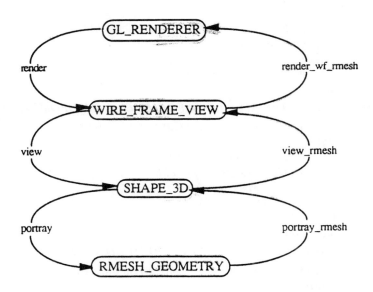

Figure 7.8: Multiple dispatching for a render feature call

As the diagram shows, rendering a single object involves setting off a chain of feature calls, passing through the view, the viewable model and its geometry, ultimately resolving to the appropriate rendering feature. In this way, the composition of the instance data structure automatically determines the rendering algorithm.

7.5.5 Dynamics and input

Analysis

Animated and interactive behavior are among the most confusing aspects of computer graphics design. These can actually be thought of together as the fundamental problem of dynamic graphics: how to modify graphical output in response to real-time input? Viewed in this way, input from the user results in interactive behavior, while input from other data sources or real-time clocks results in animated behavior.

The first problem a sequential application (i.e. a single process with one thread of control) has to solve is the multiplexing between different asynchronous input sources and the handling of those various inputs in a consistent temporal order. The most common way to do this is to have a central input-gathering algorithm responsible for selecting between several input queues (such as the windowing system, various devices, and inter-process communication channels) and extracting each input event in the proper time order, resulting in a single time-ordered queue of input events which can be handled sequentially. Assuming such a purely input-event-driven model, the basic dynamic behavior algorithm then takes the form of an loop as follows:

Initialize the application and select input channels;

from *start* ***until*** *over* ***loop***

    Go into wait state;

    Wake up when input arrives;

    Respond to input

end

In such a structure, the dynamic behavior is implemented in the section *Respond to input*. The most natural object-oriented way to model a workstation with multiple input devices is for each input device (e.g. Mouse, Spaceball) to be represented as a separate instance of a particular input device class. Given such a model, the first thing that has to be done in responding to an input event is to interpret the type of input data received, and update accordingly the object representing the source of this data. If, for example, when the application receives an input indicating that the user moved the mouse, the state of the mouse object has to be updated.

Once the input device objects are updated, the state of the application has been changed and some action has to be performed to respond to this input event, implementing in this way the dynamic behavior of the program. So, for example, if we want the virtual camera in our scene to move when the user moves his SpaceBall, some mechanism must be used to implement this dynamic behavior. An obvious way to do this is to implement some feature in the *CAMERA* class that could be called every time the state of the SpaceBall changes. However, for the same reasons that led to the separation of rendering operation described in the previous section, it is better to move the code implementing the dynamic behavior into a separate object, called a *controller*. In this case, in order to change the behavior of our virtual camera, we simply have to call the appropriate feature of its associated controller object. We call these controller objects dynamic objects because they change their state in response to external input.

Just as the encapsulation of an object's graphical appearance allows higher-level graphical assemblies to be constructed from graphical components, an assembly's dynamic behavior can be built up from the behavior of its dynamic components. To do this effectively, a mechanism must be used to represent the changes of state of dynamic objects in response to input and to represent the dependencies among these objects so they can be updated. We call these changes of state *events*, and consider the problem of updating dependent objects to be the problem of proper distribution of events between objects.

Object model

The dynamic behavior of an application, as described in the previous section, requires the creation of two sets of classes: a first cluster for maintaining and multiplexing between multiple input channels and a second cluster for representing and distributing events.

The design of the input cluster is represented in the following diagram:

Figure 7.9: Classes for input multiplexing and inter-process communication

The design of this set of classes is adapted from the set of inter-process communication classes developed by Matt Hillman [Hillman 1991] and partially reuses most of its components.

Objects of class *NET_NODE* can form and accept socket connections with other processes, and multiplex between all of these when waiting for input. It is through these connections, represented by *NET_CONNECTION* objects, that asynchronous inputs from various input devices, from the window system, and from remote processes arrive to the application. These inputs are represented by objects of type *NET_MESSAGE* which are able to both read from and write to a network connection. On top of these basic classes, several extensions are implemented by means of specialized connection objects and messages: one of these is the user interface toolkit presented in the next section.

Events and their distribution are modeled using a cluster of classes whose principal components are shown in the following diagram:

Three types of objects are used in modeling the dynamic behavior of our applications: these are events, handlers, and dynamic objects. Dynamic objects maintain a list of possible types of events it can sent out to other objects, that is, a list of instances

Figure 7.10. The dynamic cluster

of a specific subclass of *EVENT* for each type of event they can transmit. An event is transmitted every time a dynamic object has to communicate a change of state, the type of event indicating what kind of state change occurred in the dynamic object. Each event instance maintains a list of handler objects, called subscribers, which are objects that want to be informed whenever the event is transmitted. These subscribers then handle the event to implement the dynamic behavior of the application.

Dynamic objects generate events by applying to the event instances they own a feature called *transmit*. This feature is implemented in each subclass of *EVENT* by applying to all the subscribers a specific handling feature having the source of the event (i.e. the dynamic object which transmitted the event) as its only parameter. For example, an event of class *BUTTON_DOWN* is transmitted by the application of the feature *handle_button_down*, and an event of class *BUTTON_UP* transmits by applying *handle_button_up*. Again, as in the rendering cluster, this distinction is done completely through the dispatching mechanism inherent to the dynamic binding, not through conditional instructions.

This representation of dynamic behavior introduces the concept of an event being a signal between two connected objects, a source and a target, much as two IC chips communicate via a signal on a connecting wire. The only information transmitted by the event itself, however, is its type, indicated by the feature called, and any other data must be explicitly queried from the source by the handler of the event. The handler can then update its internal state and perform actions accordingly to the changes of state in the source objects and its programmed behavior. Secondary events can be transmitted by handlers that are themselves dynamic objects, the complex behavior of an application being in this way encoded in the graph of connections traversed by the events.

Dynamic objects are very important concept in our system design: graphics applications written inside our framework can in fact be thought of as big networks of dynamic objects that transmit events and handle them in real time.

Object design

Objects that can handle events are instances of descendants of the *HANDLER* class. Several deferred subclasses of *HANDLER* exist, each one defining an general object that can handle a certain type or collection of types of events. Specific implementations of handlers are obtained by writing classes that inherit from the general handlers and redefine the specific features associated with the desired events. One example is the *FLIGHT_C* controller, which is used to move three-dimensional objects using a flying vehicle metaphor:

```
class FLIGHT_C inherit
    H_VALUE
            redefine
                    handle_new_transform
            end
feature
    target: NODE_3D;
    set_target (other: like target ) is
            do
                    target := other;
            end;
feature {NONE}
    handle_new_transform (source: T_TRANSFORM) is
            -- Handles the event by moving target using a flying vehicle metaphor
            -- No action if no target.
            require
                    source /= Void
            do
                    if target /= Void then
                            target.set_global_trans f (
                                    source.value * source.delta_local * source.value.inverse *
                                    target.global_transf);
                    end
            end -- handle_new_transform
end; -- class FLIGHT_C
```

This class inherits from *H_VALUE* which is a subclass of *HANDLER* capable of handling events that indicate changes in some values, and redefines the feature *handle_new_transform* to perform the required actions when an event is transmitted indicating that a new transformation object is available.

7.5.6 User interface

The goal of the user interface cluster is to provide the typical interactive capabilities associated with modern graphics workstations, namely a mouse, a windowing system, and standard types of interaction widgets, like text input, sliders, and buttons. We also wanted to encapsulate in an object-oriented way some of the newer 3D input devices such as the SpaceBall or the DataGlove.

This was, in fact, the goal of an earlier development effort by our group to create a user-interface toolkit, called the Fifth Dimension Toolkit, for use in our laboratory [Turner 1990]. When that project started, we had no access to an object-oriented language, so we developed a technique for doing object-oriented programming in C, mentioned earlier. In designing this toolkit, which was inspired to a large extent by the

NextStep AppKit [Thompson 1989], we consciously tried to make as purely object-oriented a design as possible.

The modeling of events, in particular, is rather innovative. NextStep's Target/Action paradigm, in which two objects communicate via an action message, with the message's source as a parameter, was extended to model all events. The concept of a centralized event queue was abandoned, replaced by a decentralized collection of event-generating objects such as a mouse object, keyboard object or window object. Therefore there is no conceptual or syntactic difference between a mouse object sending an event when it is moved, and a button widget sending an event when it is pressed.

One particularly powerful feature of the toolkit is an interface builder application, which allows panels of widgets to be arranged and their attributes edited interactively. The resulting user-interface panels can then be stored in a human-readable (and editable) ASCII file and loaded in by an application program at run-time.

Given this functionality required by the animation system, and given the fact that numerous other application programs had already been developed using the 5D Toolkit, we were reluctant to start over from scratch in Eiffel. We therefore considered encapsulating the toolkit in a Eiffel class. This presented some problems, however, since encapsulating an object-oriented software library is considerably more difficult that a non-object-oriented one. Unlike the BLAS and LAPACK routines, which do not maintain their own data structures or state, an object-oriented software library allocates memory and sets up a network of interrelated data structures. The encapsulating Eiffel code, therefore, must either duplicate all of an object's internal data structures itself, with its attendant problems of consistency, or it must separately encapsulate each of the objects maintained by the encapsulated object. The problem was further complicated for us by the event distribution mechanism, in which any dynamic object can send an event to any other object. Since we wanted our Eiffel objects to receive events from the 5D Toolkit objects, an event translating mechanism had to be built.

Our solution was to associate a parallel Eiffel instance of a single class, *UI*, for every instance of every type of toolkit object. Since the 5D toolkit objects are dynamically typed, the single *UI* class encapsulating all the toolkit functionality is appropriate. Most of the toolkit objects are lower level, however, and do not need to be directly accessed by Eiffel. Therefore a mechanism was devised so that the parallel Eiffel *UI* object for each toolkit object is created only on demand when it is needed in the Eiffel application. Later when it is no longer used on the Eiffel side, it is garbage-collected by Eiffel even though the toolkit object still remains. An interface was also build so that toolkit events are translated into Eiffel events as they occur. Because the Eiffel types of events were inspired by the toolkit, this was not too difficult, but the problem of mapping one system of user-interface event types onto another is in general not trivial. Finally, we integrated the toolkit's Display class, which is the main source of toolkit events, into the Eiffel inter-process communication classes so that toolkit events could be interleaved in with events from other processes.

7.6 BUILDING THE APPLICATION

Our key framing application is implemented by constructing a root class which assembles the classes making up the different clusters described in the previous section.

The first part of the application is devoted to the initialization of its data structures, and all the panels of user interface objects are loaded from files created by the user-interface builder. Windows are created to contain these panels and to display three-dimensional scenes. The visibility state of the different windows is then set according to the initial state of the program. A top-level handler class implements the commands which, in response to user input, instantiate the various graphical and dynamic objects that make up the animated scene.

To the user, the animation system appears as a collection of windows displaying either a three-dimensional scene or a control panel. Any desired combination of windows may be made visible at any given time. The principal windows are as follows:

- The two **three-dimensional viewing windows** display images of the scene as perceived by virtual cameras. A first window shows the view from a working camera, and is used for interaction: in this window, the animator builds his scene by creating a hierarchy of nodes and attaching them together. Nodes can be selected directly by clicking on them with the mouse. The second window is viewed from the animation camera: it is used for real time play-back and for defining camera motion.

- The **transit window** is the three-dimensional equivalent of the Macintosh clipboard and is used when loading models from files and for cut and paste operations like moving sub-hierarchy in the tree.

- The **node window** permits control of various parameters of the currently selected node like the rendering type, the visibility of the node etc.

- The **spline window** controls various properties of the animation path of the currently selected node. The animator may change the start time of a spline, or edit the spline through the use of a control panel to add, insert, delete or replace key values.

- The **playback window** is used for controlling the real-time playback of animations. It is resembles a control panel very similar to that of a VCR, offering operations such as moving frame by frame, controlling the animation speed and so on.

Once the interface objects have been created, controllers are then attached to the different widgets and devices using the subscription mechanism presented earlier in the chapter. Specific widgets are identified inside the panels created by the interface builder by using their names.

The interactive behavior of the application is encoded inside the controllers that respond to events generated by input devices, by interaction widgets or by other controllers. Some of the controllers that were written are general purpose and reusable in other applications (an example being the flying vehicle controller previously presented). Some others, like controllers that change the event subscription bindings between widgets and other controllers in order to change the behavior of the application, are quite application-specific and hard to reuse. We are currently working on refining our model for dynamic behavior by adding more general event routing classes in order to further simplify the programming of such controllers.

Once the static structure and the initial binding of controllers to widgets and devices is set, the event loop is started. Events generated by the various input devices propagate through the bindings and controllers perform the required actions.

The input devices currently used by the application are a SpaceBall, a mouse and a dial box. The mouse is used to select nodes and to specify position and orientation in the 3D space using a trackball metaphor, the SpaceBall is used to manipulate cameras, lights and nodes using various metaphors, while the dial box is used to control some continuous parameters such as scaling and color.

When the animator selects a graphical object, appropriate controllers are bound to it and the various interaction panels display the relevant information concerning the current selected node.

For the dial box, the action of selecting an object may also change the controller tied to the device as the parameter controlled by each dial depends on the type of selected object. If a shape is selected the dial box acts on the scaling parameters of its node, while in the case of a camera the dials control the field of view and the clipping planes.

By default the SpaceBall controls the camera of the window, while the mouse through its trackball controller object controls the currently selected node. Using a menu, the animator can modify these default bindings and change the control metaphor for the selected node or the current camera.

An animation is defined by specifying key points. To define an animation, the user has to attach a spline to the selected node. Then he moves the node with the SpaceBall or the trackball and presses on the SpaceBall button (or on the new key button of the spline window), to record the current state of the selected node as the position of the new key.

7.7 DISCUSSION

In undertaking the project of building a key-frame animation system, we were interested in answering several important questions about the use of object-oriented technology:

- Is it possible to use an object-oriented approach to build an application, or does this methodology only lead to building tools for building tools for building tools?
- Is it possible to develop reusable components as a side effect of using an object-oriented methodology when building applications?
- Is a pure object-oriented approach usable for such an high-performance system as an interactive animation application?

These questions aim at knowing if object-oriented techniques are really adequate to face with the problems of building real world applications.

7.7.1 Building object-oriented applications

The experience we had with the key-frame animation project showed us the feasibility of building large applications using a complete object-oriented methodology for all of its components, at least in the field of dynamic graphics.

Our approach for building the application was to start by defining the problem we wanted to solve, in this case the creation of a key framing application, and to analyze this informal problem statement in order to identify its principal components. Before starting to build this application, we already had some experience in the field of computer graphics and object-oriented design, and this clearly guided us in the identification of the relevant class clusters that would make compose the application.

These components were later analyzed, and clusters of classes were created by defining at first their static structure (inheritance and instance relations) and later their functional behavior. This process was reiterated several times until a satisfactory solution was found. Once the cluster of classes was completed, the application was built by assembling in a proper way its components. This phase also led to several passes of refinement on the design process and to the modification of the basic clusters design.

Even though the approach of decomposing a software project around the objects it manipulates is more "natural", software design still remains a difficult task and much time has to be spent in discussing the conception of applications.

We feel that most of the problem in using object-oriented techniques is to shift conceptually the design from the functional decomposition approach, in which the basic unit of modularization is the algorithm, to a data decomposition approach, in which the basic unit of modularization is the data structure. This shift usually requires some effort for people trained to use traditional methods.

From our point of view object-oriented techniques are often incompatible with more traditional ones. It is most of the time confusing to mix object-oriented and traditional functional decomposition techniques, and we therefore prefer to use a pure language like Eiffel instead of mixed paradigm languages such as C++ or Objective-C. However, the ability to call traditional languages from Eiffel was extremely useful for reusing existing libraries.

7.7.2 Building reusable components

The bottom-up approach that object-oriented design favors for building applications leads to the creation of software systems that are large assemblies of basic components. The question is: are the components designed during the creation of an application reusable?

From our experience, we can give a quite affirmative answer. Most of the components created for the key framing application are currently being reused in such different applications as a neural network simulator, a distributed virtual reality system, and a system for simulating the physical behavior of elastically deformable surfaces.

However, we have to admit that components are not usually reusable from the beginning, and some effort is always needed to make them general enough to be able to exploit them in different applications.

The first step for making a component reusable is to have it usable. To test this fact, client applications need to be written and feedback obtained so as to ameliorate the design. For this reason, we have the impression that the approach of building test applications in order to obtain a first draft of class libraries is necessary, and for most non-trivial class libraries preferable to directly building components from first principles.

 Another advantage of object-oriented techniques is that it is possible to exploit the similarity of structure of all application in a field by creating frameworks that define and implement the object-oriented design of an entire system such that its major components are modeled by abstract classes. High level classes of these frameworks define the general protocol and handle the default behavior, which is usually appropriate for most of the cases. Only application-specific differences have to be implemented by the designer through the use of subclassing and redefinition to customize the application. The reuse of abstract design which is offered by this solution is even more important than the obvious reuse of code.

Several well known application frameworks exist, especially in the field of user interfaces. Examples are: Smalltalk's MVC ([Krasner 1988]), Apple Computer's MacApp ([Schmucker 1986]), and the University of Zurich's ET++ ([Weinand 1989]).

Our dynamic, modeling, and rendering clusters are a first step towards building a framework for our interactive three-dimensional graphics applications, but much work still remain to be done to make this framework general enough for the creation of future applications.

7.7.3 About performance

Performance is an important issue in building dynamic graphics program. Optimization reasons are often used as an excuse for not using pure object- oriented techniques for the development of such applications, and choosing languages that offer the possibility of freely mixing the procedural and the object-oriented paradigm such as C++ ([Stroustrup 1986]) or Objective-C ([Cox 1986]).

The development of the key-frame system showed us that high performance applications can be obtained using a pure object-oriented language such as Eiffel without compromising the design. Our animation system is able to render fully shaded scenes containing several thousands of polygons at interactive speed (more than ten refreshes per second) on a Silicon Graphics Iris, and allows the user to edit and animate three-dimensional shapes using a complete direct manipulation metaphor.

The fact that the language is purely object-oriented and statically typed allows the compiler to perform important optimizations (such as inlining, unneeded code removal, and simplification of routine calls), so to obtain a high-performance code without having to compromise with the purity of the design. Optimization of several important aspects of our software system was often obtained by creating specialized subclasses that handle special cases.

The availability of a garbage collector for Eiffel allowed us to simplify algorithms and data structures obtaining therefore a more compact and efficient code. The collector is incremental and was therefore possible to be used in our interactive programs without disturbing the user. By carefully designing our components so as to minimize the creation of temporary objects, we are able to contain the cost of object allocation and deallocation in our software system to under 10%. Our previous experience with the development of a user interface toolkit using an object-oriented extension of C showed us the importance of these memory issues: in this previous system a great deal of design effort was spent in defining and maintaining appropriate data structures and storage schemes in order to properly destroy unreferenced objects.

A key factor for the success of our project was the ability to interface our Eiffel classes with pre-existing libraries written in other languages. This was done by defining a clear interface between these external libraries and the Eiffel world and did not disturb the object- oriented nature of the system.

7.8 CONCLUSIONS

The challenge of building dynamic graphics applications that realize the full potential of modern computer graphics hardware remains immense. Object-oriented design techniques, however, provide a significant advance toward the creation of reusable and extensible software components and assemblies for dynamic graphics construction.

Our experience with using a pure object-oriented approach and implementation language for building a key-frame animation system was very satisfying and showed us that these techniques are well suited for creating high-performance applications made of assemblies of reusable components in the field of dynamic graphics.

Most of the components that were created during this project are still being reused and extended for our current work, making it possible for us to concentrate our efforts in solving the specific problems of new application domains.

We are therefore continuing to use Eiffel and object-oriented techniques for our current research work, which focuses on the fields of neural networks, cooperative work for animation, and physically-based simulation of deformable models.

8

Semantic and logical object tool

**Thierry Beauchesne, Thierry Caminel,
Sylvain Dupont and Lilian Druilhe
Dialexis S.A.
Toulouse (France)**

The activity of Dialexis (formally Dialogics) company focuses mainly on developing knowledge base systems. Dialexis has acquired a broad experience in using various expert system shells. Currently, we develop our own tools based on a set of reusable artificial intelligence software components (Eiffel classes) as design tools. The **S**emantic and **L**ogical **O**bject **T**ool (S.L.O.T.) expert system shell is now a complete artificial intelligence development system.

S.L.O.T. has been used successfully in two large applications so far. The first one deals with road surface failure detection. The second one is a user assistant system, that helps to assess start-up companies.

This chapter is structured as follows. Part 1 (section 8.1 to 8.7) describes the system and presents examples of knowledge bases and their implementations in S.L.O.T. Part 2 (8.8 to 8.11) discusses various issues within the object-oriented framework and some of the potential applications.

Part 1: System Description

Artificial intelligence (AI) is an experimental discipline that tries to define a theory of intelligent behaviour in order to implement intelligent machine agents [Boy 1990]. In practice an expert system is constituted of three main parts : a *knowledge base*, an *inference engine* and a *control processing mechanism*. An inference engine is the logic process on allowing to reach a goal from known facts. An inference engine is managed by the control processing mechanism. The most common applications area of AI technique are *problem-solving* and *common-sense knowledge representation*.

One of the most useful paradigms for knowledge representation is the *semantic network*. A semantic network [Quillian 1968] [Woods 1973] is an oriented graph in which the nodes are objects in the universe of the discourse and edges represent binary relations between objects.

The **S**emantic and **L**ogical **O**bject **T**ool (S.L.O.T.) is an object-oriented expert system development tool. One of its features is that knowledge can be represented in a semantic network format. Objects can be either semantically related or independent. Basic objects of the system are the representations of the semantic network elements: nodes are represented by objects called frames, and links are represented by objects called *Slots*.

8.1 MAIN FEATURES OF S.L.O.T.

Our first aim was to develop a set of reusable AI software components. We needed an object-oriented language because of the object oriented structure of the system, and we had to implement powerful abstractions as active objects and sources of knowledge (see section 8.3). Furthermore we planned to add many features (fuzzy logic, first order logic, multi-users, graphical user interface, ...). to the original kernel, so we needed a greatly expandable language to develop it in an open architecture.

For these reasons, S.L.O.T. is developed in Eiffel [Meyer 1988, 1992]. The object-oriented approach and structure of this language as well as its reliability suited our implementation needs best. S.L.O.T. includes a wide range of possibilities for representing knowledge that may be used for implementing *simple* or *complex* reasoning. In addition to propositional logic and its object-oriented structure, S.L.O.T. includes the following characteristics:

  - − Decision trees, i.e., structures that allow assignment of a value to an object when specified conditions are satisfied.
  - − Algebraic expressions, e.g., (car.size + 2)*3.
  - − Object descriptions, i.e. structures that allow specification of an object within specified conditions.
  - − Calls to C or Eiffel functions.
  - − Multi-user facilities.

– Explicit conclusion text designing system.
– Rule-by-rule control of the reasoning in forward and backward chaining; backward chaining is the default.
– First-order logic reasoning.
– Fuzzy logic reasoning.
– Belief revision.
– Reasoning explanation system.

It is also possible to implement integrated applications where S.L.O.T. can be connected to any C or Eiffel programs because the application interface is both Eiffel and C.

8.2 STRUCTURE OF THE KNOWLEDGE BASE

8.2.1 Description of the knowledge base

Frames are the main symbolic objects of the knowledge base. They have properties that define slots. All these objects are unique in the knowledge base.

The knowledge base includes the following elements:

• A set of frames and a set of properties defining a set of slots.
• A set of features that allow manipulation of slots.

Features include rules, decision trees, default values, slot descriptions, etc. It is easy to add other features because each one is considered as an independent information source.

8.2.2 The slot object

The slot is the main abstraction of this system. It is an active object which is able to reach its value by itself and to react to any change of its value. A slot may be non-valued and act to reach its value by activating knowledge sources. Therefore there is no explicit inference engine, all its functions being performed by the slot objects.

A slot is the association of a property to a frame. It represents a link of the semantic network. It is the only object that has a value.

A slot has a specific behaviour. It includes a number of facets that make explicit descriptive or behavioural modalities. The syntax for a slot is:

frame.property (e.g. : manager.missing_experiences)

Slot values can be of three different types:

• integer
• boolean
• frame_set (this symbolic type permits the assignment of a set of frames called a

frame_set)

A semantic network is built by assigning a value of the frame_set type to a slot. For instance:

car.passenger := John, Arthur, Mary; -- assign a set of three frames
                                        -- to a *car.passenger* slot.

John.eye_color := blue -- assign a set of one frame to a *John.eye_color* slot.

This example shows the implementation of the semantic network using the object paradigm. The frame object (*John*) both may **be** a value and may **have** values through its properties.

Slot facet

In addition to rules and decision trees, the *facet* tool is also available. It allows the manipulation of slot features. Slot facets may be knowledge sources.

Its syntax is:

```
SLOT_FACET ::= "slot" SLOT
    default -> value
    enumeration : FRAME_SET
    description : DESCRITION
    question : "text"
    conclusion : CONCLUSION
    tolerance : numeric value
end
```

A slot object can be used with or without explicit declarations. But it has to be declared in order to make its facets usable.

Here is an example, which is part of the second application using S.L.O.T. The aim of this application is to provide a diagnosis of new business projects. It is made of two main parts; the first one is a financial analysis and second the one is a descriptive analysis of the different components of the company (human factors, market, product etc.). This example analyses the possibly incomplete experience of the new manager.

```
-- Slot declarations involve needed slot facets
slot new_manager.experience
-- facet enumeration to restrict at a set of values
    enumeration : commercial,
                production_technique,
                scientific,
                knowledge_of_professional_environment,
                management
-- facet question : the system displays that question when it needs the value of this slot
-- question : "What is the experience of the new_manager?"
end;
```

8.2.3 Frames

A frame represents a semantic object in the knowledge base. It is identified by its name. A frame is a data structure that represents a typical object [Minsky 1975]. It only receives values from its properties. A frame can be compared to a data sheet including boxes to fill in. These boxes correspond to slots and characterise properties.

For instance, the following knowledge base is defined by two frames and one property:

Two frames: *new_manager*, *management*
One property: *experience*
new_manager:= *management*   : is a non-valid statement (a frame cannot receive values)
new_manager.experience:= management : is a valid statement (a slot can receive values)

8.2.4 Property

A property is the name of a link in the semantic network. The same property may characterise several frames. Each property is unique and global in the knowledge base.

8.3 SOURCES OF KNOWLEDGE

Each slot object has an ordered set of sources of knowledge. The default order priority is defined as follows :

highest priority	rule
	decision trees
	slot description
	explicit question
	default value
lowest priority	default question

8.3.1 Rules

A rule includes a pattern in its left-hand side and a list of actions in its right-hand side. It can be fired by either forward or backward chaining.

A pattern is a sequence of conjunctive tests. The truth value of a pattern is defined by a sequential evaluation of its tests. The truth value is the minimum (in the fuzzy logic reuse) among the truth values of all the tests.

A test includes a left hand side, a boolean operator and a right hand side.

Right-hand sides and left-hand sides can be instantiated by the following objects: Slot, Variable, Slot_Val, Variable.Property, Expression.

An action_list is a list of actions. An action is either an assignment or a call to an external function. An assignment includes a left-hand side and a right-hand side, such as:

A_LHS <– {Slot, Var_Prop}
A_RHS <– {Slot, Variable, Slot_Val, Expression}

Example :

This rule searches the difference between the required experience for the new firm and the actual experience of the manager.

```
rule missing_experiences
    variables : -- variable declaration
         ?x : experience.list -- variable world restriction.
    if -- 2 tests in the lhs part of this rule using first order logic
    (
         firm.required_experience  = ?x    & -- this test is true for each instance of 'x' equal to
                                             -- firm.required_experience
         new_manager.experience  /= ?x    -- this test is true for each instance of 'x' different
                                             -- from new_manager.experience
    )
    then -- assignment of each instance of the variable 'x' equal to firm.required_experience and
         -- different from new_manager.experience.
         new_manager.missing_experience := ?x
    end;
```

8.3.2 Decision tree

Nodes of a decision tree are tests and its terminal nodes are values. Its function is to assign values to its associated slot. It is implemented as an imbedded if-then-else sequence.

This decision tree searches the required experience of the firm with a combination of any conditions. The slot *firm.required_experience* fires this **decision tree** when it needs its value.

```
d3 firm.required_experience
(
-- the    required_experience    of    firm    is    equal    to    knowledge_of_professional_
-- environment if the sector of product is equal to creation.
    if product.sector = creation then knowledge_of_professional_environment
    if product.sector =developing then
    (
        if true = true then commercial, management
-- the required_experience of firm is equal to knowledge_of_professional_environment
-- if the sector of product is equal to creation and competitive_edge of firm is weak.
        if entreprise.competitive_edge = weak then knowledge_of_professional_environment
    );
```

```
    if product.sector = maturity
    then (
-- the required_experience of firm is equal to knowledge_of_professional_environment
-- if the sector of product is equal to maturity etc.
        if true = true then knowledge_of_professional_environment
        if entreprise.competitive_edge = strong then production_technique
        if entreprise.competitive_edge = medium then production_technique, management
        if entreprise.competitive_edge = weak then management
    );
    if product.sector = downfall then management, knowledge_of_professional_environment
    if product.differentiation = production_mode, functions, services
    then knowledge_of_professional_environment
    if product.differentiation = price then production_technique, management
    if product.differentiation = sale_technique
    then commercial, knowledge_of_professional_environment
) ;
```

8.3.3 Default value

A default value is the value that the slot gets when it is not specified by the reasoning. Its priority ranking is lower than the other sources.

For instance:

```
-- if the system is unable to know which experience the manager is missing, it is
-- assigned to none.
    slot new_manager.missing_experience
        default –> none
    end;
```

8.3.4 Slot description

A slot description is a source allowing the assignment of a value of an object (slot) after a description defined by a set of slot rules. For instance:

```
    slot firm.size
        description
        -- This description assigns the value small to the size of the firm if its staff_number
        -- during the third years is lower than 20 and its sales is lower than $1000,000.
    (
            year_3.staff_number < 20 {30} ;
            year_3.sales < 1000000
    )
    –> large
    (
            year_3.staff_number > 100 {30} ;
```

```
            year_3.sales > 5000000
        )
        -> small
        default -> medium
    end;
```

8.3.5 Question

A question is a facet including a text that will be displayed each time the system asks a value from the user. If the facet question does not exist then a default question will be built by the system automatically.

For instance:

explicit question :

```
    slot product.differentiation
        question: "How different is the product?"
    end;
```

default question : built as : what is the *'property'* of *'frame'*

> "What is the differentiation of product ?"

```
    slot product.sector
        question: "In which sector is the activity of product"
    end;

    slot firm.competitive_edge
        question: "What is the competitive edge of the product?"
    end;
```

8.4 OTHER FEATURES

8.4.1 Conclusion

The conclusion is a text that is displayed after answering to the evaluation of a slot. It is possible to build a text as a function of the values of a slot.

For instance:

```
    -- Goal slot provides conclusion text with two facets : facet conclusion and facet text
    slot new_manager.missing_experience
        text (
            when scientific -> {"scientific",
                when commercial, production_technique, management,
    knowledge_of_professional_environment -> {", " }},
            when commercial -> {"commercial",
                when production_technique, management, knowledge_of_professional_
```

```
environment-> {" and " }},
      when management-> {"of management",
            when production_technique,knowledge_of_professional_environment
-> {" and " }},
      when production_technique -> {"in production technique",
            when knowledge_of_professional_environment -> {" and " }},
      when knowledge_of_professional_environment -> {" knowledge of professional
      environment"}
   )
   conclusion (when none ->
   {"The new manager has a sufficient experience to reach his project."},
      when knowledge_of_professional_environment, commercial, management,
production_technique ->
   {"The new manager lacks the experiences ",current,"."},rc)
end;
```

The *text facet* provides its text when a *conclusion facet* invokes the slot owner of that *text facet*. Here the slot is called into its own *conclusion facet* by the *current* keyword.

An example of conclusion text displayed:

The new manager lacks the experience in management and in production technique.

8.4.2 Explanation system

The explanation system provides a text in natural language. It works like the conclusion text system, which means the knowledge base designer has to write it. The syntax is similar to that of the conclusion facet. Explanation sentences must be written within rules, decision trees and any knowledge sources. An explanation text is delimited by two '%'

For example :

The rule missing experience with its explanation text :

```
rule missing_experience
   variables :   ?x : experience.list
   %"To define which experience the new manager, is lacking",
   " we have to find which experience is required for the project to succeed",
   " and then compared to the experience of the new manager. ",rc%
   if (
         firm.required_experience = ?x
         %" The new project requires ",
         firm.required_experience,
         " as experience.",rc,%                              &
         new_manager.experience                 /= ?x
         %" The new manager has ",
         new_manager.experience,
         " as experience.",rc,%
```

```
)
%"  And then,"%
then
    new_manager.missing_experience := ?x
            %"the new manager lacks ",
            new_manager.experience,
            " as experience", rc%
end;
```

The explanation text displayed is :

> *To define which experience the new manager is lacking, we have to find which experience is required for the project succeed, and then compare it to the experience of the new manager.*
> *The new project requires management and production technique as experience.*
> *The new manager has scientific as experience*
> *And then the new manager lacks management and production technique as experience.*

8.5 REASONING CAPABILITIES

8.5.1 Uncertainty representation and management

Truth values are represented by integers between zero and one hundred. To compute each truth value, fuzzy logic facets (tolerance, likelihood coefficient, etc.) are attached to each fuzzy object (frame, numerical value, etc.). In S.L.O.T., a likelihood coefficient between 0 and 10 is given to each object of symbolic type and a tolerance between 0 and d 100 to each object of numerical type [Zadeh 1979].

For an equality test the formula is the following : the truth value is null if the left value (of the equality) is the same as the right value plus or minus a percentage of tolerance [Dubois 1988].

The tolerance value is normalised (i.e., redefined between 0 and 1) for the truth value test.

For instance, the equality test between val1 and val2 uses the formulas :

if val1 > val2 then

$$\text{truth} = \frac{100}{\text{tolerance}} (\text{tolerance} + 1 - \frac{\text{val1}}{\text{val2}})$$

if val1 < val2 then

$$\text{truth} = \frac{100}{\text{tolerance}} (\text{tolerance} - 1 + \frac{\text{val1}}{\text{val2}})$$

A tolerance equal to 1 (100) represents an interval with a lower bound of 0 and an upper bound of twice the value of right and side of the test (val2).

For tests involving symbolic values, unlike numeric values, a certainty factor is associated with each symbolic value.

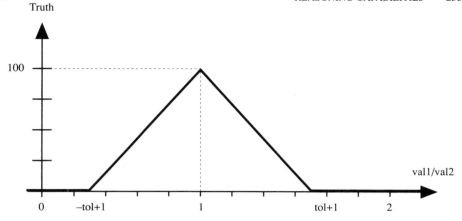

Figure 8.1: Equality test between numerical values

The result of a symbolic equality test is the intersection of both sets of frames. The resulting truth value of the test is the maximum of the certainty coefficient of each frame involved in the intersection.

For instance let consider the following sets :

red {8}, green, blue{3} and red{6}, blue{7}, yellow{4}

The intersection is:

red{6}, blue{3}

The likelihood coefficient of the equality test is the maximum of the coefficients of the frames of the resulting intersection set.

In the previous example, a likelihood coefficient of 6 is obtained.

In this system a test matches when the resulting coefficient is greater than a threshold.

8.5.2 First order logic

In order to take into account a reasoning based on first order logic(FOL), variables and an unification mechanism are available. They are adapted to the network structure of the system. This allows classical calculation in FOL, navigation through the network and simulation of the inference by inheritance. A *variable* is implemented as a set of frames.

All order 1 objects are only instantiated with symbolic values. *Variables* are instantiated with the world. The world is a set of all *frames* in the knowledge base. The syntax is:

VARIABLE ::= '?'identifier

A variable can be composed with a property as in *variable.property*. In this case it is instantiated by a set of *slots* which have the same property, and *frames* which are instances of the variable.

For instance : ?x.color request all the slots that have a colour.

8.6 USER INTERFACE

The expert system designer must write the knowledge base in text format files using the appropriate syntax with a text editor. Then the text files are then compiled by S.L.O.T. If the compilation succeeds, the system provides an interactive shell using a command language including any statements of the knowledge base description language and, in addition, any specific commands.

Some usual commands are :

– LIST, syntax : list [| all | FRAME]

The list command displays the value of the slots associated to the specified *frame*. If the *frame* is not specified or if the *all* keyword is used then the whole knowledge base is displayed.

– ASSIGNMENT, syntax: slot ":=" SLOT_VAL

Assign a value (integer, symbolic, or logical value) to a slot

– EVALUATE, syntax : eval SLOT

The eval command is the main command that starts the inference engine. Once the inference is started, S.L.O.T. asks the user to give all missing values of the slots that are necessary for the evaluation until it provides the result.

– RESET, syntax: reset SLOT | all

The reset command assigns one or all slots to NOT_EVALUATED status.

8.7 BUILDING A KNOWLEDGE BASE

A declarative language is available to build the knowledge base. It includes the syntactic structures that have been described already. The knowledge base is compiled by the system that produces resulting Eiffel objects.

8.7.1 Semantic network

The inheritance link *isa* does not yet have a specific implementation; it is a normal property but it is possible to simulate the inheritance of value by writing a F.O.L. rule.

For instance:

```
rule
    if ( ?x.isa = car )
    then
            ?x.number_of_wheels := car.number_of_wheels;
            ?x.has_engine := car.has_engine
end;
```

With this rule, the *number_of_wheels* of all instances of *car* inherits the value from all properties associated to *car*.

The example of figure 8.2 (page 256) shows how a *semantic network* should be represented with the S.L.O.T. declarative language. This is more a fact base than a knowledge base. This *semantic* network was drawn in the S.L.O.T. way; there is one link from one frame to several frames, thus we can see the difference between a *frame* (car, passenger, red etc.) and *frame_set*. A *frame* should never directly be a value; a symbolic value is always of the *frame_set* type. So one *property* (color) may be attached to several *frames* (car, shirt) defining several *slots* (car.color, shirt.color).

8.7.2 Implementation of the example in S.L.O.T. language

Frames in the KB
    VEHICULE, CAR, MARY, SHIRT_1, SHIRT_2, SHIRT, RED, GREEN

Properties in the KB
    COLOR, PASSENGER, SIZE, WEARS, ISA

Building Knowledge base
```
CAR.PASSENGER := [JOHN, MARY]
CAR.COLOR := [RED, GREEN]
CAR.ISA := [VEHICULE]
JOHN.SIZE := 5'3"
JOHN.WEARS := SHIRT_1
MARY.SIZE := 5'4"
MARY.WEARS := SHIRT_2
SHIRT_1.COLOR := GREEN
SHIRT_1.ISA := SHIRT
SHIRT_2.COLOR := RED
SHIRT_2.ISA := SHIRT
```

8.7.3 Interpretation

A car that is RED and GREEN is a VEHICULE. PASSENGERS of this CAR are JOHN and MARY. JOHN is 5 feet 3 inches tall and wears a GREEN SHIRT. MARY is 5 feet 4 inches tall and wears a RED SHIRT.

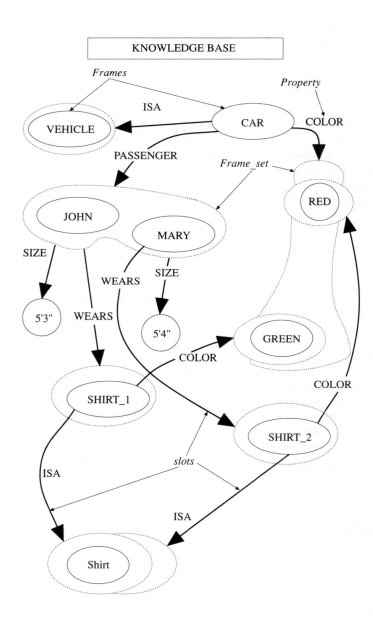

Figure 8. 2: Example of semantic network

Part 2: Design

S.L.O.T. is composed of two parts: the parser that compiles the knowledge base, and the inference engine that includes and processes all the classes of objects defining the knowledge base (slot, rule, property, and so on...).

Text files including the knowledge base are compiled. The result of this compilation is the expert system. The expert system allows queries directly from a user (test mode) or indirectly from an other system via an interface (application mode). Several queries are possible : evaluation of a slot , display of slot values etc.

8.8 COMPILING THE KNOWLEDGE BASE

The compiler performs a lexical and syntactic analysis of the KB. The lexical analysis is performed using the LEX tool provided by the UNIX system. The syntactic analysis is performed within each object.

8.8.1 Lexical analysis

Due to performance constraints the S.L.O.T. lexical analyzer has been built around the lexical analyser LEX of UNIX. Various lexical types are described using the LEX syntax. LEX generates a C source file from this description. This file includes in addition several C functions that allow to interface it with Eiffel.

In practice, the *LEX_UNIX* class is the interface between C and Eiffel. Routines of this class (such as: *get a token*, *text of the last token*) call only the corresponding C functions. This class transforms information from C to Eiffel objects, instances of a class called *TOKEN*. It substitutes itself to the *LEXICAL* class of the Eiffel library (the interface of *LEX-UNIX* is almost the same as the interface of *LEXICAL*). The functions of the *LEXICAL* class are replaced by calls to *yy_lex* functions.

```
class LEX_UNIX feature

    token_type : INTEGER;
            -- Type of the last parsed token.

    end_of_text: BOOLEAN ;
                -- Is the end of text reached ?
    get_token is
                -- Get the next token
        do
            if (lex_end_of_text=1) then
                end_of_text := true
            end ;
            token_type := lex_token_type;
            token_line_number := lex_token_line_number ;
```

                    last_token.set_val (token_type ,

                        token_line_number,

                        0, -- keyword

                        lex_last_string_read);

end;

token_type, set_file, set_string, get_token, fill_token,
last_string_read, file_name,
keyword_code, token_line_number, end_of_text,
last_token, reset_data,
problem ...

lex_token_type : INTEGER **is external langage** *"C"* **end**;
lex_token_line_number : INTEGER **is external langage** *"C"* **end**;
lex_end_of_text : INTEGER **is external langage** *"C"* **end**;

   ...

8.8.2 Syntactic Analysis

This part of the compilation is entirely performed in Eiffel. It uses the lexical analyser defined in 8.8.1. It tries to identify various constructs in this Knowledge Base.

Various typed words are extracted from the text and stored in an array of *TOKENS* in the *INPUT_UNIX CLASS*. This step is not needed for all types of compilation. However a backtracking mechanism is necessary to allow re-examination of the word list. This will be presented later in this chapter.

The parser class is fed with words and their characteristics via the *INPUT_UNIX* class, and offers capabilities that allow to analyse terminals of the description language of the knowledge base, such as identifier, keyword separator, etc.

In contrast to methods used in finite state automata (FSA) (for instance), compilation in S.L.O.T. uses a top-down method. Furthermore, S.L.O.T. includes Eiffel classes that correspond to the various syntactic constructs. For instance, the *RULE* class corresponds to the rules used in the knowledge base. The *PARSEABLE* class includes a deferred feature *parse_current* defining all compilable objects. The *PARSEABLE* class include also all characteristics that are needed to validate a compilable object. A **new compilable object** is created by defining a class that inherits from the *PARSEABLE* class. In particular, the *PARSEABLE* class includes an attribute called *PARSER* that is unique and common to all compilable objects (it is declared with the **once** keyword). Our parser works like the Eiffel library parser but, unlike it, it builds the parsed objects directly. For this reason and because we have no complex syntax we chose to develop our own parser.

Each class describing compilable objects must also include a *parse_current* routine (deferred feature inherited from *PARSEABLE*) that describes in a procedural manner the grammar rule of compilation. This approach is quite logical: only an object representing a rule (instance of the *RULE* class) needs to know how to compile a rule.

```
class RULE inherit
    PARSEABLE ;
    SOURCE ;
    TOOL_CONST ;
    KB ;
feature {MULTIPLICAND, PATTERN, OPERAND, TEST}
        -- List of variables used in the rule.
    var_list : VAR_LIST ;
        -- Left Hand Side
    lhs: PATTERN ;
        -- Right Hand Side
    rhs : ACTIONS_LIST ;
        -- Forward chaining possible ? (default = no)
    forward_control : BOOLEAN;
        -- Backward chaining possible ? (default = yes)
    backward_control : BOOLEAN;
        -- Rule id;
    id : STRING;
```

In its *parse_current* routine, the RULE class compiles a rule such as :

```
--Parsing :
parse_current: BOOLEAN is
        do
                kb.set_rule(Current);
                var_list.Forget ;
                with_var := false ;
                --Syntactic analysis
                if parser.parse_keyword("rule")
                        and then parser.parse_id
                        and then parse_optional_control
                        and then parse_var_declaration
                        and then parse_explanation_links
                        and then parse_explanation(first_explanation)
                        and then parser.parse_keyword("if")
                then
                        !!id.make(1);
                        id.append ("rule : ") ;
                        id.append (parser.pop_id);

                        kb.push_var_list(var_list);
        -- Parsing rule body (PATTERN and ACTIONS_LIST) .
                        lhs.Create ;
        -- parser.parse_obj (lhs) invoke ACTIONS_LIST class parse_current routine
                        if parser.parse_obj (lhs)                and then
                          parse_explanation(second_explanation)  and then
                          parser.parse_keyword("then")           and then
```

```
        parse_actions                              and then
        parser.parse_keyword("end")
    then
            Result := true;
            compile; -- semantic analysis and inference control
    end;
        kb.pop_var_list;
        if not var_list.empty then
            with_var := true
    end
        end
end
```

```
compile is
-- To create links between the current rule and slots
    do
        if backward_control then
            rhs.link_slots_to_source(current)
        end;
        if forward_control then
            lhs.link_slots_to_rule(current)
        end
    end
```

Elementary entities are compiled using the *PARSER* class. Each class may use other classes that correspond to compilable objects to write its routine *parse_current*.

Each class that inherits from *PARSEABLE* stores the data output of the compilation process. This data will be subsequently evaluated. In fact each class also includes evaluation methods. Thus, the *RULE* class includes a method that compiles a rule, attributes that store data output of the compilation process with respect to this rule, and methods that manage the formatting of data needed for the evaluation of the rule. Thus, an instance of the *RULE* class will include everything necessary to a rule.

A model of each object that requests a syntactic construct (rule, d3, test etc. ..) is created uniquely using the once clause and stored in a *choice* table implemented as a polymorphic list. There is a *choice* table for each node of the syntactic tree. The syntactic analysis is performed using the *parse_current* function of each object model that is cloned in the knowledge base if the analysis is performed correctly. For instance, in the knowledge base, we can find at a given level (syntactic tree node) either a *RULE* class, a decision tree (*D3* class), or a description of slot (*SLOT_DESC* class). All these classes inherit from the *PARSEABLE* class; a polymorphic list of them is built (*choice* table). Using this polymorphic list has several advantages; in particular:

• For the compilation process, it is sufficient to compile the first element of the list, eventually the second, etc., until a success is reached. Between two unsuccessful trials, a backtracking in the word sequence is needed. If the end of the list is reached without success then a syntax error is generated.

- To add or delete a syntactic construct, it is sufficient to add or delete an element in the polymorphic list (*choice* table). This allows to build easily new syntactic constructs to extend the language.

8.9 SOFTWARE ARCHITECTURE OF S.L.O.T.

The main class fires the parser that will activate the command interpreter. The knowledge base is entirely included in a class called *KB* that is global to the entire system. The knowledge base class includes the list of frames and the list of properties (figure 8.3) constituting the knowledge base. Their uniqueness is guaranteed thanks to the use of the HASH_TABLE class from the Eiffel library.

As mentioned earlier there are four main abstractions: frame, properties, slot, and sources, therefore there are four main classes called *FRAME*, *PROPERTY*, *SLOT* and *SOURCE*. Each frame includes a set of slots that corresponds to the properties associated to them. Slots are unique in the knowledge base, but they are local in the frames. Frames and properties are global to the system.

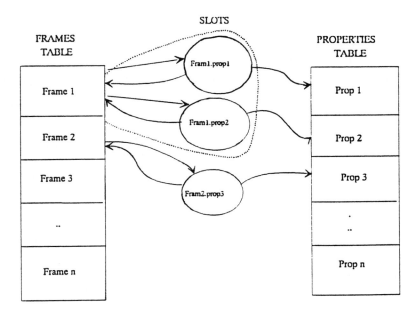

Figure 8.3: Knowledge base architecture

8.9.1 Slot classes

The slot concept is implemented by a generic class *SLOT[T–>SIMPLE_DATA]*. The *T* generic parameter stands for actual types that are descendants of the *SIMPLE_DATA* class. There are three generic derivations of slot classes, *SLOT[NUM_DATA]* (numeric slot), *SLOT[BOOLEAN]* (boolean slot), *SLOT[FRAME_SET]* (symbolic slot) with respect to the type of the slot associated property. Slots are derivated during the parsing process; this implies two consequences. First, the slot class has no *parse_current* feature. Second, the properties must be declared with their type before their attached slot is used. We replaced the *parse_current* feature by a global function from the *PARSER* class called *parse_slot*. Each slot includes its attached frame and property. The slot object includes a sorted sources list. Thus it can fire each item of its sources list to get value. In backward chaining reasoning, a slot object includes all rules that include it on their right-hand sides.

Any slot class features, such as :

*value : T is **do** ... **end**;*

status : integer ;

could have one value among *NOT_EVAL*, *KNOWN*, *NOT_KNOWN* and *IN_EVALUATION*.

sources : SORTED_LIST [SOURCE]

*eval : INTEGER is **do** ... **end**;* To fire all sources until the status changes to *KNOWN* or *NOT_KNOWN*.

apply_op(op : INTEGER,data : DATA) ; to apply a logical operator (such as =,>,< ...) to the current slot value with data.

A slot can be considered as a datum such as an integer or a boolean because the test format is *:DATA* operator *DATA*. Data may be instantiated by slot, integer, frame_set or boolean object.

For instance :

car.size > 3 , John.age > Mary.age or *red = car.color;*

For this reason, class SLOT inherits from the *DATA* class (figure 8.5).

Sources

A *sources* object is an ordered list (ordered by priority) of objects necessary to the evaluation of a slot in backward chaining (*SORTED_LIST[SOURCE]* class) (figure 8.4). The *eval* function of a current slot fires each source by an interaction loop of its sources list, so it first fires the higher priority sources. The source list may include one of the following objects (decreasing priorities):

- A rule: a slot owns a rule in its list of sources when it is in the left part of this rule in order for this rule to be chosen in backward chaining.

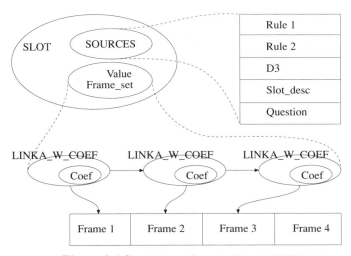

Figure 8.4 Structure of symbolic slot Eiffel object

- A decision tree *d3*: a decision tree is always attached to a slot. A decision tree that is attached to a slot constitutes a source of it.
- A default value.
- A question; the question has the lowest priority level of the sources. If a slot does not have any source, a default question will be built, with lower priority level than the explicit question, as follows : for a slot *frame.prop –>* the *prop* of *frame*

Possible values represent the accumulation of all values of the slot that are in the right parts of tests and assignments, or in the "then" parts of the decision trees, as well as in the affectation parts of slots descriptions.

Dependencies are represented by a list of rules that must be fired in forward chaining. In this case, the slot must be in the left part of the rule.

Used sources are a list of sources that are actually used to evaluate the slot. This list will be useful only after the evaluation of the slot, to explain the reasoning.

Each slot has an attribute called *value*, represented by a table of values provided by users (*USER-VAL*). Each element of this table consists of a value of the *SIMPLE-DATA* type and a state (*KNOWN, UNKNOWN* etc.) that characterises the slot for a specific user. Symbolic values are represented by the assignment of frames to a slot value (figure 8.4). Note that each frame is unique in the knowledge base. As a consequence, the likelihood coefficient is located in the *LINKABLE* class that is redefined as *LINKA-W-COEF*. The *FRAME-SET* class, that implements a set of frames, uses *LINKA-W-COEF* as an element instead of *LINKABLE*. This class can inherit from the *LINKED-LIST* class of the Eiffel library by redefining the type of the first-element feature using anchored declaration, such as shown in figure 8.5.

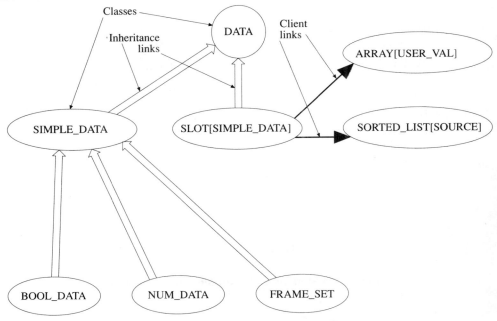

Figure 8.5: Architecture of DATA classes

8.10 INFERENCE MECHANISM

The inference mechanism is the same for all objects. In all cases, an object is evaluated first, then its value is used either for a test or for an action. An object can be evaluated by any source object. As a reminder, a slot source makes it possible to determine the value of this slot, and by extension a property source is a rule including this property acting on a variable in the action part: the source of a property is then the potential source of all slots that include this property. A property source is necessarily a rule because it is the only construct that allows to use variables. In Eiffel, this leads to the design of a *SOURCE* class that is inherited by *RULE, D3, QUESTION*, etc. Thus, it is possible to build polymorphic lists. Arbitrary priorities have been defined among sources. The sources can be listed by decreasing order as follows : rules (*RULE* class) decision trees (D3 class) slot descriptions (*D_RULE_SET*) - rules with variables - default values (*DEFAULT_VAL* class) - questions (*QUESTION* Class) An object of the Slot class has an ordered list of sources. If this list has several sources of the same priority, they remain in the same original order. In our case, the *SOURCE* class inherits from the *PART_COMPAR* class of the library so that the objects instance of the *SOURCE* class can be compared to each other. Then an order within the *SOURCE* class is created by defining the primitive "<". The current source is less than it is necessary to define another source if its priority is lower. This network of objects allows the execution of the knowledge base. The current version of S.L.O.T. is being developed for diagnostic applications and works in backward chaining.

8.10.1 Backward chaining

In order to manage the evaluation of a slot, a state is associated with a slot :

- NOT_EVALUATED: the slot is not yet deduced by the system, nor given by the user.
- KNOWN: the slot value has been either deduced or given. KNOWN is the only state.
- NOT KNOWN: this state is possible in two cases: the user does not know the slot value and declares NOT KNOWN; the system tried to deduce the slot value but did not succeed. A slot that has been evaluated is either KNOWN or NOT KNOWN.

The slot is the only entity within the system that can be evaluated. Indeed, it is the only entity to have a value. The user can ask the evaluation of a slot by using the command "Eval frame property" When this command is invoked, the inference engine is started:

- A value is assigned to a slot if the system is able to deduce it in the current context; the state of the slot is set to *KNOWN*.
- The state of the slot is set to *NOT_KNOWN* if no value can be deduced.
- No change if the slot has been already evaluated.

In general the system attempts to reach the goal (evaluate the slot) either by examining the fact base or by trying to deduce it from the available sources. Note that in applying these sources may introduce other goals. This process is repeated until the system reaches goals that can be easily deduced from the fact base, or that are given by the user after a question.

Let us use an example to detail this process :

```
rule plug-it-in
    if (
        recorder.problem= impossible-recording &
        recorder not-plugged-in = true
    )
    then
        recorder.solution : = plug_in
    end;
slot recorder.problem
   description
    (recording.quality= bad)
        –>bad_quality_image,
    (try.recording=no-reaction)
        –>recording impossible
end;
slot recorder.solution
    default : call_the_repair_man
end ;
```

slot recorder.not_plugged_in
question : "is the recorder plugged in?"
end ;

Typically this KB in invoked by the following statement :
    eval recorder.

The system starts by finding the Eiffel object of the Slot class that corresponds to the slot involved in the evaluation. This is performed using a special object of the *KB-INFO* class that can be seen as the "door" of the knowledge base. In the previous example, this object is the slot "recorder.solutions".

This slot is then asked to evaluate itself. It includes an ordered list of sources as we have already described it. Note that each attempt by a source is sent to this source and confirmed by changing the slot state.

In the previous example, the slot "recorder.solutions" attempts to apply the rule "plug-it -in", and if this rule does not give any result it takes the available default value.

Evaluation algorithms working on objects of the *RULE*, *PATTERN*, and *TEST* classes are presented in figure 8.6. Note that for a list of tests, a likelihood coefficient is first calculated on the sub-list of tests (it can be empty) when all entities have a *KNOWN* state. This avoids the need to add useless goals.

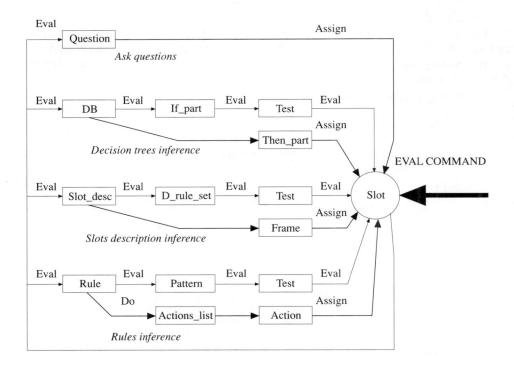

Figure 8.6: Inference principle

8.10.2 Evaluation of objects

Let us take a rule as example. The evaluation of a rule starts by the evaluation of its PATTERN. This results in a sequential evaluation of each test. As a test is composed of a left part, an operator, and a right part, such as:

LHS op RHS.

The evaluation of a test is processed as follows: its left part is evaluated, its right part is evaluated, and the operator is applied to the results of these two evaluations. both left and right parts have the *DATA* type. Thus, they can be simple data or high level data such as slots and variables. The *DATA* class includes a deferred feature *apply-op* (*data* : *DATA*, *op* : *INTEGER*) that attempts to apply the operator *op* to the value of its own data. Each heir of the *DATA* class must define the feature *apply-op*. Thus, calculation of the truth value is performed as follows :

truth = rhs. apply-op (rhs, op);

Note that this evaluation process may introduce other goals. Indeed, if the rhs or lhs is a slot it will be evaluated and other sources (d3, rule ...) will be fired.

In our expert system of recorder maintenance, the rule "plug-it-in" fires the evaluation of the slot "recorder.problem". Its condition part (pattern) has two tests :

(1) recorder.problem = impossible-recording
(2) recorder.not_plugged_in=true

Both of these tests are evaluated :

− The first test fires the evaluations of the slot recorder.problem, this slot attempts to deduce its value from its slot description source :

slot recorder.problem
  description
    (recording.quality= bad)
       −>bad_quality_image,
    (try.recording=no-reaction)
       −>recording impossible
  end;

− The second test fires the evaluations of the slot recorder.not_plugged_in this slot attempts to deduce its value from its question source :

slot recorder.not_plugged_in
  question : "is the recorder plugged in?"
  end ;

Other goals are added when the tests are examined. In the example, the corresponding slots are 'recording.quality' and 'try.recording'. The same mechanism is carried out on these slots.

The second test leads to the evaluation of a question. This causes the display of the following string :

is the recorder plugged in?

At this point, the user has the following alternatives :

– Type '*' if he needs to get information on the type of the expected answer.

    boolean value (will be answered by the system)

– Type '?' if he does not know the value.

–true or false.

If the rule "plug_it_in" does not reach any conclusion the slot "recorder.solution' attempts to evaluate the default value.

This example illustrates mechanisms related to rules, default values and questions. Two other sources have not been used in the example: the execution of an Eiffel function ; a decision tree. A knowledge base may include a call to an Eiffel function that has been written for the application, e.g. , display of a drawing.

8.10.3. Decision tree d3

The syntax of a decision tree shows the recursive structure of its grammar. this structure will be implemented using Eiffel objects as follows :

It syntax is:

Dtrees ::= d3 Slot If_Part_List

If_Part_List ::= '(' {If_Part} ')'

If_Part ::= if TEST then THEN_PART

THEN_PART ::= FRAME_SET I IF_PART_LIST

```
    d3 car.passenger
       ( if car.type = sport_car then
              ( if car.color = red then John
                else Mary
                )
       )
    end;
```

The result of the compilation is presented in figure 8.7. This structure is possible because a *THEN_PART* class has been defined, its children are: a set of frames *FRAME_SET* (terminal modes) or a list *IF_PART_LIST* (tree description). Attributes "then-part" and "else-part" of the objects of the *IF_PART* class are both of the *THEN_PART* class.

The algorithm is then :

Attempt to evaluate a decision tree (d3) :

– Find values (*SIMPLE_DATA*) corresponding to terminal nodes; this is performed by evaluating the list of IF branches (*IF_PART_LIST*);

– If this set is not empty then assign them to the *slot* that becomes known ;

Attempt to evaluate the list of IF branches (*IF_PART_LIST*). To each branch :

– Evaluate the test

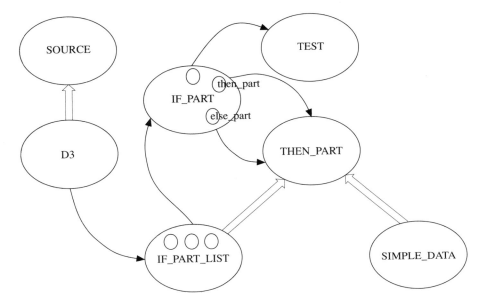

Figure 8.7: Structure of the decision tree

- If the result is positive then find verified data (*SIMPLE_DATA* class) in the sub-tree (*THEN_PART* class) ;
- Store these data with the ones that are already verified ;

else

- Evaluate the ELSE part (same process as above, class *THEN_PART*) ;
- Store these data.

This recursive mechanism stops when terminal modes are reached, i.e., objects of the *FRAME_SET* class (children of the *THEN_PART* class). These objects return as results.

8.11 CONCLUSION

This chapter did not aim to describe in depth all the possibilities of S.L.O.T. as well as possible implementations. The main goal was to illustrate an example of systems that were implemented using the object-oriented approach.. S.L.O.T. has been design to be applied in very different domains. This is possible because the main feature of S.L.O.T. is its extendibility that comes from the object-oriented approach and, in particular, from the use of Eiffel.

Bibliography

[Ackroyd 1991]
M. Ackroyd and D. Daum, "Graphical Notation for Object-Oriented Design and Programming", *Journal of Object-Oriented Programming*, January 1991.

[Allen 1985]
J.F. Allen, "Maintaining Knowledge about Temporal Intervals", in *Readings in Knowledge Representation*, ed. H.J. Levesque, pp. 509-521, Morgan Kaufman, 1985.

[Anderson 1990]
E. Anderson, Z. Bai, C. Bischof, J. Denmel, J. Dongarra, J. DuCroz, A. Greenbaum, S. Hammarling, A. McKenney and D. Sorensen, "A Portable Linear Algebra Library for High-Performance Computers", Lapack Working Note 20, University of Tennessee, Computer Science Department, University of Tennessee, 1990.

[Balkenende 1990]
R. Balkenende, "ProMod Graphical Query Tool", BI-90-042, TNO Building and Construction Research, Rijswijk (The Netherlands), June 1990.

[Balthazaar 1985]
Carmel Balthazaar, Alex Gray and Ted Lawson, "An Object-Oriented Temporal Model Embodied as Eiffel Software Components", in *Proceedings of TOOLS 91*, pp. 249-257, May 1985.

[Barbic 1985]
F. Barbic and B. Pernici, "Time Modelling in Office Information Systems", in *Proceedings of ACM SIGMOD Conference*, pp. 51-61, May 1985.

[Belina 1989]
F. Belina and D. Hogrefe, *The CCITT Specification and Description Language SDL*, pp. 311-341, Elsevier Science Publishers B.V. (North-Holland), 1989.

[Berard 1990]
Edward V. Berard, "Creation of, and Conversion to, Object-Oriented Requirements", Usenet Posting to comp.object, April 29, 1990.

[Berard 1990]
Edward V. Berard, "Life-Cycle Approcaches", *Hotline of Object-Oriented Technology*, vol. 1, p. 6, 1990.

[Boehm 1988]
Barry W. Boehm, "A Spiral Model of Software Development and Enhancement", *IEEE Computer*, vol. 21, p. 5, 1988.

[Booch 1991]
Grady Booch, *Object-Oriented Design with Applications*, Benjamin-Cummings, 1991.

[Boulic 1991]
R. Boulic and O. Renault, "3D Hierarchies for Animation", in *New Trends in Animation and Visualization*, John Wiley and Sons, 1991.

[Boy 1991]
Guy Boy, *Intelligent Assistant Systems*, Academic Press Ltd., 1991.

[Britannica 1974]
"*Calendar* article", in *Encyclopaedia Britannica*, Encyclopaedia Britannica Inc., London, 1974.

[Brooks 1982]
Fred P. Brooks, *The Mythical Man-Month*, Addison-Wesley, 1982.

[Cheng 1989]
K.E. Cheng and L.N. Jackson, "MELBA+: A Telecommunications CASE Tool Using SDL", in *Proceedings of IREECON 1989*, pp. 447-450, 1989.

[Cheng 1989]
K.E. Cheng and L.N. Jackson, "MELBA+: An SDL Software Engineering Environment", in *SDL 1989: The Language at Work*, ed. O. Faergemand, M.M. Marques, Elsevier Science Publishers B.V. (North-Holland), 1989.

[Clifford 1983]
J. Clifford and D. Warren, "Formal Semantics for Time in Databases", *Transactions on on Database Systems*, vol. 8, no. 2, pp. 214-254, 1983.

[Coad 1991]
Peter Coad and Edward N. Yourdon, *Object-Oriented Analysis*, Prentice Hall, 1991.

[Connell 1989]
Connell and Shafer, *Structured Rapid Prototyping*, Yourdon Press (Prentice Hall), Englewood Cliffs (N.J.), 1989.

[Cook 1989]
William R. Cook, "A Proposal for Making Eiffel Type-safe", in *Proceedings of ECOOP 89*, ed. S. Cook, 1989.

[Cox 1986]
Brad J. Cox, *Object-Oriented Programming: An Evolutionary Approach*, Addison-Wesley, Reading (Massachusetts), 1986.

[Delisle 1991]
D. Delisle and L. Pelamourgues, "B-USDB and How it Works", *IEEE Spectrum*, August 1991.

[DeMay 1991]
V. DeMay, "Flexible Graphic Design System", in *Object Composition*, pp. 145-155, Université de Genève, 1991.

[de Bruijn 1991]
W.J. de Bruijn, "EXIS Reference Manual version 1.1", BI-91-187, TNO Building and Construction Research, Rijswijk (The Netherlands), November 1991.

[Dubois 1988]
D. Dubois and H. Prade, *Theory of Possibility*, Masson, 1988.

[Ellis 1990]
Margaret A. Ellis and Bjarne Stroustrup, *The Annotated C++ Reference Manual*, Addison-Wesley, 1990.

[Fleischer 1988]
K. Fleischer and A. Witkin, "A Modeling Testbed", in *Proceedings of Graphics Interface 1988*, pp. 127-137, 1988.

[Gadia 1986]
S.K. Gadia, "Weak Temporal Relations", in *Proceedings for Fifth ACM SIGMOD Conference on Principles of Database Systems*, pp. 70-77, 1986.

[Genman 1984]
S. Genman and D. Genman, "Stochastic Relaxation, Gibbs Distribution and the Bayesian Restoration of Images", in *IEEE Proceedings of Pattern Analysis and Machine Intelligence*, vol. PAMI-6, pp. 721-741, 1984.

[Gielingh 1988]
W.F. Gielingh, "General AEC Reference Model (GARM)", BI-88-150, TNO Building and Construction Research, 1988.

[Gindre 1989]
Cyrille Gindre and Frédérique Sada, "A Development in Eiffel: Design and Implementation of a Network Simulator", *Journal of Object-Oriented Programming*, May-June 1989.

[Gobbetti 1991]
Enrico Gobbetti and Russell Turner, "Object-Oriented Design of Dynamic Graphics Applications", in *New Trends in Animation and Visualization*, John Wiley, 1991.

[Goguen 1978]
J.A. Goguen, J.W. Thatcher and E.G. Wagner, "An Initial Algebra Approach to the Specification, Correctness and Implementation of Abstract Data Types", in *Current Trends in Programming Methodology*, ed. Raymond T. Yeh, vol. 4, pp. 80-149, Prentice Hall, Englewood Cliffs (N.J.), 1978.

[Grant 1986]
E. Grant, P. Amburn and T. Whitted, "Exploiting classes in Modeling and Display Software", *IEEE Computer Graphics and Applications*, vol. 6, no. 11, 1986.

[Grune 1989]
D. Grune, B. Berliner and J. Polk, *Manual page for the CVS sytem*, July 1989.

[Hajnicz 1989]
E. Hajnicz, "Absolute Dates and Relative Dates in an Inferential System on Temporal Dependencies Between Events", *International Journal of Man-Machine Studies*, vol. 30, pp. 537-549, 1989.

[Hajnicz 1990]
E. Hajnicz, "Role of the Present in Temporal Representation in Artificial Intelligence", *International Journal of Man-Machine Studies*, vol. 32, pp. 263-274, 1990.

[Hedelman 1984]
H. Hedelman, "A Data Flow Approach to Procedural Modeling", *IEEE Computer Graphics and Applications*, vol. 6, no. 11, 1984.

[Hillman 1990]
M.F. Hillman, "A Network Programming Package in Eiffel", in *Proceedings of TOOLS 2*, pp. 541-551, SOL/Angkor, Paris, 1990.

[Ingalls 1986]
D.H.H. Ingalls, "A Simple Technique for Handling Multiple Polymorphism", in *Proceedings of OOPSLA (ACM Object-Oriented Programming Systems and Applications)*, 1986.

[ISO 1990]
International Standards Organization, "Exchange of Product Model Data – Part II: The EXPRESS Language", Document CD 10303-11, ISO TC 184/SC4 N64, July 1990.

[ISO 1991]
> International Standards Organization, "Product Data Representation and Exchange – Part 2: Clear Text Encoding of the Exchange Structure", Document CD 10303-21, ISO TC 184/SC4 N78, March 1991.

[Jepsen 1983]
> D.W. Jepsen and C.D. Gelatt, "Macro Placement by Monte Carlo Annealing", in *Proceedings of International Conference on Computer Design*, pp. 495-498, Port Chester (N.Y.), 1983.

[Johnson 1989]
> D.S. Johnson, C.R. Aragon, L.A. McGeoch and C. Schevon, "Optimization by Simulated Annealing: An Experimental Evaluation; Part 1, Graph Partitioning", *Operations Research*, vol. 37, no. 6, November 1989.

[Johnson 1990]
> Paul A. Johnson, "Report on the Emacs Object-Oriented Browser", Internal document Y/240/1402, GEC-Marconi Research, July 1990.

[Johnson 1990]
> Paul A. Johnson, "Private Communication Concerning Fine Grain Inheritance and the Sibling-Supertype Rule", Internal document Y/240/1810, November 1990.

[Johnson 1991]
> Paul A. Johnson and C.S. Rees, "Reusability Through Fine Grain Inheritance", *Software – Practice and Experience*, April 1991.

[Johnson 1991a]
> Paul A. Johnson, "Simulated Annealing for System Building", Internal document Y/240/1672, January 1991.

[Johnson 1991b]
> Paul A. Johnson, "Maintaining Consistent Cross-References in Eiffel", in *Proceedings of the Eighth International Eiffel User Conference*, March 1991.

[Jones 1980]
> C.B. Jones, *Systematic Software Development Using VDM*, Prentice Hall International, Hemel Hempstead, 1980.

[Jones 1980a]
> S. Jones and P.J. Mason, "Handling the Time Dimension in a Database", in *Proceedings of International Conference on Databases*, pp. 65-83, 1980.

[Kernighan 1978]
> Brian W. Kernighan and Dennis M. Ritchie, *The C Programming Language*, Prentice Hall, Englewood Cliffs (N.J.), 1978.

[Kirkley 1991]
> J.R. Kirkley and B.K. Seitz, "STEP Framework, Concepts and Principles", Draft document, ISO TC 184/SC4/WG5.P 1, March 1991.

[Laarhoven 1987]
P.J.M. van Laarhoven and E.H.L. Aarts, *Simulated Annealing: Theory and Practice*, Kluwer Academic Publishers, Dordrecht (The Netherlands), 1987.

[Lamport 1978]
Leslie Lamport, "Time, Clocks and the Ordering of Events in Distributed Systems", *Communications of the ACM*, vol. 21, no. 7, pp. 558-565, 1978.

[Lawson 1979]
H. Lawson and K. Kincaid, "Basic Linear Algebra Subprograms for FORTRAN Usage", *ACM Transactions on Mathematical Software*, vol. 5, pp. 308-323, 1979.

[Linton 1989]
M.A. Linton, J.M. Vlissides and P.R. Calder, "Composing User Interfaces with InterViews", *IEEE Computer*, vol. 22, no. 2, 1989.

[Luiten 1991]
G.T. Luiten, "Development and Implementation of Multi-Layered Project Models", Second International Workshop on Computer Building Representation for Integration, Aix-les-Bains (France), June 1991.

[Metropolis]
W. Metropolis, A. Rosenbluth, M. Rosenbluth, A. Teller and E. Teller, "Equation of State Calculations by Fast Computing Machines", *J. Chem. Phys.*, vol. 21, pp. 1087-1092.

[Meyer 1987]
Bertrand Meyer, "Reusability: The Case for Object-Oriented Design", *IEEE Software*, vol. 4, no. 2, pp. 50-64, March 1987.

[Meyer 1988]
Bertrand Meyer, *Object-Oriented Software Construction*, Prentice Hall International, Hemel Hempstead, 1988.

[Meyer 1989]
Bertrand Meyer et al., "Eiffel: The Libraries", Technical report TR-EI-7/LI, Interactive Software Engineering, Santa Barbara (Calif.), 1989.

[Meyer 1989a]
Bertrand Meyer, "Eiffel: The Language", Technical report TR-EI-17/RM, Interactive Software Engineering, Santa Barbara (Calif.), 1989. (Describes version 2 of the language; superseded by [Meyer 1992].)

[Meyer 1990]
Bertrand Meyer, "Tools for the new culture: lessons from the Design of the Eiffel Libraries", *Communications of the ACM*, vol. 33, no. 9, pp. 69-88, 1990.

[Meyer 1990a]
Bertrand Meyer et al., "Eiffel: The Environment", Technical report TR-EI-5/UM, Interactive Software Engineering, Santa Barbara (Calif.), 1990.

[Meyer 1990b]
Bertrand Meyer, "The New Culture of Software Development", *Journal of Object-Oriented Programming*, November-December 1990.

[Meyer 1992]
Bertrand Meyer, *Eiffel: The Language*, Prentice Hall International, Hemel Hempstead, 1992. (Supersedes [Meyer 1989a].)

[Meyer 1992a]
Bertrand Meyer, "Applying "Design by Contract"", *IEEE Computer*, vol. 25, no. 10, pp. 40-51, October 1992.

[Meyer 1993]
Bertrand Meyer, "What is an Object-Oriented Environment?", *Journal of Object-Oriented Programming*, July-August 1993.

[Minsky 1975]
Marvin Minsky, "A Framework for Representing Knowledge", in *The Psychology of Computer Vision*, ed. Winston, Prentice Hall, Englewood Cliffs (N.J.), 1975.

[Neighbors 1984]
J.M. Neighbors, "The Draco Approach to Constructing Software from Reusable Components", *IEEE Transactions on Software Engineering*, vol. 10, no. 5, pp. 574-588, 1984.

[Nerson 1991]
Jean-Marc Nerson, "Extending Eiffel toward Object-Oriented Analysis and Design", in *Proceedings of TOOLS USA 91*, 1991.

[Nerson 1993]
Jean-Marc Nerson and Kim Walden, *Object-Oriented Architectures: Analysis and Design of Reliable Systems*, Prentice Hall International, Hemel Hempstead, 1993. To appear.

[Nijssen 1989]
G.M. Nijssen and Halpin, *Conceptual Schema and Relational Database Design*, Prentice Hall, Englewood Cliffs (N.J.), 1989.

[Nobecourt 1988]
P. Nobecourt, Colette Rolland and J.Y. Lingat, "Temporal Management in an Extended Relational DBMS", in *Proceedings of BNCOD 6*, pp. 87-123, 1988.

[Omohundro]
Steve M. Omohundro and Bob Weiner, *eiffel.el: Major Mode for Editing Eiffel Code*, Interactive Software Engineering, Santa Barbara (Calif.). Available by FTP from tut.cis.ohio-state.edu.

[Parnas 1986]
David L. Parnas, "A Rational Design Process: How and Why to Fake It", *IEEE Transactions on Software Engineering*, vol. 12, no. 2, pp. 251-257, 1986.

[Parsaye 1989]

K. Parsaye, M. Chignel, S. Khoshafian and H. Wong, *Intelligent Databases*, Wiley & Sons, 1989.

[Paulk 1991]

M.C. Paulk, B. Curtis, E. Averill, J. Bamberger, T. Kasse, M. Konrad, J. Perdue, C. Weber and J. Withey, "Capability Maturity Model for Software", Technical Report, CMU/SEI-91-TR-24, Software Engineering Institute, Pittsburgh (Penn.), 1991.

[Press 1988]

W.H. Press, B.P. Flanery, S.A. Teukolsky and W.T. Vetterling, *Numerical Recipes in C*, p. 343, Cambridge University Press, 1988.

[Prieto -Diaz 1987]

R. Prieto-Diaz, "Domain Analysis for Reusability", in *Proceedings of Compsac 1987*, 1987.

[Quillian 1968]

M. Ross Quillian, "Semantic Memory", in *Semantic Information Processing*, ed. M. Minsky, pp. 216-260, MIT Press, Cambridge (Mass.), 1968.

[Rumbaugh 1991]

J. Rumbaugh, M. Blaha, W. Premerlaini, F. Eddy and W. Lorensen, *Object-Oriented Modelling and Design*, Prentice Hall, Englewood Cliffs (N.J.), 1991.

[Sadeghi 1988]

R. Sadeghi, W.B. Samson and S.M. Deen, "HQL – A Historical Query Language", in *Proceedings of BNCOD 6*, pp. 69-86, 1988.

[Sarada 1990]

N.L. Sarada, "Algebra and Query Language for a Historical Data Model", *The Computer Journal*, vol. 33, no. 1, pp. 11-18, 1990.

[Schmucker 1986]

Kurt Schmucker, *Object-Oriented Programming for the Macintosh*, Hayden, 1986.

[Shoemake 1985]

Kurt Shoemake, "Animating Rotation with Quaternion Curves", *Computer Graphics*, vol. 19, no. 3, pp. 245-254, 1985.

[Snodgrass 1985]

Richard Snodgrass and I. Ahn, "A Taxonomy of Time in Databases", in *Proceedings of ACM SIGMOD Conference*, pp. 236-246, March 1985.

[Snodgrass 1987]

Richard Snodgrass, "The Temporal Query Language TQUEL", *ACM Transactions on Database Systems*, vol. 12, no. 2, pp. 247-298, 1987.

[Sombe 1989]
Lea Sombe, *Raisonnement sur les Informations incomplètes en Intelligence Artificielle*, 1989.

[Stallman 1988]
Richard M. Stallman, *GNU Emacs 18.55*, Free Software Foundation, August 1988.

[Standish 1984]
Tim A. Standish, "An Essay on Software Reuse", *IEEE Transactions on Software Engineering*, vol. 10, no. 5, pp. 494-497, 1984.

[Stroustrup 1986]
Bjarne Stroustrup, "An Overview of C++", *SIGPLAN Notices*, vol. 21, no. 10, pp. 7-18, 1986.

[Sun]
"Programming Utilities and Libraries", Part number 800-3847-10, Sun Microsystems, Mountain View (Calif.).

[Telesoft 1990]
"TeleUSE Reference Manual", 1.1, Telesoft AB, Linkoping, Sweden, 1990.

[Thompson 1989]
T. Thompson, "The Next Step", *BYTE*, vol. 14, no. 3, pp. 365-369, 1989.

[TOOLS 1989-1993]
TOOLS 1 to 11: Technology of Object-Oriented Languages and Systems, Prentice Hall (from volume 4 on), 1989-1993. 11 volumes so far. Volumes 1 to 3 published by SOL/Angkor, Paris.

[Turner 1990]
Russell Turner, Enrico Gobbetti, Francis Balaguer, Angelo Mangili, Daniel Thalmann and Nadia Magnenat-Thalmann, "An Object-Oriented Methodology Using Dynamic Variables for Animation and Scientific Visualization ", in *Proceedings of Computer Graphics International 1990*, pp. 317-328, Springer-Verlag, 1990.

[Vogel 1991]
T. Vogel, "Configurable Graphical Editor", DTDL Reference Manual, Release 1.2, TNO Institute of Applied Computer Science, Delft (The Netherlands), February 1991.

[Wegner 1984]
Peter Wegner, "Capital-Intensive Software Technology", *IEEE Software*, pp. 7-45, July 1984.

[Weinand 1989]
André Weinand, E. Gamma and R. Marty, "Design and Implementation of ET++, a Seamless Object-Oriented Application Framework", *Structured Programming*, vol. 10, no. 2, pp. 63-87, 1989.

[Willems 1990]

P.H. Willems, "Road Model Kernel", BI-89-831(E), TNO Building and Construction Research, Rijswijk (The Netherlands), January 1990.

[Willems 1991]

P.H. Willems, "A Framework for Evolutionary Information Model Development", in *CIV Seminar: The Computer Integrated Future*, Eindhoven (The Netherlands), September 1991.

[Winston 1984]

Patrick H. Winston, *Artificial Intelligence*, Addison Wesley, 1984.

[Wirfs-Brock 1990]

Rebecca Wirfs-Brock, B. Wilerson and Lauren Weiner, *Designing Object-Oriented Software*, Prentice Hall, Englewood Cliffs (N.J.), 1990.

[Wirth 1977]

Niklaus Wirth, *Communications of the ACM*, pp. 822-823, November 1977.

[Wirth 1985]

Niklaus Wirth, *Programming in Modula-2* , Springer-Verlag, 1985.

[Woods 1975]

William A. Woods, "What's a Link? Foundations for Semantic Networks", in *Representation and Understanding*, ed. A. Collins, pp. 35-82, Academic Press, New York, 1975.

[Zadeh 1978]

L.A. Zadeh, *Fuzzy Set as a Basis for a Theory of Possibility*, 1978.

[Zelkowitz 1984]

Marvin V. Zelkowitz, Raymond T. Yeh, Richard G. Hamlet, John D. Gannon and Victor D. Basili, "Software Engineering Practices in the US and Japan", *IEEE Computer*, vol. 17, no. 6, pp. 57-66, June 1984.